Computer accounting systems

Tutorial

Michael Fardon

Debbie Board (consultant)

Published by Osborne Books Limited
Unit 1B Everoak Estate
Bromyard Road, Worcester WR2 5HP
Tel 01905 748071
Email books@osbornebooks.co.uk
Website www.osbornebooks.co.uk

Design by Laura Ingham

Printed by CPI Group (UK) Limited, Croydon, CR0 4YY, on environmentally friendly, acid-free paper from managed forests.

British Library Cataloguing in Publication Data
A catalogue record for this book is available from the British Library

ISBN 978 1909173 132

Contents

Acknowledgements

The author wishes to thank the following for their help with the reading, production and design of the text: Maz Loton, Jon Moore, Cathy Turner and Charli Wilson. Particular thanks must go to Debbie Board for the updating of the text for this new edition and for test running the Sage tasks. The author also wishes to thank Hania Lee for further test running of the Sage and reading of the text.

Thanks are also due to Microsoft UK and to Sage (UK) Limited for their kind permission to use screen images within the text. It should be noted that Osborne Books Limited is a company which operates completely independently of Sage (UK) Limited.

Authors

Michael Fardon has extensive teaching experience of a wide range of banking, business and accountancy courses at Worcester College of Technology where he also set up and ran computer accounting courses, using Sage software. He now specialises in writing business and financial texts and is General Editor at Osborne Books. He is also an educational consultant and has worked extensively in the areas of vocational business curriculum development.

Debbie Board spent twenty-six years in the commercial sector before becoming a teacher and assessor of accounting in further education. While working in the commercial sector she was responsible as director and office manager for the introduction of computerised accounting in a multi-million pound business. She currently works in South Devon as a part-time AAT tutor and as the accounts manager of a small independent tool hire company.

Introduction

what this book covers

This book has been written specifically to cover the 'Computerised accounting' Unit which is mandatory for the revised (2013) AAT Level 2 Certificate in Accounting.

The book contains clear and practical explanations of how to set up and run a Sage system. The Sage system (Version 18) has been chosen as it is widely used both by businesses and by training providers.

A Case Study – Pronto Supplies Limited – runs through the chapters. The Activities at the end of each chapter contain short questions to help consolidate learning and inputting tasks to develop Sage inputting skills. Answers to the short questions and printouts of the Sage input are included at the end of the book to enable students to check progress.

A further extended activity 'Interlingo Translation Services' is included at the end of the book for further practice in computer input.

AAT Sample Assessment – important note

This edition incorporates the 2013 AAT sample assessment material. Tutors and students are strongly advised to consult the latest 'Computerised Accounting' guidance material from the AAT website before preparing for the assessment.

Introduction to computer accounting

this chapter covers...

■ *Computer systems involve:*
- *hardware – the equipment*
- *software – the programs that run the computers*

■ *There are a number of different types of computer programs used by businesses and other organisations: word processing, databases, spreadsheets, email management, accounting packages*

■ *The structure of a Computer Accounting program is based on manual bookkeeping systems. It includes the Sales Ledger, Purchase Ledger, Cash Book and Nominal Ledger*

■ *Computers require input of data – which can either be carried out manually from sources such as financial documents or can be imported from other computer systems.*

■ *Computers also output data in the form of 'hard copy' printouts and electronic data which can be emailed or exported to other computer programs.*

COMPUTER HARDWARE

Computer **hardware** is the equipment on which the programs will be run.

There are two main ways of setting up the hardware – a standalone system and a network.

standalone system

A typical standalone system uses a single computer with a screen, mouse, a hard disk for data storage and a printer. This computer is likely to be linked to the internet by phone line. This type of system is useful for a small business when only one person needs to operate the computer at any one time.

network and intranet

A **network** comprises a number of computer workstations linked to a server (which holds all the data) and other equipment such as printers and scanners. This type of system is likely to be used by a larger business or organisation (such as a college IT centre) where a number of operators need to access the system and its data at the same time. A network will often give employees direct access to the internet through an **internet** service provider.

When a network is set up, it is also possible to establish an **intranet**. This is an internal website which operates through the network and enables employees to share data, documents and internal web pages. An intranet cannot be accessed by unauthorised outsiders (except for 'hackers' who are successful in breaking in).

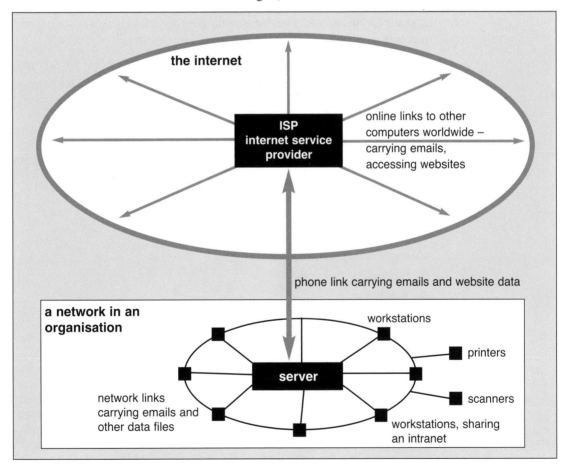

printers

All computer systems need a printer to produce 'hard copy' such as letters, financial documents and management reports. Inkjet or laser printers can produce high quality copies as required.

data storage and back-up

It is very important that the data held by the computer is backed up regularly and stored away from the premises or transmitted to another location. Data can be backed up onto a variety of storage media, eg tape, portable hard disk, USB memory stick, CD and DVD. All systems should therefore have some form of data storage facility or be able to transmit data to another location.

COMPUTER SOFTWARE

Windows operating systems

The program – the **software** – that makes a computer work is known as the operating system. Most business computers are PCs (personal computers) and laptops which run the Windows operating system.

Standard 'off-the-shelf' accounting programs such as Sage 50 are also designed for use on Windows, and it is this system which we will refer to and illustrate when explaining computer accounting in this book.

types of software

The different types of software used in businesses and other organisations are listed below:

- word processing
- databases
- spreadsheets
- email managers
- accounting packages
- web browsers

INTRODUCTION TO COMPUTER ACCOUNTING PACKAGES

a growth area

Although some organisations, particularly small businesses, still use paper-based accounting systems, most are now operating computerised accounting systems.

Small and medium-sized businesses can buy 'off-the-shelf' accounting programs from suppliers such as Sage while larger businesses may opt to have custom-designed programs. Computer accounting programs are easy to use and can automate operations such as invoicing which take so much time and effort in a manual system.

links with traditional bookkeeping

If you are studying on a bookkeeping or accounting course, your study is likely to concentrate initially on paper-based systems. The reason for this is that when you use a paper-based system you have to do all the work manually and so you can understand the theory that underlies the system: you prepare the documents, make entries in the accounts, balance the cash book, and so on. You know where all the figures are entered, and why they are entered. If you know how a paper-based system works, you will be in a much better position to be able to understand the operation of a computer-based system.

comparison with other computer programs

Computer accounting packages – such as the Sage 50 series of products – make use of many of the functions of the other types of computer program.

Most computer accounting packages contain:

- word processing functions – eg the facility to write memos and notes

- a series of databases – eg details of customers, stock items held

- calculation facilities – eg invoices where the operator inputs figures and the program automatically generates VAT amounts and totals

- charting and graphing facilities – eg charting of activity on a customer account

FEATURES OF COMPUTER ACCOUNTING

facilities

A typical computer accounting program will offer a number of facilities:

- on-screen input and printout of sales invoices and credit notes
- automatic updating of customer accounts with sales transactions
- recording of suppliers' invoices
- automatic updating of supplier accounts with details of purchases
- recording of money paid into bank or cash accounts
- recording of payments to suppliers and for expenses

Payroll can also be computerised – using a separate program.

management reports

A computer accounting program can provide instant reports for management, for example:

- an aged debtors' summary – showing who owes you what and for what periods of time
- activity reports on customer and supplier accounts
- activity reports on expenses accounts

advantages of a computer accounting program

Computer accounting programs are popular because they offer a number of distinct advantages over paper-based systems:

- they save time and therefore money
- they tend to be more accurate because they rely on single-entry input (one amount per transaction) rather than double-entry bookkeeping
- they can provide the managers of the organisation with a clear and up-to-date picture of what is happening

computer accounting and ledgers

The 'ledgers' of a business are basically the books of the business. 'The ledgers' is a term used to describe the way the accounts of the business are grouped into different sections.

There are four main ledgers in a traditional accounting system:

- **sales ledger** contains the accounts of receivables (debtors), ie customers
- **purchases ledger** contains the accounts of payables (creditors), ie suppliers
- **cash book** contains the main cash book and the petty cash book
- **nominal ledger** (also called general or main ledger) contains the remaining accounts, eg expenses (including purchases), income (including sales), assets, loans, inventory (stock), VAT

A diagram illustrating these ledgers is shown on the next page. The structure of a computer accounting system is based on these ledgers. It may also include stock control and be linked to a payroll processing program.

A ledger-based computer system is designed to be user-friendly in Windows software. In Sage 50 regular tasks can be performed by clicking on the TASK options on the vertical panel on the left of the screen. These options change according to the module button selected at the bottom of the panel. The full range of modules within Sage (shown opposite) is accessed through the

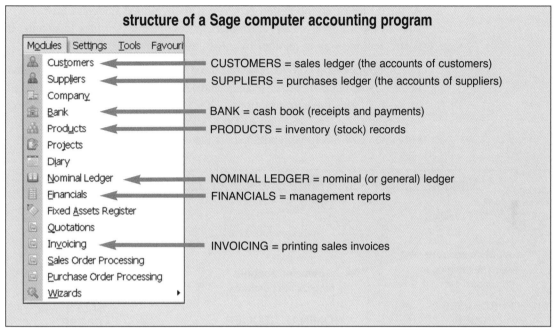

structure of a Sage computer accounting program

Modules | Settings | Tools | Favouri

- Customers ← CUSTOMERS = sales ledger (the accounts of customers)
- Suppliers ← SUPPLIERS = purchases ledger (the accounts of suppliers)
- Company
- Bank ← BANK = cash book (receipts and payments)
- Products ← PRODUCTS = inventory (stock) records
- Projects
- Diary
- Nominal Ledger ← NOMINAL LEDGER = nominal (or general) ledger
- Financials ← FINANCIALS = management reports
- Fixed Assets Register
- Quotations
- Invoicing ← INVOICING = printing sales invoices
- Sales Order Processing
- Purchase Order Processing
- Wizards ▶

MODULES drop-down menu on the menu bar. The notes to the side explain what the various modules are. Note that computer accounting packages vary in levels of sophistication; you may be working with one that does not include product records or invoice printing.

Please note that the screens shown in these chapters may not necessarily be exactly the same as those on your computer because programs are regularly updated. This should not be a problem, however, because the basic principles of using the software are likely to remain exactly the same.

computerised ledgers – an integrated system

Before we look at the various functions on the toolbar, it is important to appreciate that a computerised ledger system is **fully integrated.** This means that when a business transaction is input on the computer it is normally recorded in two accounts at the same time, although only one amount is entered. Take the three transactions shown in the diagram on the next page:

- a business buys from a supplier on credit (ie the business gets the goods but will pay later)
- a business sells to a customer on credit (ie the business sells the goods but will receive payment later)
- a business pays an advertising bill

At the centre of an integrated program is the Nominal Ledger which deals with all the accounts except customers' accounts and suppliers' accounts. It is affected one way or another by most transactions.

The diagram below shows how the three 'ledgers' link with the Nominal Ledger. Note in each case how an account in the Nominal Ledger is affected by each of the three transactions. This is the double-entry bookkeeping system at work. The advantage of the computer system is that in each case only one entry has to be made. Life is made a great deal simpler this way!

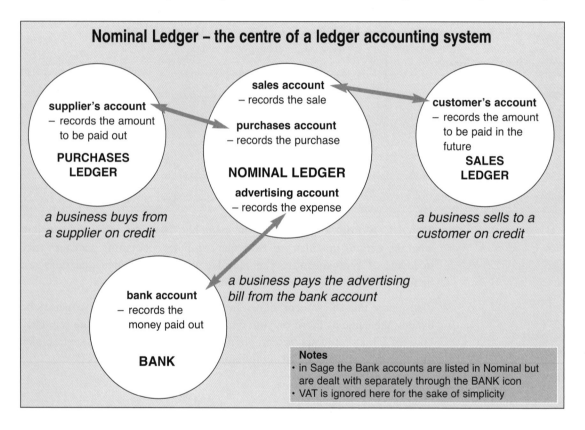

INPUT INTO A COMPUTER ACCOUNTING PACKAGE

manual input

Input into a computer accounting package is normally made direct on screen from source documents or other data. If you are not familiar with financial documents, please read pages 73 to 77 before proceeding any further.

Typical transactions which form the 'bread and butter' of computer accounting input include:

- processing **sales invoices**, often in runs of several transactions known as 'batches' – the invoices are either produced before input or they can be input and printed out by the computer

- inputting **credit notes** from authorised documentation which says why the credit note has to be issued and a refund made – again the credit notes may be produced separately and used as a basis for input, or they may be printed out by the computer

- inputting **bank receipts** (money paid into the bank) – for example cheques or BACS payments received from customers in settlement of accounts due

- inputting details of **new customer accounts** – this is the input of text onto what is effectively a database screen in the computer accounting package

There are, of course, many other types of transactions which you will input on the computer, but these are common examples. We will cover the input procedures in much greater detail in the individual chapters of this book.

importing data

Text files such as Customer and Supplier details can be imported into a computer accounting package from other programs such as Microsoft Office or other accounting programs.

authorisation and checking

Each organisation will have its own procedures to make sure that the data input is accurate and authorised. Source documents – invoices received, for example – may have a stamp placed on them with boxes for the initials of

- the person checking the document

- the person authorising the input – often as part of a 'batch' of invoices

- the computer operator

- the person who checks the input against the source document

This ensures that accuracy is maintained. Each individual takes responsibility for a particular stage in the process and any errors can be traced to that individual.

OUTPUT FROM A COMPUTER ACCOUNTING PACKAGE

Output of data from a computer accounting package can take a number of different formats and can be used in a number of different ways.

printouts

The familiar form of data output from a computer is the paper printout. This is often referred to as 'hard copy'. There are a number of different forms of printout:

- day-to-day lists of items processed, eg a list of invoices produced on a particular day, a list of cheques issued to pay suppliers

- financial documents such as invoices and credit notes

- reports for management, eg activity reports on accounts, aged debtors analysis (a list of who owes what – highlighting overdue accounts)

A printout of sales invoices produced is shown below.

Pronto Supplies Limited

Day Books: Customer Invoices (Detailed)

Transaction From: 1	**N/C From:**	
Transaction To: 99,999,999	**N/C To:** 99999999	

Dept From: 0
Dept To: 999

Tran No.	Type	Date	A/C Ref	N/C	Inv Ref	Dept.	Details	Net Amount	Tax Amount	T/C	Gross Amount	V	B
48	SI	05/02/2013	JB001	4000	10023	0	Hardware	400.00	80.00	T1	480.00	N	-
49	SI	06/02/2013	CH001	4000	10024	0	Hardware	16.00	3.20	T1	19.20	N	-
50	SI	06/02/2013	CR001	4001	10025	0	Software	450.00	90.00	T1	540.00	N	-
51	SI	08/02/2013	KD001	4002	10026	0	Consultancy	120.00	24.00	T1	144.00	N	-
							Totals:	986.00	197.20		1,183.20		

emailed data

Most current computer accounting packages have the facility for data to be exported to an email management program so that it can be emailed direct to the person who needs the information. Sage, for example, allows you to send invoices and statements direct to customers. Printouts and reports previewed on screen can be emailed directly to external email addresses.

exporting data direct to other programs

Most computer accounting packages also allow you to export data to spreadsheet and word processing programs. Sage allows you to:

- export data to a Microsoft Excel spreadsheet, eg a list of the nominal accounts and their balances – this data will be placed direct into a spreadsheet grid from the Sage screen and can then be manipulated as required

- email reports in various formats from reports previewed on-screen

- export data in the form of a mailmerge to a Microsoft Word word processing file – for example, if a business wants to send a letter advertising a new product to all its customers, it can export the names and addresses from the customer details in the computer accounting program to a letter file in Word which will then print out personalised letters to all the customers

- export data files to your accountant

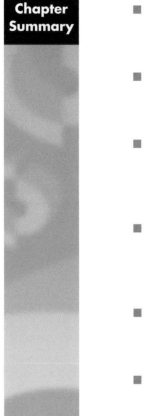

Chapter Summary

■ Organisations using computer systems can either use a single standalone machine or a network of computers linked on an intranet. Many computers or systems are now linked externally to the internet.

■ Computer accounting programs combine the functions of a number of different programs – they act as database and spreadsheet and can generate text and data for use in other programs.

■ A computer accounting program can record financial transactions, generate financial documents, provide management with financial reports and generally make running and managing the finances of any organisation a more efficient process.

■ Computer accounting programs are based on the ledger system of bookkeeping and link together accounts for customers (Sales Ledger), suppliers (Purchases Ledger), bank (Cash Book) and other payments, receipts and items owned or owed by the organisation (Nominal Ledger).

■ Input into a computer accounting program is normally carried out manually on the keyboard. Many programs will now accept data imported from other programs.

■ Output from a computer accounting program can be on paper (hard copy), or sent by email or direct to other programs, a spreadsheet for example.

Key Terms	**hardware**	the computer equipment on which the computer programs run
	software	the computer programs which enable the computer to work and carry out its functions
	intranet	a linked network of computers within an organisation
	internet	computers linked up externally by phone line with other computers on the worldwide web (www)
	ledgers	the books of the accounting system which contain individual accounts – the Sales Ledger, for example, contains the individual accounts of customers who buy on credit (ie they pay later)
	integrated system	a computerised accounting system which links together all the ledgers and accounts so that a transaction on one account will always be mirrored in another account
	double-entry bookkeeping	the method of manual bookkeeping from which the integrated system has been developed – it involves the making of two entries in the accounts for every financial transaction
	hard copy	a paper document containing data – often a printout from a computer
	data export	the transfer of data from one computer program to another

2 Looking after the computer data

this chapter covers...

- *Before looking in detail at the setting up of a computer accounting system it is important to establish the principles of good housekeeping for computers. In other words, knowing how to look after the computer software and avoid losing the data held on it.*

- *The issues we will look at in this chapter include:*

  - *the use of passwords and access rights to the computer accounting system*

  - *logging onto the computer and dealing with dates*

  - *saving and backing up data*

  - *restoring data in Sage*

  - *software problems*

COMPUTER CARE

An organisation that uses computers will have invested thousands of pounds in buying equipment and in training staff to operate it. A business that fails to look after the data that it holds is potentially throwing this money down the drain.

What are the dangers to the data? In this chapter we look at the importance of protecting the data from viruses, hackers and unauthorised access from employees.

USING PASSWORDS

Before getting going on the computer you are likely to have to use **passwords** to enable you to gain access to:

- the computer itself, for example if you are using a workstation on a network – this is a **system password**

■ particular computer programs, some of which may enable you to access sensitive or confidential information – eg the accounting software – this is a **software password**

We will deal with the security aspect of passwords later in this chapter. We will concentrate here on the practical aspects of passwords as part of the starting up procedure.

system passwords – logging on

If you are working on a network you have to 'log on' as a user before you can use a computer workstation. You may have to give a user name and also a unique password. The user name will normally show on the screen as you input it, but the password will show as a series of dots or asterisks. The example below shows someone logging onto a computer in the production department.

logging onto the system

software passwords – accessing a program

Passwords are also needed to protect sensitive and confidential data held on the computer system. This is particularly important in the areas of staff records and also in the case of financial data processed by computer accounting programs.

One solution to the problem of unauthorised employees gaining access to sensitive financial data is the use of **passwords** to gain access to the computer program. Many larger businesses will employ a number of people who need to operate the computer accounting system; they will be issued with an appropriate password. Businesses can also set up **access rights** which restrict certain employees to certain activities and prevent them from accessing more sensitive areas such as the making of payments from the bank account.

When an employee comes to operate, for example, a Sage computer accounting package, he or she will be asked to 'log on'. In the example from Sage 50 shown on the next page a person called Tom enters his log on name and a password (COBBLY).

LOGGING ON AND DEALING WITH DATES

the different dates

One potential problem area for the operator of a computer accounting system is the use of dates when inputting. There are a number of dates that need to be borne in mind:

- the actual date – most people can manage this concept
- the **system date** – this is the date that the computer thinks is the actual date – the computer is normally right
- the **program date** – the date which you can instruct the accounting software to use as the actual date
- the **financial year** start date – the month in which the financial year of the business starts

logging on and using dates

When you log on and start using the computer accounting software, you should check that the date shown at the bottom of the screen is the date you want to use for your input.

The date shown here will be allocated to any transactions that you input into the computer. Normally this is the **system date** (the date the computer thinks it is).

You should then ask yourself if you want your transactions to be allocated any other date. This might be the case if . . .

- you are inputting a batch of transactions which went through last week – for example a number of cheques received from customers – and you want the transactions to show on the records as going through last week
- you are in a training situation and you have been given a specific date for input

If you are using Sage software in these cases you should change the **program date** through the SETTINGS menu. The program date lets you set any date to be 'today's date'.

This new date will appear against every transaction you make that day and will remain in force until you exit from the program, after which it reverts to the system (actual) date.

financial year

A business will use a financial year for accounting purposes. The financial year, like the calendar year, may run from January through to December. But the financial year can start anytime during the year; some businesses end their financial year on 31 March or 30 June, for example. When setting up the data in a computer accounting program you have to state when the financial year starts. In Sage this is done from the SETTINGS menu:

The financial year is important for the management of the business. The end-of-year routines run on the computer provide the data from which the end-of-year financial statements and management reports can be produced.

SAVING AND BACK-UP

The computer accounting program you are using will tell you when to Save your work. This is normally done after inputting a group of transactions and before passing on to the next task.

backing-up files

You will also need to **back-up** the data generated by the computer. There is no set rule about when you should do this, but it should be at least at the end of every day and preferably when you have completed a long run of inputting.

back-up media

If you are working on a network, you can normally save to your files, to your work station's hard disk and also to the server. If you have a standalone computer system, the back-up files should be saved to some form of storage device. This may take the form of a disk drive in the workstation itself or it may be an external drive.

Data can be backed up onto a variety of media:

- writable or rewritable CDs (cheap and disposable)
- tape drive
- portable hard disk drive
- writable or rewritable DVDs
- USB memory stick

Another back-up option is to send files by email and keep them secure at a remote location, although this option might be limited by file size.

back-up in Sage

Back-up in Sage is carried out from the FILE menu, or on the prompt when you close down. The screen gives you a choice of file name (by default the date) and asks to which drive you want the data saved. In the Sage screen shown at the top of the next page it is an external USB drive.

If you are using Sage you are recommended to run the ERROR CHECKING routine from MAINTENANCE (from the FILE menu) before backing up. This will check the data files and ensure that you do not back-up any corrupted data. The screen after a check looks like this:

back-up policy

It is important that an organisation works out a systematic policy for back-up of its data. This should involve:

■ more than one back-up held at any one time

■ back-up media held off the premises

■ periodic back-up (eg back-ups at the end of each month) stored securely

One solution is for the business to keep a set of back-up media (eg tapes) for each working day, labelled with the name of the day.

At the end of each working day the data is backed up on the appropriate back-up media, which are kept securely on site, preferably under lock and key.

As a further security measure, a second set of back-ups could be kept as an off-site security back-up. These would be backed up at the end of each day and taken off-site by an employee.

With this system in place the business has double security for its valuable data.

It should also be mentioned that the back-up media should be replaced periodically (every three months, for example) as they wear out in time and the data can become corrupted.

restoring data from a back-up

In the unfortunate event that the accounting data on your computer has been lost or corrupted, you can **restore** the data from an earlier date from the appropriate back-up media. This is carried out in Sage from RESTORE in the FILE menu. Note that all the data is restored in this process; it is not possible to restore selected files. You should then run ERROR CHECKING routine from FILE MAINTENANCE to make sure the restored data is not corrupted.

SOFTWARE PROBLEMS

Software problems can occur. If it is a case of not knowing how to carry out a particular operation, refer the matter to someone who does. Help is always at hand through HELP menus, on-line support or telephone technical support to which the business is likely to have subscribed. If a program crashes, it may be necessary to restart the computer. If the program refuses to work after repeated attempts, it may have become corrupted, in which case it may need to be re-installed.

corrupted, deleted or overwritten data files

Problems can also be caused if a data file

- becomes **corrupt**, ie it becomes unusable and will not open or print, or both

- gets **deleted** by accident or by a malicious computer virus

- is accidentally **overwritten** by an older version of a file, and in the process wipes out the work you may have done on the file

In these cases you have to rely on being able to restore your back-up files.

virus protection

Computers are vulnerable to viruses. A **virus** is a destructive program which can be introduced into the computer either from a disk, USB memory stick, an internet download, email attachment or from another computer.

Some viruses are relatively harmless and may merely display messages on the screen, others can be very damaging and destroy operating systems and data, putting the computer system completely out of action. Most computers are now sold already installed with virus protection software which will:

- establish a firewall to repel viruses

- check for existing viruses

- destroy known viruses

- check for damage to files on the hard disk

- repair damage to files on the hard disk where possible

This software should be run and updated regularly so that it can deal with the latest viruses.

precautions against viruses

There are a number of precautions which you can take against viruses:

- be wary of opening any unidentified email attachments which arrive

- use protective software to inspect any disk or memory stick received from an outside source before opening up any file saved onto it

- make sure that your protective software is up to date – very often they will update automatically over the internet

If your protective software announces that you have a virus, you should report it at once in your workplace and stop using your computer.

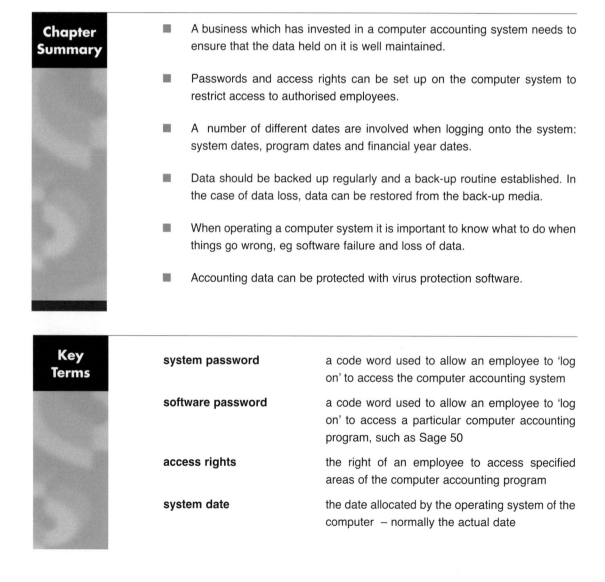

Chapter Summary

- A business which has invested in a computer accounting system needs to ensure that the data held on it is well maintained.

- Passwords and access rights can be set up on the computer system to restrict access to authorised employees.

- A number of different dates are involved when logging onto the system: system dates, program dates and financial year dates.

- Data should be backed up regularly and a back-up routine established. In the case of data loss, data can be restored from the back-up media.

- When operating a computer system it is important to know what to do when things go wrong, eg software failure and loss of data.

- Accounting data can be protected with virus protection software.

Key Terms

system password	a code word used to allow an employee to 'log on' to access the computer accounting system
software password	a code word used to allow an employee to 'log on' to access a particular computer accounting program, such as Sage 50
access rights	the right of an employee to access specified areas of the computer accounting program
system date	the date allocated by the operating system of the computer – normally the actual date

program date	the date which you can tell the computer accounting software to use as 'today's' date
financial year	the twelve month period used by the business to record its financial transactions
back-up	to copy the computer data onto a separate storage medium in order to ensure that the data is not lost
restore	to copy the back-up data back onto the computer when the original data has been lost or corrupted
corrupt data	data which has become unusable
virus	a computer program introduced into the computer system which then disrupts or destroys the operation of the system

Activities

2.1 Explain how passwords and access rights to accounting software help protect computer data.

2.2 Explain the difference between a system date and a program date used on a computer accounting program such as Sage.

2.3 Write down a suggested back-up policy for an office which runs a computer accounting system.

2.4 You are running a check on your computer accounting data at the end of the day before carrying out the back-up routine. The message appears on screen that a number of your data files have become corrupted. You normally back-up your data daily at the end of the day. Explain what you would do to rescue your data and bring the computer accounting records up to date.

2.5 You hear from a friend working for another business that their computer systems have had a catastrophic crash following infection by a virus which came in over the internet. Describe the measures you could take to safeguard against a similar catastrophe to your own systems.

3 Setting up the company in Sage

this chapter covers...

■ Setting up a computer accounting program for a business or other organisation will take some time, but as long as the correct data is entered in the correct format there should be no problem.

■ We will assume here that the organisation setting up the computer accounting program is a business. Sage software always calls a business a 'company' – so we will adopt that term.

■ The chapter introduces a Case Study business – Pronto Supplies Limited – which will be used throughout this book to show how computer accounting works.

■ There is plenty of help around when you are setting up accounts on the computer. In Sage, for example, there is the user guide, the 'Help' function, and on-screen step-by-step instruction procedures known as 'Wizards'.

■ The data that will have to be input includes:

- the 'company' details such as name and address, financial year and VAT status

- the customer details and any sales transactions already carried out

- the supplier details and any purchases transactions already carried out

- details of accounts for income and expenses, assets (items owned), liabilities (loans) and capital (money put in by the owner) – this is all contained in the nominal ledger

■ This chapter concentrates on setting up the company details. The other data – customer and supplier details and balances and the nominal ledger – will be covered in the next two chapters.

important note
AAT assessments will require the setting up of company details and financial year, together with the ability to set the software date (p26). Assistance can be given by the training provider because set-up does not form part of the standards, but it is useful for candidates to know how to enter set-up details.

WHERE ARE YOU STARTING FROM?

If you are reading this book you are likely to be in one of two situations:

1   You are in a real business and looking for guidance in setting up a computer accounting system.

2   You are a student in a training situation and will have the program already set up for you on a training centre network. You will be given exercises to practise the various functions of a computer accounting program.

In the first case – the real business – you may be starting from scratch and will have to go through the whole installation and set-up procedure. This is not at all difficult. The software itself will take you through the various steps.

In the second case – the training centre situation – the computer may already have accounting records on it, possibly another student's work. You will need to refer to your training provider on how to set up your data.

The Case Study which follows on the next page – Pronto Supplies Limited – assumes that you are in business setting up computer accounts for the first time using Sage software. It is important for your studies that you know how this is done, even if you may not carry out in the training centre all the procedures explained in the Case Study.

WHY SAGE AND WHICH SAGE?

Osborne Books (the publisher of this book) has chosen Sage software for this book for two very good reasons:

1   Sage software is widely used in business and is recognised as a user-friendly and reliable product.

2   Osborne Books has used Sage itself for over fifteen years and is well used to the way it works.

The Sage software used as a basis for this book is Sage 50 Accounts Professional 2012 (Version 18). The screens displayed in this book are taken from this version by kind permission of Sage (UK) Limited.

screen illustrations

It should be appreciated that some training centres and businesses may be using older and slightly different versions and so some of the screens may look slightly different. This does not matter however: using Sage is like driving different models of car – the controls may be located in slightly different places and the dashboard may not look exactly the same, but the controls are still there and they still do the same thing. So if the screens shown here look unfamiliar, examine them carefully and you will see that they will contain the same (or very similar) Sage icons and functions as the version you are using.

PRONTO SUPPLIES LIMITED:
SETTING UP THE COMPANY IN SAGE

the business

Pronto Supplies is a limited company run by Tom Cox who has worked as a computer consultant for over ten years. Pronto Supplies provides local businesses and other organisations with computer hardware, software and consumables needed in offices. It also provides consultancy for computer set-ups through its proprietor, Tom Cox. Pronto Supplies has eight employees in total. The business is situated on an industrial estate, at Unit 17 Severnvale Estate, Broadwater Road, Mereford, Wyvern, MR1 6TF.

the accounting system

Pronto Supplies Limited started business on 1 January 2013. The business is registered for VAT (ie it charges VAT on its sales) and after a month of using a manual accounting system Tom has decided to transfer the accounts to Sage 50 software and sign up for a year's telephone technical support. Tom has also decided to put his payroll onto the computer, but this will be run on a separate Sage program.

Tom has chosen Sage 50 because it will enable him to:

- record the invoices issued to his customers to whom he sells on credit

- pay his suppliers on the due date

- keep a record of his bank receipts and payments

- record his income and expenses, business assets and loans in a nominal ledger

In short he will have an integrated computer accounting package which will enable him to:

- record all his financial transactions

- print out reports

- manage his business finances

- save time (and money) in running his accounting system

getting started

Tom has decided to use just one machine in the office to run Sage and so he has bought a 'single user' package together with telephone technical support for a year.

He installs the program from his CD and uses the ActiveSetup Wizard to take him through the procedure.

Note

A Wizard is a series of dialogue boxes on the screen which take you step-by-step through a particular procedure. The ActiveSetup Wizard is one of a number of Wizards in Sage. Wizards generally appear automatically on screen when you need to carry out a complicated procedure.

The ActiveSetup Wizard takes Tom through a series of screens by which he can personalise Sage to his business. In the first he chooses to set up a new company as shown below.

ActiveSetup

Sage Accounts - Company Set-up

1 Welcome

Welcome to Sage 50 Accounts

Please select one of the following to set-up a new company in Sage 50 Accounts:

⊙ Set-up a new company

○ Use an existing company stored on your network

○ Restore data from a backup file

Your company will be created in the following location.

C:\DOCUMENTS AND SETTINGS\ALL USERS\APPLICATION DATA\SAGE\ACCOUNTS\20   change

Next he must enter his company details

ActiveSetup

Sage Accounts - Company Set-up

1 Welcome
2 Network Sharing
3 **Company Details**
4 Business Type
5 Financial Year
6 VAT
7 Currency
8 Confirm Details

Enter Company Details

Company Name :	Pronto Supplies Limited
Street 1 :	Unit 17 Severnvale Estate
Street 2 :	Broadwater Road
Town :	Mereford
County :	Wyvern
Post Code :	MR1 6TF
Country :	United Kingdom GB
Telephone Number :	01908 748071
Fax Number :	01908 748951
Email Address :	mail@prontosupplies.co.uk
Website Address :	www.prontosupplies.co.uk

As Pronto Supplies is a limited company, in the next screen Tom chooses the "Limited Company" option. The list of accounts will cover all his business needs such as sales, purchases, bank accounts and expenses.

ActiveSetup

Sage Accounts - Company Set-up

1. Welcome
2. Network Sharing
3. Company Details
4. **Business Type**
5. Financial Year
6. VAT
7. Currency
8. Confirm Details

Select Business ?

Select a type of business that most closely matches your own. If your business type is not listed, please consult your accountant.

- ○ Sole Trader
- ○ Partnership
- ◉ Limited Company
- ○ Charity
- ○ I don't want to setup based on a business type
- ○ I want to use a predefined business type:

Description
This creates nominal codes and Profit & Loss / Balance Sheet reports specifically designed for a Limited Company

[Browse]

Next he sets up his financial year start date: January 2013

1. Welcome
2. Network Sharing
3. Company Details
4. Business Type
5. **Financial Year**
6. VAT
7. Currency

Select Financial Year ?

Choose when your company financial year begins. If you are not sure when your financial year begins, please contact your accountant for guidance before you proceed any further.

Month   January

Year   2013

Financial year range

01 January 2013 - 31 December 2013

The next two screens require Tom to enter the business VAT details and the currency he trades in. Finally he must enter the serial number and activation key provided by Sage to activate the program.

1. Welcome
2. Network Sharing
3. Company Details
4. Business Type
5. Financial Year

Select VAT Details

Is your company VAT registered?   ◉ Yes   ○ No

Enter your VAT registration number   404 7106 52   ?

VAT Scheme   Standard VAT   ?

Enter your standard VAT rate %   20.00   ?

1. Welcome
2. Network Sharing
3. Company Details
4. Business Type

Select Currency ?

Select the currency your accounts will be prepared in.

If the currency is not shown in the list select Unlisted Currency.

Base Currency   Pound Sterling

Tom must now confirm the details he has entered.

Sage Accounts - Company Set-up

① Welcome	**Create**
② Network Sharing	You must confirm that the key details below are correct. Click Back to make changes or click Create to create your company.
③ Company Details	
④ Business Type	**What you have entered**
⑤ Financial Year	Share location: \\ACER9410\SAGE2012
⑥ VAT	Share this folder? Yes
⑦ Currency	Company Name: Pronto Supplies Limited
⑧ **Confirm Details**	Business Type: Limited Company
	Financial Year: 01 January 2013 - 31 December 2013
	VAT Scheme: Standard VAT
	Currency: Pound Sterling

Tom should now check his VAT codes. This is done by selecting CONFIGURATION from the SETTINGS menu. This shows the various tax codes used, eg T1 for standard rate transactions, T0 for zero-rated transactions (eg sales of books). The screen appears as follows . . .

Configuration Editor

Custom Fields		Dispute Reasons		Credit Control		Project
General	Chart of Accounts	Terms	**Tax Codes**	Account Status	Products	Fixe

Tax Codes

Sage 50 Accounts helps you to keep track of VAT with a comprehensive set of tax codes. These tax codes are set-up by default when you install the program, and you will not normally need to change any of the settings.

If you do need to modify any of the tax codes, you can do this below.

For more information on VAT and tax codes, visit the HM Revenue and Customs web site - just select "HM Revenue and Customs" from the WebLinks menu.

Code	Rate	In Use	EC Sales	EC Purchases	Description
T0	0.00	Y	N	N	Zero rated transactions
T1	20.00	Y	N	N	Standard rated transactions
T2	0.00	Y	N	N	Exempt transactions
T3	0.00	Y	N	N	
T4	0.00	Y	Y	N	Sales of goods to VAT registered customers ...
T5	5.00	Y	N	N	Lower Rate
T6	0.00	Y	N	N	

Edit

Tom can at any time check and amend if necessary his company details. This is done in COMPANY PREFERENCES which can also be found in the SETTINGS menu. This screen is illustrated on the next page.

There are a number of tabs, including 'Address'. The address entered here will automatically be printed by the program, as required, on business documents such as invoices and credit notes. Tom has the option to enter a different delivery address, but this is unlikely in his case, as all the deliveries from his suppliers will be made to his warehouse at Unit 17 Severnvale Estate. He decides not to bother with this option.

He also does not enter anything into the other tabs as he does not need these facilities at present.

The third tab 'Parameters' provides Tom with a number of options. Most of these he will not have to worry about at the moment.

Tom's COMPANY PREFERENCES screen appears as follows . . .

Company Preferences

VAT				Sage Pay	
Details	Labels	Parameters	Reporting	Accountant	Budgeting

Name	Pronto Supplies Limited
Street1	Unit 17 Severnvale Estate
Street2	Broadwater Road
Town	Mereford
County	Wyvern
Post Code	MR1 6TF
Country Code	United Kingdom GB
Telephone	01908 748071
Fax	01908 748951
Email	mail@prontosupplies.co.uk
Website	www.prontosupplies.co.uk
Credit Ref No	
DUNS Number	

Delivery Addresses...

HELP!

Tom now has his business details set up on the computer but he still has to install his account balances and get to know how the system works. Sage provides a number of facilities which help the user when he or she needs information: wizards, a user guide, and an on-screen Help function.

wizards

Wizards, as seen in the Case Study, help the user step-by-step through difficult procedures. We will encounter wizards in later chapters.

user guide

The Sage User Guide is a useful reference source. It can be accessed from within the program and printed if required. Less experienced users may find on-screen guidance more helpful.

on-screen Help

On-screen help can be accessed through either the HELP menu or by pressing the F1 function key. It works with three tabs, all of which will enable the user to access information. Look at the diagram below.

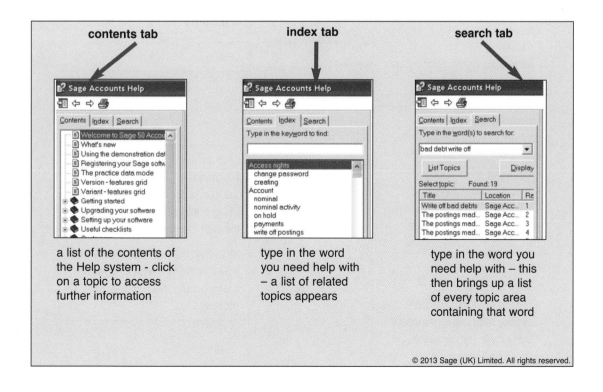

contents tab

a list of the contents of the Help system - click on a topic to access further information

index tab

type in the word you need help with – a list of related topics appears

search tab

type in the word you need help with – this then brings up a list of every topic area containing that word

TRANSFERRING DATA INTO SAGE

When a business first sets up a computer accounting system a substantial amount of data will need to be transferred onto the computer, even if the business is in its first week of trading. A summary of this data is shown in the diagram below.

The images shown in the diagram are the icons on the Sage desktop which represent the different operating areas of the program. As you can see they relate to the ledger structure of a manual bookkeeping system.

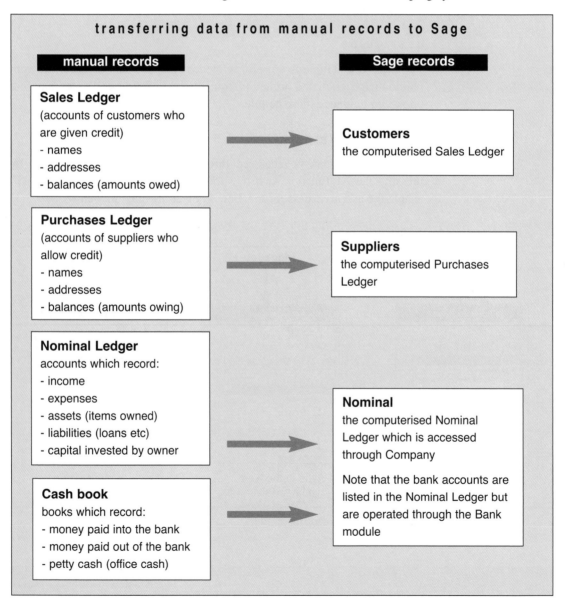

transferring data from manual records to Sage

manual records

Sage records

Sales Ledger
(accounts of customers who are given credit)
- names
- addresses
- balances (amounts owed)

Customers
the computerised Sales Ledger

Purchases Ledger
(accounts of suppliers who allow credit)
- names
- addresses
- balances (amounts owing)

Suppliers
the computerised Purchases Ledger

Nominal Ledger
accounts which record:
- income
- expenses
- assets (items owned)
- liabilities (loans etc)
- capital invested by owner

Nominal
the computerised Nominal Ledger which is accessed through Company

Note that the bank accounts are listed in the Nominal Ledger but are operated through the Bank module

Cash book
books which record:
- money paid into the bank
- money paid out of the bank
- petty cash (office cash)

Chapter Summary

- ■ A business setting up a Sage computer accounting program for the first time will have to enter the details of the company on-screen, for example

  - the program serial number and Activation Key code

  - the start date of the financial year of the business

  - the business VAT registration number and VAT Status (where applicable)

  - the business name and address

  - any passwords that are needed.

- ■ The business will also be required to enter the 'chart of accounts' that it requires – this is the list of Nominal accounts which will automatically be set up on the system.

- ■ The business can make use of the on-screen Wizard and other 'Help' functions in the set-up process. The index is the most useful of these.

- ■ The business will need to enter details and balances of its customers, suppliers and its Nominal Accounts (the other accounts). These are covered in the next two chapters.

Key Terms

Wizard	on-screen dialogue boxes in a Sage program which take you step-by-step through complex procedures
sales ledger	the accounts of customers to whom a business sells on credit - in Sage this part of the accounting system is known as 'Customers'
purchases ledger	the accounts of suppliers from whom a business buys on credit - in Sage this part of the accounting system is known as 'Suppliers'
nominal ledger	the remaining accounts in the accounting system which are not Customers or Suppliers, eg income, expenses, assets, liabilities – in Sage this is known as 'Nominal'
chart of accounts	the structure of the nominal accounts, which groups accounts into categories such as Sales, Purchases, Overheads . . . and so on

Activities

3.1 Describe the sources of assistance that are available to Alan Bramley who is setting up a Sage system for the first time.

3.2 Helen Egremont is setting up a Sage system for the first time. What details will have to be input before any account balances can be transferred?

3.3 James Greave has been trading for six months using a manual double-entry bookkeeping system. Into what part of a Sage system will the following ledgers be transferred?

(a) Sales Ledger

(b) Purchases Ledger

(c) Nominal Ledger

PRONTO SUPPLIES LIMITED INPUTTING TASK

important notes

1   This activity involves you in setting up a new company in Sage and inputting live data into the computer. If you are asked to do this, remember to Save your data and keep any printouts as you progress through subsequent tasks.

2   It may be that the Company has already been set up for you on the computer or that you have to carry out a 'Restore' operation to set up the company. If this is the case, you should ignore these two tasks.

Task 1

Set the program date as 31 January 2013. Set up the company details of Pronto Supplies Limited in Sage. The details are:

Address/contact	Unit 17 Severnvale Estate, Broadwater Road, Mereford, Wyvern, MR1 6TF.
	Tel 01908 748071, Fax 01908 748951
	Email mail@prontosupplies.co.uk
	www.prontosupplies.co.uk
Financial year start:	January 2013 (if not already input)
VAT Registration number	404 7106 52
Chart of Accounts:	General Business – Standard Accounts

Task 2

Check the business details in the first tab of COMPANY PREFERENCES in SETTINGS.

Now check that the Details tab in COMPANY PREFERENCES matches the screen on page 30. Make any amendments if you need to.

Reminder! Have you made a back-up?

4 Setting up records for customers and suppliers

this chapter covers...

■ The term 'Customers' is a word which in Sage means people to whom a business sells on credit. In other words, the goods or services are supplied straightaway and the customer is allowed to pay at a specified later date – often a month or more later. Another term for a credit customer is a 'receivable' (debtor).

■ A business keeps running accounts for the amounts owed by individual customers – much as a bank keeps accounts for its customers. The accounts are maintained by the business in the 'Sales Ledger'.

■ The term 'Suppliers' is a word which in Sage means people from whom a business buys on credit. In other words, the goods or services are supplied straightaway and the business is allowed to pay at a specified later date. Another term for a credit supplier is a 'payable' (creditor).

■ A business keeps running accounts for the amounts owed to individual suppliers. The accounts are maintained by the business in the 'Purchases Ledger'.

■ This chapter continues the Pronto Supplies Limited Case Study and shows how the business sets up its Customer and Supplier records on the computer.

■ When the accounts have been set up on the computer the business will need to input the amounts owed by Customers and owing to Suppliers.

■ The next step – dealt with in the next chapter – is to input the Nominal Ledger accounts. When this has been done, the set up is complete and the system will be ready for the input of transactions such as sales and purchases.

CASH AND CREDIT SALES

cash and credit – the difference

When businesses such as manufacturers, shops and travel agents sell their products, they will either get their money straightaway, or they will receive the money after an agreed time period. The first type of sale is a **cash sale**, the second is a **credit sale**. These can be defined further as:

cash sale
A sale of a product where the money is received straightaway – this can include payment in cash, or by cheque or by credit card and debit card. The word 'cash' means 'immediate' – it does not mean only notes and coins.

credit sale
A sale of a product where the sale is agreed and the goods or services are supplied but the buyer pays at a later date agreed at the time of the sale.

buying and selling for cash and on credit

Businesses are likely to get involved in cash and credit sales not only when they are selling their products but also when they are buying. Some goods and services will be bought for cash and some on credit. Buying and selling are just two sides of the same operation.

You will see from this that it is the nature of the business that will decide what type of sales and purchases it makes. A supermarket, for example, will sell almost entirely for cash – the cash and cheques and credit/debit card payments come in at the checkouts – and it will buy from its suppliers on credit and pay them later. It should therefore always have money in hand – which is a good situation to be in for a business.

SETTING UP CUSTOMER ACCOUNTS

accounting records for customers

Customers who buy from a business on credit are known as **receivables** (**debtors**) because they owe money to the business and the business will in due course 'receive' it.

The amounts owed by customers are recorded in individual customer accounts in the **Sales Ledger**. In double-entry terms these customer account balances are **debit balances**.

The total of all the customer (receivable/debtor) accounts in the Sales Ledger is recorded in an account known as **Debtors Control Account**. This is the total amount owing by the customers of a business.

accounting records for suppliers

When a business purchases goods and services from its suppliers on credit the suppliers are known as **payables** (**creditors**) because the business owes them money and has to 'pay' them.

The amounts owed to suppliers (payables/creditors) are recorded in individual supplier accounts in the **Purchases Ledger**. In double-entry terms these customer account balances are **credit balances**.

The total of all the supplier accounts in the Purchases Ledger is known as **Creditors Control Account**. This is the total amount owing to the suppliers of a business.

All this is summarised in the table set out below.

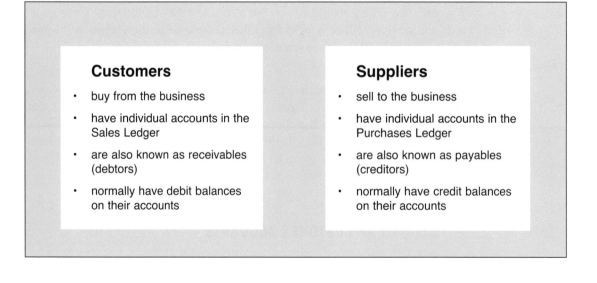

Customers

- buy from the business
- have individual accounts in the Sales Ledger
- are also known as receivables (debtors)
- normally have debit balances on their accounts

Suppliers

- sell to the business
- have individual accounts in the Purchases Ledger
- are also known as payables (creditors)
- normally have credit balances on their accounts

credit limits

When a business is opening a new account it will need to establish a credit limit. A **credit limit** is the maximum amount of credit a seller is willing to grant to a customer. For example if a credit limit of £5,000 is set up by the seller, the customer can owe up to £5,000 at any one time – for example two invoices of £2,500. A well-managed business will keep an eye on situations where a credit limit might be exceeded.

credit terms

The seller will need to establish its **terms** of trading with its customers and the customer will have to agree. The terms are normally set out on the invoice (the invoice is the document issued when the goods or services are sold and supplied). They include:

- **trade discount** given to the customer based on the selling price, for example a customer with a 30% trade discount will pay £70 for goods costing £100, ie £100 minus £30 (30% discount)

- the **payment terms** – the length of credit allowed to the customer, ie the number of days the customer is allowed to wait before paying up – this is commonly 30 days after the invoice date

- **settlement discount** (also known as **cash discount**) sometimes given to a customer who settles up early within a specified number of days, for example a 2.5% reduction for settlement within 7 days

day-to-day customer/supplier information

A business will need information on file relating to its day-to-day dealings with customers and suppliers. For example:

- the name and address of the customer

- telephone and fax numbers, email, and website address (if there is one)

- contact names

- credit limit, trade discount, payment terms and any settlement discount agreed

setting up the accounts in Sage

As you will see from the last three pages, there is a great deal of information that has to be input when setting up accounts for customers and suppliers on a computer accounting program such as Sage.

In the Case Study which follows on page 41 we will follow the steps taken by Pronto Supplies Limited in setting up its Customers and Suppliers records.

SETTING UP THE COMPUTER FILES

There are two methods in Sage for setting up new records for customers or suppliers. If, for example, you wanted to set up a new Customer account you could . . .

1 Go to the CUSTOMERS screen and click on NEW. You will be given a Wizard to take you through the procedure.

2 Go to the CUSTOMERS screen and click on RECORD. You will be given blank screens to complete, but with no Wizard guidance.

The Wizard screen is shown below and the second method is illustrated in the Case Study, as the process is very simple.

Whether you are using the Wizard or just setting up a new record through RECORD, you will need to have to hand all the customer details you have on file. These are the type of details covered earlier in this chapter.

customer and supplier reference codes

You will see from the Wizard screen shown above that you need to decide on a unique reference code for each customer and supplier account. This code can be letters, numbers, or a mixture of both. If letters are used they are often an abbreviation of the account name. This process, using both letters and numbers, will be illustrated in the Case Study.

customer and supplier record defaults

If you are setting up a number of customer and supplier accounts it is possible that the terms agreed – discounts and payment periods – will be the same for each customer or supplier account. To save you entering these in each and every account (which can take a lot of time!) you can establish a default set of terms which will apply to all accounts. These can be set up from the 'Terms' tab of the CONFIGURATION EDITOR in SETTINGS.

It is also important to establish the standard VAT rate to be used in transactions (currently 20%) and also the default account number used for sales to customers (usually account number 4000). This is carried out from the 'Record' tab in CUSTOMER DEFAULTS in SETTINGS. In the illustration below note the default VAT code (T1, 20%) and the 'Def. N/C' default Sales Account number 4000 (N/C stands for 'Nominal Code').

PRONTO SUPPLIES LIMITED: SETTING UP CUSTOMERS AND SUPPLIERS IN SAGE

Tom Cox at Pronto Supplies has decided to input his customer and supplier records into the computer first, and will then afterwards input the Nominal balances.

During the month of January Tom had set up accounts for customers and suppliers which at the end of the month (31 January) have balances as follows:

Customers   6 accounts in the Sales Ledger   Total now outstanding £29,534

Suppliers   3 accounts in the Purchases Ledger   Total now outstanding £18,750

Tom has kept the relevant financial documents – sales and purchase invoices and purchase order forms – in two separate files marked 'Credit Sales' and 'Credit Purchases'. The accounts are as follows:

customers

account reference	account name	amount outstanding (£)
JB001	John Butler & Associates	5,500.00
CH001	Charisma Design	2,400.00
CR001	Crowmatic Ltd	3,234.00
DB001	David Boossey	3,400.00
KD001	Kay Denz	6,500.00
LG001	L Garr & Co	8,500.00
Total	(Debtors Control Account)	29,534.00

suppliers

account reference	account name	amount outstanding (£)
DE001	Delco PLC	5,750.00
EL001	Electron Supplies	8,500.00
MA001	MacCity	4,500.00
Total	(Creditors Control Account)	18,750.00

entering the customer defaults

Tom sets his program date to 31 January 2013. He decides that he will save time by setting up his standard terms in the CONFIGURATION EDITOR in SETTINGS:

Payment due days	30 days
Terms of payment	Payment 30 days of invoice

He also checks his default VAT code (T1) and rate (20%) and Sales Account number (4000) in CUSTOMER DEFAULTS (reached through SETTINGS):

VAT rate	Standard rate of 20% (this is Tax Code T1)
Default nominal code	4000
	(Note that this is his computer hardware Sales Account, which accounts for most of his sales to customers; Tom will later allocate further separate sales account numbers for sales of computer software and computer consultancy services)

Tom decides not to set a default credit limit as this will vary from customer to customer and will be input with the individual customer details.

Note also that as Tom has not long been in business he does not allow **discounts** on his sales nor receive discounts on his purchases. These will be negotiated as time goes on.

entering customer details and opening balances

Tom will now enter the details and the opening balance for each customer. He does this by clicking on RECORD in CUSTOMERS. The first customer to input is John Butler & Associates. The information he wants to input (including the invoice issued in January) is as follows:

Account name	John Butler & Associates
Account reference	JB001
Address	24 Shaw Street Mereford MR4 6KJ
Contact name	John Butler

Telephone 01908 824342, Fax 01908 824295, Email mail@jbutler.co.uk www.jbutler.co.uk

Credit limit £10,000

Invoice reference 10013 for £5,500.00 issued on 05 01 13

Tom inputs the data on the 'Details' screen, checks the data and then Saves.

He now has to input the details of the invoice which he had issued on 5 January and which has not yet been paid. He does this by clicking the O/B button which brings up the screen shown on the next page. When prompted to Save the new record, Tom clicks 'Yes'.

The data Tom inputs into the above screen are:

Ref: the invoice number

Date: the date the invoice was issued

Type: the transaction was the issue of an invoice

Gross: the total amount of the invoice

Having saved this data, Tom will go to the CREDIT CONTROL screen and input the credit limit, the payment period and the terms, and tick the box marked 'Terms Agreed' and then Save again. Some of these details may already be on screen if Tom has used the CONFIGURATION EDITOR (see page 41).

Tom will now repeat this process with the other five customer records, checking carefully as he goes and saving each record as it is created.

entering supplier details and opening balances

Tom can now carry out the same process for supplier details and opening balances. He will first ensure that the Supplier Defaults in SETTINGS include T1 as the default tax code and 5000 as the default Nominal Account number.

He sets up his Supplier Accounts by clicking on RECORD in SUPPLIERS. The first supplier to input is Delco PLC. The information he wants to input (including the invoice issued by the supplier) is as follows:

Account name	Delco PLC
Account reference	DE001
Address	Delco House
	Otto Way
	New Milton
	SR1 6TF
Contact name	Nina Patel

Telephone 01722 295875, Fax 01722 295611, Email sales@delco.co.uk www.delco.co.uk

Credit limit granted £10,000, payment terms 30 days of invoice date

Invoice reference 4563 for £5,750.00 issued by Delco PLC on 04 01 13

Tom will now input the supplier details and opening balances, starting with Delco PLC. The completed Delco PLC details screen is shown below.

Supplier - Delco PLC

Details | Defaults | Credit Control | Purchases | Orders | Graphs | Activity | Bank | Communications | Memo

Account Details

A/C:	DE001
Company name:	Delco PLC
Balance:	5750.00

Registered address

Street1	Delco House
Street2	Otto Way
Town	New Milton
County	
Post Code	SR1 6TF
Country	United Kingdom GB
VAT Number	

Addresses & Contacts...

Contact information

Contact name:	Nina Patel
Trade contact:	
Telephone:	01722 295875
Telephone 2:	
Fax:	01722 295611
Website:	www.delco.co.uk

Email Settings

| Email: | sales@delco.co.uk |

I send letters, remittances, etc to this supplier via email ☐

I send orders to this supplier via Transaction Email ☐

Tom will now input the credit limit and payment terms agreed on the CREDIT CONTROL screen of the Supplier record. These are not held as defaults because they may well vary from supplier to supplier. The 'Terms Agreed' box will also be ticked.

Supplier - Delco PLC

| Details | Defaults | Credit Control | Purchases | Orders | Graphs | Activity | Bank | Communications | Memo |

Terms

Credit Limit	10000.00
Settlement Due	0 Days
Sett.Discount	0.00
Payment Due	0 Days
Trading Terms Text	30 days of invoice date
Credit Reference	
Bureau	
Priority Supplier	☐
Credit Position	Good
Account status	0 Open
DUNS Number	

Credit Review

A/C Opened	31/01/2013
Last Credit Review	/ /
Next Credit Review	/ /
Application Date	/ /
Date Received	/ /
Memo:	

Tom will now repeat this process with the other supplier records, checking carefully as he goes and saving each record as it is created.

the final checks

Tom will need to ensure that his input is correct and that the customer and supplier accounts are accurate.

Tom will now check the individual account entries by comparing his original paper-based records with reports printed from CUSTOMERS and SUPPLIERS.

The input of customer invoices can be checked from the Day Books: Customer Invoices (Summary) report, which can be printed from the list of reports accessed through the REPORTS icon on the CUSTOMERS menu bar.

Pronto Supplies Limited
Day Books: Customer Invoices (Summary)

Customer From:
Customer To: ZZZZZZZZ

Transaction From: 1
Transaction To: 99,999,999

Tran No.	Items	Tp	Date	A/C Ref	Inv Ref	Details	Net Amount	Tax Amount	Gross Amount
1	1	SI	05/01/2013	JB001	10013	Opening Balance	5,500.00	0.00	5,500.00
2	1	SI	05/01/2013	CH001	10014	Opening Balance	2,400.00	0.00	2,400.00
3	1	SI	09/01/2013	CR001	10015	Opening Balance	3,234.00	0.00	3,234.00
4	1	SI	10/01/2013	DB001	10016	Opening Balance	3,400.00	0.00	3,400.00
5	1	SI	10/01/2013	KD001	10017	Opening Balance	6,500.00	0.00	6,500.00
6	1	SI	17/01/2013	LG001	10019	Opening Balance	8,500.00	0.00	8,500.00
						Totals:	29,534.00	0.00	29,534.00

The input of supplier invoices can be checked from the Day Books: Supplier Invoices (Summary) report accessed through REPORTS on the SUPPLIERS menu bar.

Pronto Supplies Limited
Day Books: Supplier Invoices (Summary)

Date From:	01/01/1980					Supplier From:		
Date To:	31/12/2019					Supplier To:	ZZZZZZZZ	
Transaction From:	1							
Transaction To:	99,999,999							

Tran No.	Item	Type	Date	A/C Ref	Inv Ref	Details	Net Amount	Tax Amount	Gross Amount
7	1	PI	04/01/2013	DE001	4563	Opening Balance	5,750.00	0.00	5,750.00
8	1	PI	05/01/2013	EL001	8122	Opening Balance	8,500.00	0.00	8,500.00
9	1	PI	09/01/2013	MA001	9252	Opening Balance	4,500.00	0.00	4,500.00
						Totals	18,750.00	0.00	18,750.00

Lastly Tom will print out a **trial balance**. He does this by clicking on COMPANY on the vertical toolbar, then FINANCIALS in the LINKS section above and finally the TRIAL icon on the horizontal toolbar. In the PERIOD box in CRITERIA he chooses 1 January 2013. A trial balance is a list of the account balances of the company. It shows the control (total) accounts as follows.

Debtors control account   £29,534 (the total of the customer invoices)

Creditors control account   £18,750 (the total of the supplier invoices)

The Suspense Account has been created automatically and shows the arithmetic difference (£10,784) between the two control accounts. It is put in automatically by the system to make the two columns balance.

Pronto Supplies Limited
Period Trial Balance

To Period: Month 1, January 2013

N/C	Name	Debit	Credit
1100	Debtors Control Account	29,534.00	
2100	Creditors Control Account		18,750.00
9998	Suspense Account		10,784.00
	Totals:	29,534.00	29,534.00

conclusion

The Customer and Supplier records are now installed and their account balances summarised in the two Control 'total' Accounts.

The trial balance is far from complete, however, and Tom's next task will be to input the Nominal Ledger balances – eg income received, expenses paid, loans, items purchased. When these items have all been entered the trial balance should 'balance' – the two columns will have the same total and the Suspense Account will disappear. This will be dealt with in the next chapter.

AMENDING RECORDS

As well as setting up customer and supplier records, an organisation operating a computer accounting system will from time-to-time need to amend its records. For example amending records:

■ to take account of changes of address, contact names, terms of supply

■ by indicating that the account is no longer active

■ by deleting the account (if the system allows you to – see next page)

amending records in Sage

The procedures in Sage are very straightforward:

■ select either CUSTOMERS or SUPPLIERS as appropriate

■ highlight the record that needs amending, click RECORD and go to the

 - DETAILS screen (for customer or supplier details) or

 - CREDIT CONTROL screen (for terms of supply, eg credit limit)

■ make the necessary change on screen

■ SAVE

In the following example, the name of a customer contact at L Garr & Co has been changed from Ted Nigmer to Win Norberry.

In the example below, the credit limit of £10,000 given to customer John Butler & Associates has been increased to £15,000.

'closing' a customer or supplier account

The question may well arise "What should we do if a customer has ceased trading, or if we no longer use a particular supplier?" The logical answer is to close the account.

Sage does not allow you to **delete** an account when there are transactions recorded on it, even if the balance is nil. Instead you should **amend** the name of the account on the Customer or Supplier Record to something anonymous like 'Closed Account' so that it cannot be used again.

If, on the other hand, the account has no transactions on it (eg it may have been opened and not used), it may be closed by clicking on the Delete button at the bottom of the DETAILS tab of the record (see below).

<table>
<tr><td rowspan="9">**Chapter Summary**</td></tr>
</table>

Chapter Summary

- Businesses buy and sell products either on a cash basis (immediate payment) or on credit (payment made later).

- The accounting records for selling on credit comprise the accounts of customers (receivables/debtors) contained in the Sales Ledger.

- The accounting records for buying on credit comprise the accounts of suppliers (payables/creditors) contained in the Purchases Ledger.

- A business will also have to agree the terms of trading with a customer – the credit limit, the level of discount and the payment period it allows.

- In the Sage accounting system the Sales Ledger is known as 'Customers' and the Purchases Ledger as 'Suppliers'.

- Setting up Customer and Supplier records in Sage involves the input of details such as names, addresses and outstanding financial transactions.

- Records set up in this way should be carefully checked against printed out reports such as the Day Book Report and the trial balance.

- Customer and Supplier records in Sage can also be amended or deleted (where allowable) as required.

Key Terms

cash sale	a sale where payment is immediate
credit sale	a sale where payment follows after an agreed period of time
receivables (debtors)	customers who owe money to a business
payables (creditors)	suppliers who are owed money by a business
debtors control account	the total of the balances of debtors' accounts
creditors control account	the total of the balances of creditors' accounts
credit terms	discounts and extended payment periods allowed to customers who make purchases
defaults	sets of data on the computer which are automatically applied

Activities

4.1 A cash sale is a sale where the only means of payment is notes and coins. True or false?

4.2 Define:

(a) a receivable (debtor)

(b) a payable (creditor)

4.3 What books of the business (ledgers) contain:

(a) receivables' (debtors') accounts

(b) payables' (creditors') accounts

4.4 What is shown in:

(a) Sales Ledger Control Account (known in Sage as Debtors Control Account)

(b) Purchases Ledger Control Account (known in Sage as Creditors Control Account)

4.5 What is the difference between a trade discount and a settlement discount?

4.6 What report shows the debit and credit balances of the accounts in an accounting system?

4.7 There are two important pieces of information (excluding financial transactions) that are missing from the computer-held customer details shown below.

What are they, and why are they important?

Account name   John Butler & Associates

Address   24 Shaw Street
Mereford
MR4 6KJ

Contact name   John Butler

Telephone 01908 824342, Fax 01908 824295, Email mail@jbutler.co.uk
www.jbutler.co.uk

4.8 Can you delete a customer or supplier record in Sage if you cease to deal with the customer or supplier?

PRONTO SUPPLIES INPUTTING TASKS

warning note!

This activity involves you in setting up Customer and Supplier records in Sage and inputting live data into the computer.

Ensure that you have changed your program date to 31 January 2013 in SETTINGS.

Also check that the Customer and Supplier Defaults are set to Nominal accounts 4000 and 5000 respectively. The default tax code should be T1 (standard rate). The Customer Defaults can also be set up for payment due days as 30 days and terms of payment 30 days of invoice.

Task 1

Enter the customer details into the Customers screens as indicated in the Case Study.

The six customer records are as follows:

JB001	**John Butler & Associates**
	24 Shaw Street
	Mereford
	MR4 6KJ

Contact name: John Butler

Telephone 01908 824342, Fax 01908 824295, Email mail@jbutler.co.uk

www.jbutler.co.uk

Credit limit £10,000

Invoice 10013 issued, 05 01 13, £5,500.00

CH001	**Charisma Design**
	36 Dingle Road
	Mereford
	MR2 8GF

Contact name: Lindsay Foster

Telephone 01908 345287, Fax 01908 345983, Email mail@charisma.co.uk

www.charisma.co.uk

Credit limit £5,000

Invoice 10014 issued, 05 01 13, £2,400.00

CR001   **Crowmatic Ltd**
             Unit 12 Severnside Estate
             Mereford
             MR3 6FD
Contact name: John Crow
Telephone 01908 674237, Fax 01908 674345, Email mail@crowmatic.co.uk
www.crowmatic.co.uk
Credit limit £5,000
Invoice 10015 issued, 09 01 13, £3,234.00

DB001   **David Boossey**
             17 Harebell Road
             Mereford Green
             MR6 4NB
Contact name: David Boossey
Telephone 01908 333981, Fax 01908 333761, Email dboossey@swoopwing.com
Credit limit £5,000
Invoice 10016 issued, 10 01 13, £3,400.00

KD001   **Kay Denz**
             The Stables
             Martley Hillside
             MR6 4FV
Contact name: Kay Denz
Telephone 01908 624945, Fax 01908 624945, Email kdenz@centra.com
Credit limit £10,000
Invoice 10017 issued,10 01 13, £6,500.00

LG001   **L Garr & Co**
             17 Broadheath Chambers
             Stourminster
             ST1 6MX
Contact name: Ted Nigmer
Telephone 01621 333691, Fax 01621 333982, Email mail@lgarr.co.uk
www.lgarr.co.uk
Credit limit £15,000
Invoice 10019 issued, 17 01 13, £8,500.00

Task 2

Enter the supplier details into the Suppliers screens as indicated in the Case Study.

The three supplier records are as follows:

DE001   Delco PLC

Delco House

Otto Way

New Milton

SR1 6TF

Contact name: Nina Patel

Telephone 01722 295875, Fax 01722 295611, Email sales@delco.co.uk

www.delco.co.uk

Credit limit £10,000, payment period 30 days.

Invoice 4563 issued, 04 01 13, £5,750.00

EL001   Electron Supplies

17 Maxim Way

Manchester

M1 5TF

Contact name: Jon Summers

Telephone 0161 6282151, Fax 0161 628161, Email sales@electronsupplies.co.uk

www.electronsupplies.co.uk

Credit limit £15,000, payment period 30 days.

Invoice 8122 issued 05 01 13, £8,500.00

MA001   MacCity

Unit 15 Elmwood Trading Estate

RoughWay

RM2 9TG

Contact name: Josh Masters

Telephone 01899 949233, Fax 01899 949331, Email sales@maccity.co.uk

www.maccity.co.uk

Credit limit £10,000, payment period 30 days.

Invoice 9252 issued 09 01 13, £4,500.00

Task 3

Print out a Day Books: Customer Invoices (Summary) report for the new Customer accounts and check and agree the amounts you have input. Check it against the printout on page 199.

Task 4

Print out a Day Books: Supplier Invoices (Summary) report for the new Supplier accounts and check and agree the amounts you have input. Check it against the printout on page 199.

Task 5

Print out a trial balance for January 2013 (by selecting Period 1. January 2013 in the Criteria screen) and check that the Debtors and Creditors Control account balances agree with the figures on page 47 and the totals shown on the Day Book reports produced in Tasks 3 and 4.

Task 6

At the end of January Ted Nigmer, who is your named contact at L Garr & Co, retires. He has been replaced by Win Norberry. You are asked to amend the customer details as appropriate.

Task 7

At the end of January, Tom of Pronto Supplies has had discussions with a good customer, J Butler & Associates, and has agreed to amend their credit limit to £15,000. You are asked to amend the customer record as appropriate.

Reminder! Have you made a back-up?

5 Setting up the nominal ledger

this chapter covers...

- In the last two chapters we have set up the company in Sage and entered details of Customers and Suppliers. All that remains to be done is to set up the Nominal Ledger on the computer.

- The Nominal Ledger contains all the other accounts in the accounting system:

    - income accounts, including Sales

    - purchases accounts for goods that the company trades in

    - expenses and overheads accounts

    - asset accounts (for items the business owns)

    - liability accounts (for items the business owes)

    - capital accounts (the investment of the business owner)

- The Nominal Ledger lists the bank accounts of the business, but they are operated through a separate BANK module, just as in a manual accounting system the bank accounts are recorded in a Cash Book, kept separately from the Nominal Ledger accounts.

- The accounts in the Nominal Ledger are set up in Sage using the structure of a 'Chart of Accounts' provided by the program. This allocates suitable reference numbers to the various accounts which are grouped in categories (eg expenses, assets, liabilities) so that the computer program knows where to find them in the system and can then provide suitable reports to management.

- One of the reports produced by the computer is the trial balance, which lists the nominal account balances in two balancing columns. When the balances of all the nominal accounts have been entered on the computer, the two columns should balance and the Suspense Account (which records any difference) should disappear.

NOMINAL ACCOUNTS

nominal accounts

An account in an accounting system records financial transactions and provides a running balance of what is left in the account at the end of each day. The **nominal ledger** accounts in any accounting system are the accounts which are not Customer accounts (sales ledger) or Supplier accounts (purchases ledger). The nominal accounts record:

- income – eg sales, rent received
- expenses – eg wages, advertising
- assets – items that a business owns or amounts that it is owed
- liabilities – money that a business owes, eg loans or creditors
- capital – money invested by the owner(s) and profits made

bank accounts

In a manual accounting system the bank accounts are kept in a separate Cash Book and are not strictly speaking part of the Nominal Ledger. In Sage the bank accounts of the business are *listed* in NOMINAL, but they are *operated* through a separate BANK module.

the default Nominal accounts

When Tom in the Case Study set up his company he chose the set of nominal accounts automatically provided by the Sage program.

If you click on the COMPANY button in the Sage opening screen the accounts are to be found in the NOMINAL opening screen (see below). You can scroll down this screen to see the whole list (summarised on the next page).

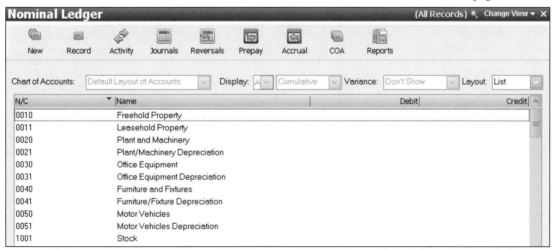

Nominal Account List

0010	Freehold Property
0011	Leasehold Property
0020	Plant and Machinery
0021	Plant/Machinery Depreciation
0030	Office Equipment
0031	Office Equipment Depreciation
0040	Furniture and Fixtures
0041	Furniture/Fixture Dpn
0050	Motor Vehicles
0051	Motor Vehicles Depreciation
1001	Stock
1002	Work in Progress
1003	Finished Goods
1004	Raw materials
1100	Debtors Control Account
1101	Sundry Debtors
1102	Other Debtors
1103	Prepayments
1104	Inter-company Debtors
1105	Provision for Credit Notes
1106	Provision for Doubtful Debts
1200	Bank Current Account
1210	Bank Deposit Account
1220	Building Society Account
1230	Petty Cash
1235	Cash Register
1240	Company Credit Card
1250	Credit Card Receipts
2100	Creditors Control Account
2101	Sundry Creditors
2102	Other Creditors
2109	Accruals
2200	Sales Tax Control Account
2201	Purchase Tax Control Acc.
2202	VAT Liability
2204	Manual Adjustments
2210	P.A.Y.E.
2211	National Insurance
2220	Net Wages
2230	Pension Fund
2300	Loans
2310	Hire Purchase
2320	Corporation Tax
2330	Mortgages
3000	Ordinary Shares
3010	Preference Shares
3060	Directors Loan Acc (Dir 1)
3061	Directors Loan Acc (Dir 2)
3100	Reserves
3101	Undistributed Reserves
3200	Profit and Loss Account
4000	Sales Type A
4001	Sales Type B
4002	Sales Type C
4009	Discounts Allowed
4010	Mgmt Charges Receivable

4099	Flat Rate – Benefit/Cost
4100	Sales Type D
4101	Sales Type E
4200	Sales of Assets
4400	Credit Charges (Late P'ments)
4900	Miscellaneous Income
4901	Royalties Received
4902	Commissions Received
4903	Insurance Claims
4904	Rent Income
4905	Distribution and Carriage
5000	Materials Purchased
5001	Materials Imported
5002	Miscellaneous Purchases
5003	Packaging
5009	Discounts Taken
5100	Carriage
5101	Import Duty
5102	Transport Insurance
5200	Opening Stock
5201	Closing Stock
6000	Productive Labour
6001	Cost of Sales Labour
6002	Sub-Contractors
6100	Sales Commissions
6200	Sales Promotions
6201	Advertising
6202	Gifts and Samples
6203	P.R.(Literature & Brochures)
6900	Miscellaneous Expenses
7000	Gross Wages
7001	Directors Salaries
7002	Directors Remuneration
7003	Staff Salaries
7004	Wages-Regular
7005	Wages-Casual
7006	Employers N.I.
7007	Employers Pensions
7008	Recruitment Expenses
7009	Adjustments
7010	SSP Reclaimed
7011	SMP Reclaimed
7012	Employers NI (Directors)
7100	Rent
7102	Water Rates
7103	General Rates
7104	Premises Insurance
7200	Electricity
7201	Gas
7202	Oil
7203	Other Heating Costs
7300	Vehicle Fuel
7301	Vehicle Repairs & Servicing
7302	Vehicle Licences
7303	Vehicle Insurance
7304	Misc Motor Expenses
7305	Congestion Charges
7306	Mileage Claims
7350	Scale Charges

7400	Travelling
7401	Car Hire
7402	Hotels
7403	U.K. Entertainment
7404	Overseas Entertainment
7405	Overseas Travelling
7406	Subsistence
7500	Printing
7501	Postage and Carriage
7502	Office Stationery
7503	Books etc
7550	Telephone and Fax
7551	Internet Charges
7552	Computers and Software
7553	Mobile Charges
7600	Legal Fees
7601	Audit Fees
7602	Accountancy Fees
7603	Consultancy Fees
7604	Professional Fees
7605	Mgt Charges Payable
7606	Software Subscriptions
7700	Equipment Hire
7701	Office Machine Maintenance
7702	Equipment Leasing
7703	Leasing Costs
7800	Repairs and Renewals
7801	Cleaning
7802	Laundry
7803	Premises Expenses
7900	Bank Interest Paid
7901	Bank Charges
7902	Currency Charges
7903	Loan Interest Paid
7904	H.P. Interest
7905	Credit Charges
7906	Exchange Rate Variance
7907	Other Interest Charges
7908	Factoring Charges
8000	Depreciation
8001	Plant/Machinery Depreciation
8002	Furniture/Fitting Depreciation
8003	Vehicle Depreciation
8004	Office Equipment Dpn
8100	Bad Debt Write Off
8102	Bad Debt Provision
8200	Donations
8201	Subscriptions
8202	Clothing Costs
8203	Training Costs
8204	Insurance
8205	Refreshments
8206	Cash Register Discrepancies
8250	Sundry Expenses
9001	Taxation
9998	Suspense Account
9999	Mispostings Account

CHART OF ACCOUNTS

If you look at the nominal account list you will see that a four digit code is given to each nominal account in the nominal ledger. These account number codes range from 0010 to 9999. Tom is very unlikely to use all these accounts and may even want to change some.

What is important, however, is that Tom – or any user of Sage – must appreciate that these accounts are organised into categories by account number. These categories are set out in the **chart of accounts.** They can be accessed in the Nominal Ledger by clicking on the COA (chart of accounts) icon and then EDIT . . .

The left hand panel shows the **categories** of account, eg Sales, Purchases. If you click on a category you will see the ranges of accounts and account numbers covered by that category displayed in the right-hand panel.

In this case the Sales category has been selected and the types of Sales listed on the right. This panel tells you that all Product Sales should have an account number between 4000 and 4099. When you set up the Customer records in the last chapter you chose 4000 as the default number (see page 41) for sales to customers.

But if you wanted to categorise customer sales (by area or type of product, for example) you could choose to have three accounts running for Product Sales: 4000 Sales Type A, 4001 Sales Type B, 4002 Sales Type C.

reports from Nominal

The Sage Nominal accounts are used as the basis for a number of computer-generated management reports telling the owner about subjects such as the profit and the value of the business. If accounts get into the wrong category, the reports will also be wrong.

a summary of categories

It may be that a new business will adopt all the default nominal accounts (see list on page 58) because it does not need any others, but if a new account has to be set up it is critical that the new account is in the right category. The business owner will therefore need to understand what the categories mean and what they include.

The nominal categories and account number ranges are:

Sales	4000 - 4999	income from sales of goods or services
Purchases	5000 - 5299	items bought to produce goods to sell
Direct Expenses	6000 - 6999	expenses directly related to producing goods
Overheads	7000 - 8299	expenses the business has to pay anyway
Taxation	9001 - 9001	corporation tax due on company profits

*These are used to produce the **income statement (profit and loss account)** which shows what profit (or loss) the business has made.*

Fixed Assets	0010 - 0059	items bought to keep in the business long-term
Current Assets	1000 - 1250	items owned by the business in the short-term
Current Liabilities	2100 - 2299	items owed by the business in the short-term
Long Term Liabilities	2300 - 2399	items owed by the business in the long-term
Capital & Reserves	3000 - 3299	the financial investment of the owner(s)

*These are used to produce the **statement of financial position (balance sheet)** which gives an idea of the value of the business. and shows the owner what is represented by the capital investment (the money put in by the owner).*

*Note that **Fixed Assets** are also known by the international term of **Non-current Assets**.*

We will now put this theory into practice with a continuation of the Pronto Supplies Limited Case Study.

Case Study

PRONTO SUPPLIES LIMITED: SETTING UP THE NOMINAL ACCOUNTS

Pronto Supplies Limited was set up in January 2013 and during that month operated a **manual** bookkeeping system using hand-written double-entry ledger accounts.

It was a busy month for Tom Cox . . .

financing	Tom paid £75,000 into the bank as ordinary share capital to start up the limited company business.
	Tom also raised a £35,000 business loan from the bank.

assets   The finance raised enabled Tom to buy:

office computers	£35,000
office equipment	£15,000
furniture for the office	£25,000

purchases   Tom bought in a substantial amount of stock during January for £69,100.

All of this stock was for resale by Pronto Supplies Limited.

sales   Tom divided his sales into three types:

Computer hardware sales
Computer software sales
Computer consultancy

overheads   Tom also had to pay fixed expenses including:

Wages	£16,230
Advertising	£12,400
Rent	£4,500
Rates	£450
Electricity	£150
Stationery	£175
Telephone	£275

Pronto Supplies Trial Balance

Tom at the end of January listed all the balances of his accounts in two columns, using a spreadsheet. This is his **trial balance** and will form the basis of the entries to the Sage system. The columns are headed up Debit (Dr) and Credit (Cr) and they have the same total. In double-entry bookkeeping each debit entry in the accounts is mirrored by a credit entry. If the bookkeeping is correct, the total of debits should be the same as the total of the credits. The spreadsheet is shown below. Note that:

- **debits** = assets and expenses   **credits** = liabilities, capital and income

- the control (total) account for debtors (receivables) shows the total amount owed by all Tom's customers; it is a debit balance because it is money owed to the business

- the control (total) account for creditors (payables) shows the total amount owed by Tom to his suppliers: it is a credit balance because it is money owed by the business

- Tom is registered with HM Revenue & Customs for Value Added Tax (VAT). This means that he has to quote his registration number on all his documents and also

    - charge VAT on his sales – this is due to HM Revenue & Customs and so is a credit balance – Sales tax control account

    - reclaim VAT on what he has bought – this is due from HM Revenue & Customs and so is a debit balance – Purchase tax control account

	A	B	C	D	E	F
1	TRIAL BALANCE		Dr	Cr		
2						
3	Plant and machinery		35000			
4	Office equipment		15000			
5	Furniture and fixtures		25000			
6	Debtors control account		29534			
7	Bank current account		14656			
8	Creditors control account			18750		
9	Sales tax control account			17920		
10	Purchase tax control account		26600			
11	Loans			35000		
12	Ordinary shares			75000		
13	Computer hardware sales			85000		
14	Computer software sales			15000		
15	Computer consultancy sales			2400		
16	Materials purchased		69100			
17	Advertising		12400			
18	Gross wages		16230			
19	Rent		4500			
20	General rates		450			
21	Electricity		150			
22	Office stationery		175			
23	Telephone		275			
24						
25	Total		249070	249070		

inputting the accounts into Sage Nominal

The date is 31 January 2013.

Tom uses his trial balance as the source document for inputting his nominal account balances. The procedure he adopts is:

1 He clicks on the COMPANY button on the vertical toolbar and examines the Nominal Accounts list which appears on the Nominal Ledger screen. He allocates the accounts in his existing books with computer account numbers as follows:

Plant and machinery	0020
Office equipment	0030
Furniture and fixtures	0040
Debtors control account	1100
Bank current account	1200
Creditors control account	2100
Sales tax control account	2200
Purchase tax control account	2201
Loans	2300
Ordinary Shares	3000
Sales type A	4000
Sales type B	4001
Sales type C	4002
Materials purchased	5000
Advertising	6201
Gross wages	7000
Rent	7100
General rates	7103
Electricity	7200
Office stationery	7502
Telephone and fax	7550

Note: Earlier versions of Sage used nominal codes 7502 and 7504 respectively for Telephone and Office stationery.

2 Tom scrolls down the screen and clicks on all the accounts that he is going to need – they then show as selected.

But – importantly – he does not click on the following two accounts:

Debtors Control Account – the total of the Customers' accounts

Creditors Control Account – the total of the Suppliers' accounts

This is because he has already input the debtors' (Customers') and creditors' (Suppliers') balances (see the last chapter). If he inputs these totals now they will be entered into the computer twice and cause havoc with the accounting records!

The NOMINAL screen is shown at the top of the next page.

3   Tom is now ready to input the balances of these accounts. To do this he will

- Select the RECORD icon which will bring up a RECORD window.

- Click on O/B on the balance box which asks him to enter the date (31/01/2013) and the balance which must go in the correct box: debits on the left, credits on the right. He should ignore the 'ref' box. The first account entry will look like the one shown left.

This record should then be saved.

Tom should repeat this for all the selected accounts (using the Next button to move to the next one), making sure that he is saving all the data as he goes along.

checking the input – the trial balance

Tom needs to check that what he has input is accurate. He needs to check his original list of balances – his trial balance (see page 62) – against the computer trial balance.

The trial balance is produced through FINANCIALS by clicking on the TRIAL icon. The printout produced is shown on the next page.

Pronto Supplies Limited
Period Trial Balance

To Period: Month 1, January 2013

N/C	Name	Debit	Credit
0020	Plant and Machinery	35,000.00	
0030	Office Equipment	15,000.00	
0040	Furniture and Fixtures	25,000.00	
1100	Debtors Control Account	29,534.00	
1200	Bank Current Account	14,656.00	
2100	Creditors Control Account		18,750.00
2200	Sales Tax Control Account		17,920.00
2201	Purchase Tax Control Account	26,600.00	
2300	Loans		35,000.00
3000	Ordinary Shares		75,000.00
4000	Sales Type A		85,000.00
4001	Sales Type B		15,000.00
4002	Sales Type C		2,400.00
5000	Materials Purchased	69,100.00	
6201	Advertising	12,400.00	
7000	Gross Wages	16,230.00	
7100	Rent	4,500.00	
7103	General Rates	450.00	
7200	Electricity	150.00	
7502	Office Stationery	175.00	
7550	Telephone and Fax	275.00	
	Totals:	249,070.00	249,070.00

Is the input accurate? Yes, because all the figures agree with the original trial balance figures and they are all in the correct column. The totals also agree.

You will see that the Suspense Account which the system created in the last chapter (see page 52) has now disappeared because the total of the debits now equals the total of the credits, as on Tom's spreadsheet shown on page 62.

Tom is now ready to input February's transactions – new sales invoices, new purchase invoices and payments in and out of the bank. These will be dealt with in the chapters that follow.

CHANGING NOMINAL ACCOUNT NAMES

It is possible to change the names of accounts in the Nominal Ledger if they do not fit in with the nature of your business. If, for example, you run a travel agency your Nominal Account names may be very different from the names used by an insurance broker.

The important point to remember is that if you change your account names they must fit in with the categories in the Chart of Accounts. You should not, for example, include an Office Rent Paid Account in the Purchases category. Much of this should be common sense.

adding new nominal accounts

Accounts can be added to the Nominal Ledger. Again, care should be taken to ensure that any new account fits into the Chart of Accounts structure (see page 59).

In the Case Study continuation below, Tom changes the names of his Sales accounts to reflect more accurately what is going on in his business. Tom also plans to offer a computer helpline to customers and so decides to add this to his sales accounts.

<table>
<tr><td>**Case Study**</td><td></td></tr>
</table>

PRONTO SUPPLIES LIMITED: CHANGING NOMINAL ACCOUNT NAMES

Tom looks at his Trial Balance (see page 65) and realises that his Sales accounts are named 'Type A' and 'Type B' and Type C'. This does not really tell him much about what he is actually selling, so he decides that he will change the names as follows:

account number	old name	new name
4000	Sales Type A	Computer hardware sales
4001	Sales Type B	Computer software sales
4002	Sales Type C	Computer consultancy

He selects the three accounts in the NOMINAL list screen, goes to RECORD in NOMINAL and overwrites the old name in the name box for each account and Saves. The amended screen for Account 4000 (Computer hardware sales) is shown below.

To add a new Nominal Account, Tom clicks RECORD and types 4003 into the N/C box. Sage recognises this as a New Account. Tom enters 'Computer helpline' in the account name box. There is no opening balance so Tom saves the new record. The new account now appears in the nominal list.

Tom now prints a Nominal List from REPORTS in NOMINAL LEDGER. This shows all the accounts available to him including his new customised accounts.

Pronto Supplies Limited
Nominal List

N/C From:
N/C To: 99999999

N/C	Name
0010	Freehold Property
0011	Leasehold Property
0020	Plant and Machinery
0021	Plant/Machinery Depreciation
0030	Office Equipment
0031	Office Equipment Depreciation
0040	Furniture and Fixtures
0041	Furniture/Fixture Depreciation
0050	Motor Vehicles
0051	Motor Vehicles Depreciation
1001	Stock
1002	Work in Progress
1003	Finished Goods
1004	Raw Materials
1100	Debtors Control Account
1101	Sundry Debtors
1102	Other Debtors
1103	Prepayments
1104	Inter-company Debtors
1105	Provision for credit notes
1106	Provision for doubtful debts
1200	Bank Current Account
1210	Bank Deposit Account
1220	Building Society Account
1230	Petty Cash
1235	Cash Register
1240	Company Credit Card
1250	Credit Card Receipts
2100	Creditors Control Account
2101	Sundry Creditors
2102	Other Creditors
2109	Accruals
2200	Sales Tax Control Account
2201	Purchase Tax Control Account
2202	VAT Liability
2204	Manual Adjustments
2210	P.A.Y.E.
2211	National Insurance
2220	Net Wages
2230	Pension Fund
2300	Loans
2301	Directors Loan Accounts (Director 1)
2302	Directors Loan Accounts (Director 2)
2310	Hire Purchase
2320	Corporation Tax
2330	Mortgages
3000	Ordinary Shares
3010	Preference Shares
3100	Reserves
3101	Undistributed Reserves
3200	Profit and Loss Account
4000	Computer hardware sales
4001	Computer software sales
4002	Computer consultancy
4003	Computer helpline
4009	Discounts Allowed
4010	Management Charges Receivable
4099	Flat Rate - Benefit/Cost
4100	Sales Type D
4101	Sales Type E
4200	Sales of Assets
4400	Credit Charges (Late Payments)

Chapter Summary

■   When a business sets up its accounts on a Sage computer accounting package it will normally set up its Customer and Supplier records first.

■   The next stage will be for the business to set up its Nominal Accounts, adopting the default list of accounts supplied by Sage in its 'Chart of Accounts' structure.

■   If the business has already started trading it should input all its Nominal Account balances (except for the Debtors and Creditors control accounts).

■   The input balances should be checked carefully against the source figures. The Sage program can produce a trial balance which will show the balances that have been input.

■   Account names can be changed and new accounts added to suit the nature of the business – but it is important that the type of account should be consistent with the appropriate category in the 'Chart of Accounts'.

Key Terms

nominal ledger
the remaining accounts in the accounting system which are not Customers or Suppliers, eg income, expenses, assets, liabilities – in Sage this is known as 'Nominal'

chart of accounts
the structure of the nominal accounts, which groups accounts into categories such as Sales, Purchases, Overheads . . . and so on

categories
subdivisions of the Chart of Accounts (eg Sales, Purchases) each of which is allocated a range of account numbers by the computer

trial balance
a list of the accounts of a business divided into two columns:

debits – mostly assets and expenses

credits – mostly income and liabilities

The two columns should have the same total, reflecting the workings of the double-entry bookkeeping system

Activities

5.1   Explain briefly what a chart of accounts is.

5.2   List the categories of account in a Chart of Accounts and write a sentence for each category, explaining what type of account that category includes.

5.3   You are transferring the manual accounting records of a company into a Sage system. The account names listed below are included in those used in the manual system. Refer to the Nominal Account list on page 58 and the categories of account numbers on page 60.

(a)   What account numbers will you allocate to these accounts?

(b)   In what categories in the chart of accounts will these accounts appear?

Complete the table below (or draw up your own table).

account name	account number	category
Freehold Property		
Office Equipment		
Motor Vehicles		
Materials Purchased		
Bank Current Account		
Creditors Control		
Directors Salaries		
Electricity		
Ordinary Shares		

PRONTO SUPPLIES INPUTTING TASKS

> **warning note!**
> This activity involves inputting live data into the computer.
> Remember to Save your data and keep your printouts as you progress through the tasks.

Task 1

Make sure the program date is set to 31 January 2013.

Open up the Nominal Ledger and select accounts in the computer Nominal Ledger list screen for the accounts included on the spreadsheet trial balance (see page 62).

But do *not* select Debtors Control Account or Creditors Control Account as they already have balances on them.

Task 2

Enter the balances from the spreadsheet trial balance (see page 62) into the appropriate Nominal Accounts as opening balances – but do not input the Debtors Control Account and the Creditors Control Account.

Make sure that debits are entered as debits and credits as credits.

Task 3

Print out a trial balance for January 2013 from the computer and check it against the trial balance on page 65 and page 214, or have it checked by your tutor. The suspense account should have disappeared.

Task 4

Change the names of the three sales accounts you have chosen as follows:

number	old name	new name
4000	Sales Type A	Computer hardware sales
4001	Sales Type B	Computer software sales
4002	Sales Type C	Computer consultancy

Task 5

Add new account number 4003 Computer helpline to the Nominal List.

Task 6

Print a Nominal List showing all accounts. Check the amended account names against the detail on page 80 of the Case Study.

Reminder! Have you made a back-up?

6 Selling to customers on credit

this chapter covers...

- A business that sells on credit will invoice the goods or services supplied and then receive payment at a later date.

- The invoice is an important document because it sets out the details of the goods or services supplied, the amount owing, and the date by which payment should be made.

- It is therefore essential that details of the invoice are entered in the computer accounting records so that the sale can be recorded and the amount owed by the customer logged into the accounting system.

- A business that sells on credit may have to issue a refund for some or all of the goods or services supplied. They may be faulty or the sale may be cancelled. As payment has not yet been made, the 'refund' takes the form of a deduction from the amount owing. The document that the seller issues in this case is a credit note.

- A credit note is dealt with by a computer accounting program in much the same way as an invoice.

- This chapter continues the Pronto Supplies Case Study and shows how details of invoices and credit notes are entered into the computer accounting records.

- The next chapter looks at how the invoices and credit notes issued by suppliers are dealt with by a computer accounting program.

BACKGROUND TO FINANCIAL DOCUMENTS

When a business sells goods or services it will use a number of different financial documents. A single sales transaction involves both seller and buyer. In this chapter we look at the situation from the point of view of the seller of the goods or services. Documents which are often used in the selling process for goods include:

- **purchase order** which the seller receives from the buyer
- **delivery note** which goes with the goods from the seller to the buyer
- **invoice** which lists the goods and tells the buyer what is owed
- **credit note** which is sent to the buyer if any refund is due
- **statement** sent by the seller to remind the buyer what is owed
- **remittance advice** sent by the buyer with the **cheque** to make payment

Study the diagram below which shows how the documents 'flow' between buyer and seller.

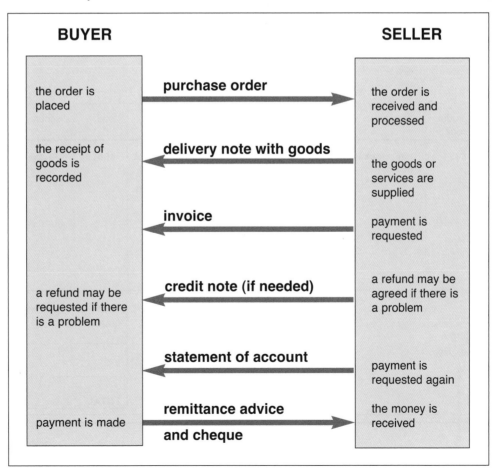

INVOICE

The main document we will deal with in this chapter is the **invoice** which is sent by the seller to the buyer to state what is owing and when it has to be paid. An invoice is illustrated below and explained on the next page.

INVOICE

DELCO PLC

Delco House, Otto Way, New Milton SR1 6TF
Tel 01722 295875 Fax 01722 295611 Email sales@delco.co.uk
VAT Reg GB 0745 4672 76

invoice to

Pronto Supplies Limited
Unit 17 Severnvale Estate
Broadwater Road
Mereford
MR1 6TF

invoice no	12309
account	3993
your reference	47609
date	02 10 13

product code	description	quantity	price	unit	total	discount %	net
Z324	Zap portable hard drive	10	40.00	box of 10	400.00	0.00	400.00

terms
30 days

goods total	400.00
VAT	80.00
TOTAL	480.00

The invoice here has been issued by Delco PLC for Zap portable hard drives ordered by Pronto Supplies on a purchase order.

The reference number quoted here is the order number on Pronto Supplies' original purchase order.

The date here is the date on which the goods have been sent. It is known as the 'invoice date'.

The date is important for calculating when the invoice is due to be paid. In this case the 'terms' (see the bottom left-hand corner of the invoice) are 30 days. This means the invoice is due to be paid within 30 days of the invoice date.

The arithmetic and details in this line must be checked very carefully by Pronto Supplies to make sure that they pay the correct amount:

- *product code* – this is the catalogue number for the hard drives which Pronto put on the original purchase order
- *description* – this describes the goods ordered – the hard drives
- *quantity* – this should be the same as the quantity on the purchase order
- *price* – this is the price of each unit shown in the next column
- *unit* is the way in which the unit is counted up and charged for, eg units (single items), or 10s, boxes (as here)
- *total* is the price multiplied by the number of units
- *discount %* is the percentage allowance (known as trade discount) given to customers who regularly deal with the supplier, ie they receive a certain percentage (eg 10%) deducted from their bill
- *net* is the amount due to the seller after deduction of trade discount, and before VAT is added on

The Goods Total is the total of the column above it. It is the final amount due to the seller before VAT is added on.

Value Added Tax (VAT) is calculated and added on – here it is 20% of the Goods Total, ie £400.00 x $\dfrac{20}{100}$ = £80.00

The VAT is then added to the Goods Total to produce the actual amount owing: £400.00 + £80.00 = £480.00

The 'terms' explain the conditions on which the goods are supplied. Here '30 days' means that Pronto has to pay within 30 days of 2 October.

CREDIT NOTE

The other document we will deal with in this chapter is the **credit note**.

The **credit note** is issued when some form of refund has to be given to the buyer of goods or services. As payment has not yet been made the credit note allows the buyer to deduct an amount from the invoice when settlement is finally made.

Note that it is never acceptable practice to change the amounts on an invoice; a credit note is always required.

The credit note illustrated below has been issued by Delco PLC because one of the boxes of Zap hard drives ordered by Pronto Supplies was faulty. Pronto Supplies has returned the box, asking for a reduction in the amount owing.

Study the document below and read the notes which follow.

CREDIT NOTE

DELCO PLC

Delco House, Otto Way, New Milton SR1 6TF
Tel 01722 295875 Fax 01722 295611 Email sales@delco.co..uk
VAT Reg GB 0745 4672 76

to

Pronto Supplies Limited Unit 17 Severnvale Estate Broadwater Road Mereford MR1 6TF		

credit note no	12157
account	3993
your reference	47609
our invoice	12309
date/tax point	10 10 13

product code	description	quantity	price	unit	total	discount %	net
Z324	Zap portable hard drives	1	40.00	box	40.00	0.00	40.00

Reason for credit
1 box of Zap hard drives received faulty and returned.

GOODS TOTAL	40.00
VAT	8.00
TOTAL	48.00

notes on the credit note

You will see from the credit note on the previous page that the credit note total is £48. This can be deducted from the invoice total (see page 74) of £480. In other words, Pronto Supplies now owes £480 minus £48 = £432.

Note in particular from the credit note opposite:

■ The format of the credit note is very much the same as the invoice.

■ The reference quoted is Pronto Supplies' purchase order number.

■ The columns (eg 'product code') are identical to those used on the invoice and work in exactly the same way.

■ VAT is also included – it has to be refunded because the goods have not now been supplied.

■ If there was any discount this should also be refunded – but there is no discount here.

■ The reason for the credit note (the 'reason for credit') is stated at the bottom of the document. Here it is a box of faulty hard drives that has been returned to Delco PLC by Pronto Supplies.

INVOICES, CREDIT NOTES AND SAGE

the bookkeeping background

The totals of invoices and credit notes have to be entered into the accounting records of a business. They record the sales and refunds made to customers who have bought on credit – the **receivables** (**debtors**) of the business (known in Sage as Customers). The amounts from these documents combine to provide the total of the **Sales Ledger**, which is the section of the accounting records which contains all the customer balances. This is recorded in the **Debtors Control Account** which tells the business how much in total is owing from customers who have bought on credit.

methods of recording invoices and credit notes

When a business uses a computer accounting program such as Sage, it will have to make sure that the details of each invoice and credit note issued are entered into the computer accounting records.

batch entry

Invoices are produced independently of the computer accounting program and the invoice details are entered into Sage on a **batch invoice** screen. A 'batch' is simply a group of items (eg a 'batch' of cakes in the oven). The term is used in this context to describe a group of invoices which are all input at one time. This may not be the day that each invoice is produced – it may be the end of the week, or even the month.

It is normal practice to add up the totals of all the actual invoices that are being input – the 'batch total' – and check this total against the invoice total calculated by the computer from the actual input. This will pick up any errors.

A batch invoice entry screen with four invoices input is shown below.

A/C	Date	Ref	Ex.Ref	N/C	Dept	Project Ref	Details	Net	T/C	VAT
JB001	05/02/2013	10023		4000	0		Hardware	400.00	T1	80.00
CH001	06/02/2013	10024		4000	0		Hardware	16.00	T1	3.20
CR001	06/02/2013	10025		4001	0		Software	450.00	T1	90.00
KD001	08/02/2013	10026		4002	0		Consultancy	120.00	T1	24.00

A/C: Kay Denz   N/C: Computer consultancy   Tax Rate: 20.00   Total: 1183.20

986.00   197.20

Save   Discard   Calc. Net   Memorise   Recall   Close

notes on the data entry columns:

- 'A/C' column contains the customer account reference
- 'Date' is the date on which each invoice was issued
- 'Ref' column is the invoice number (note that they are consecutive)
- 'Ex.Ref' is optional – it could be used for the purchase order number
- 'N/C' column is the Nominal Account code which specifies which type of sale is involved
- 'Dept' is 0 by default and is not used here
- 'Project Ref' is optional and is not used here
- 'Details' describes the goods that have been sold

- 'Net' is the amount of the invoice before VAT is added on
- 'T/C' is the tax code which sets up the VAT rate that applies – here T1 refers to Standard Rate VAT, and is the default rate set up in Customer Preferences in SETTINGS
- 'VAT' is calculated automatically

When the operator has completed the input and checked the batch totals with the computer totals, the batched invoices can be saved.

computer printed invoices

Most versions of Sage include an invoice production function which requires the business to input the details of each invoice on screen. The computer system can then print out the invoices on the office printer.

---

important note: treatment of invoicing in this book

In this book we will concentrate on the batch entry method of recording invoices and credit notes.

Case Study

PRONTO SUPPLIES LIMITED: PROCESSING SALES INVOICES AND CREDIT NOTES

Tom Cox runs Pronto Supplies Limited which provides computer hardware, software and consultancy services. At the end of January he input his Nominal Accounts and his Customer and Supplier details and balances into his Sage accounting program. He has set up four Sales Accounts in his Nominal Ledger:

Computer hardware sales	Account number 4000
Computer software sales	Account number 4001
Computer consultancy	Account number 4002
Computer helpline	Account number 4003

It is now February 8, the end of the first full trading week. Tom needs to input

- the sales invoices he has issued to his customers
- the credit notes he has issued to his customers

He has the documents on file and has collected them in two batches . . .

SALES INVOICES ISSUED

invoice	name	date	details	net amount	VAT
10023	John Butler & Associates	5/02/13	Hardware	400.00	80.00
10024	Charisma Design	6/02/13	Hardware	16.00	3.20
10025	Crowmatic Ltd	6/02/13	Software	450.00	90.00
10026	Kay Denz	8/02/13	Consultancy	120.00	24.00
Subtotals				986.00	197.20
Batch total					1183.20

CREDIT NOTES ISSUED

credit note	name	date	details	net amount	VAT
551	David Boossey	6/02/13	Software returned	450.00	90.00
552	L Garr & Co	6/02/13	Hardware returned	40.00	8.00
Subtotals				490.00	98.00
Batch total					588.00

batch invoice entry

Tom will start by opening up the CUSTOMERS screen in Sage and clicking on the INVOICE icon. This will show the screen shown below. He will then:

- identify the account references for each of the four customers
- enter each invoice on a new line
- take the data from the invoice: date, invoice no ('Ref'), product details and amounts
- enter the appropriate Sales account number ('N/C') for the type of sale
- enter the T1 tax code for standard rate VAT and check that the VAT amount calculated on screen is the same as on the invoice

When the input is complete Tom should check his original batch totals (Net, VAT and Total) against the computer totals. Once he is happy that his input is correct he should SAVE.

Batch Customer Invoices

A/C Kay Denz
N/C Computer consultancy

the batch total → Tax Rate 20.00
Total 1183.20

A/C	Date	Ref	Ex.Ref	N/C	Dept	Project Ref	Details	Net	T/C	VAT
JB001	05/02/2013	10023		4000	0		Hardware	400.00	T1	80.00
CH001	06/02/2013	10024		4000	0		Hardware	16.00	T1	3.20
CR001	06/02/2013	10025		4001	0		Software	450.00	T1	90.00
KD001	08/02/2013	10026		4002	0		Consultancy	120.00	T1	24.00

the VAT total of the batch
the net total of the batch → 986.00 → 197.20

Save Discard Calc. Net Memorise Recall Close

checking the invoices are on the system

As a further check Tom could print out a Day Book Report. This can be obtained through the REPORTS icon on the CUSTOMERS menu bar. The title of the report is 'Day Books: Customer Invoices (Detailed)'. The report appears as follows:

Pronto Supplies Limited
Day Books: Customer Invoices (Detailed)

Transaction From:	1				N/C From:	
Transaction To:	99,999,999				N/C To:	99999999
Dept From:	0					
Dept To:	999					

Tran No.	Type	Date	A/C Ref	N/C	Inv Ref	Dept.	Details	Net Amount	Tax Amount	T/C	Gross Amount	V	B
48	SI	05/02/2013	JB001	4000	10023	0	Hardware	400.00	80.00	T1	480.00	N	-
49	SI	06/02/2013	CH001	4000	10024	0	Hardware	16.00	3.20	T1	19.20	N	-
50	SI	06/02/2013	CR001	4001	10025	0	Software	450.00	90.00	T1	540.00	N	-
51	SI	08/02/2013	KD001	4002	10026	0	Consultancy	120.00	24.00	T1	144.00	N	-
							Totals:	986.00	197.20		1,183.20		

batch credit note entry

Tom will input the details from the two credit notes in much the same way as he processed the invoices. He will start by opening up the CUSTOMERS screen in Sage and clicking on the CREDIT icon. This will show the screen shown below. He will then identify the account references for each of the two customers and the Sales account numbers and input the credit note details as shown on the screen. When the input is complete Tom should check his original batch totals (Net, VAT and Total) against the computer totals. Once he is happy that his input is correct he should SAVE.

Batch Customer Credits

A/C	L Garr & Co		Tax Rate	20.00
N/C	Computer hardware sales		Total	588.00

A/C	Date	Credit No	Ex.Ref	N/C	Dept	Project Ref	Details	Net	T/C	VAT
DB001	06/02/2013	551		4001	0		Software ret..	450.00	T1	90.00
LG001	06/02/2013	552		4000	0		Hardware re...	40.00	T1	8.00
								490.00		98.00

Save	Discard	Calc. Net	Memorise	Recall		Close

checking the credit notes are on the system

As a further check Tom could print out a Day Book Report for Credit notes. This can be obtained through the REPORTS icon on the CUSTOMERS toolbar. The title of the report is 'Day Books: Customer Credits (Detailed)'.

The report appears as follows:

Pronto Supplies Limited

Day Books: Customer Credits (Detailed)

Date From:	06/02/2013							Customer From:		
Date To:	06/02/2013							Customer To:	ZZZZZZZZ	
Transaction From:	1							N/C From:		
Transaction To:	99,999,999							N/C To:	99999999	
Dept From:	0									
Dept To:	999									

Tran No.	Type	Date	A/C Ref	N/C	Inv Ref	Dept.	Details	Net Amount	Tax Amount	T/C	Gross Amount	V	B
52	SC	06/02/2013	DB001	4001	551	0	Software returned	450.00	90.00	T1	540.00	N	-
53	SC	06/02/2013	LG001	4000	552	0	Hardware returned	40.00	8.00	T1	48.00	N	-
							Totals:	490.00	98.00		588.00		

<table>
<tr><td>**Chapter Summary**</td><td>

■ When a business sells on credit it will issue an invoice to the buyer. This sets out the amount owing and the date by which it has to be paid.

■ When a business has to make a refund to a customer to whom it sells on credit it will issue a credit note to the customer. This sets out the amount by which the amount owing is reduced.

■ Sales invoices and credit notes are part of the 'flow of documents' which occurs when a sale is made on credit. The full list is purchase order, delivery note, invoice, credit note, statement, remittance advice and cheque. Not all of these will be used all of the time.

■ The details of invoices and credit notes must be entered into the accounting records of a business. If a computer program is used the details will be input on screen.

■ Computer accounting programs will either print out the invoices after input, or will need to have the details of existing invoices input, commonly in batches.

■ It is essential to check the details of invoices and credit notes which have been input. This can be done by printing out a Daybook Report.

</td></tr>
</table>

Key Terms		
	credit sale	a sale made where payment is due at a later date
	receivables (debtors)	customers who owe money to a business
	sales ledger	the part of the accounting system where the customer accounts are kept – it records the amounts that are owed to the business
	purchase order	the financial document which requests the supply of goods or services and specifies exactly what is required
	invoice	the financial document which sets out the details of the goods sold or services provided, the amount owing and the date by which the amount is due
	credit note	the financial document – normally issued when goods are returned – which reduces the amount owing by the customer
	batch	a group of documents, eg invoices or credit notes
	batch entry	the input of a number of documents in a group

Activities

6.1 Place the following documents in the order in which they are likely to be used in a transaction in which goods are sold on credit.

statement

invoice

purchase order

delivery note

cheque

credit note

6.2 A delivery note will always be used in a sale made on credit. True or false?

6.3 A credit note will always be used in a sale made on credit. True or false?

6.4 List two important pieces of information that the invoice will provide to the purchaser of goods or services.

6.5 Give a definition of the 'receivables' (debtors) of a business.

6.6 Where in the accounting records of a business will the receivables' (debtors') balances be found?

6.7 What arithmetic checks should be made when inputting details of invoices and credit notes into a computer accounting system?

6.8 What details would you expect to enter when inputting details of each invoice into a computer accounting system?

6.9 What difference does the tax code make when inputting details of an invoice or credit note into a computer accounting system?

PRONTO SUPPLIES INPUTTING TASKS

warning note!

This activity involves inputting live data into the computer.

Remember to Save your data and keep your printouts as you progress through the tasks.

Task 1

Making sure that you have set the program date to 8 February 2013, enter the following invoice details into the computer. Check your totals before saving and print out a Day Books: Customer Invoices (Detailed) Report to confirm the data that you have saved. You can limit the transactions shown on the report by selecting the transaction date range in 'report criteria' (here 5 to 8 Feb). Check this report against the report on page 81.

SALES INVOICES ISSUED					
invoice	name	date	details	net amount	VAT
10023	John Butler & Associates	5/02/13	Hardware	400.00	80.00
10024	Charisma Design	6/02/13	Hardware	16.00	3.20
10025	Crowmatic Ltd	6/02/13	Software	450.00	90.00
10026	Kay Denz	8/02/13	Consultancy	120.00	24.00
Subtotals				986.00	197.20
Batch total					1183.20

Task 2

Enter the following credit note details into the computer. Check your totals before saving and print out a Day Books: Customer Credits (Detailed) Report, date range 6 Feb only. Check this report against the report on page 82.

CREDIT NOTES ISSUED					
credit note	name	date	details	net amount	VAT
551	David Boossey	6/02/13	Software returned	450.00	90.00
552	L Garr & Co	6/02/13	Hardware returned	40.00	8.00
Subtotals				490.00	98.00
Batch total					588.00

Task 3

It is now 16 February 2013. Change your program date setting. You have a further batch of invoices to process. Enter the details into the computer. Check your totals before saving and print out a Day Books: Customer Invoices (Detailed) Report (12 to 16 Feb) and check it against the report on page 81.

account	invoice date	number	details	net	VAT
John Butler & Associates	12/02/13	10027	Consultancy	120.00	24.00
David Boossey	13/02/13	10028	Hardware	600.00	120.00
L Garr & Co	16/02/13	10029	Hardware	180.00	36.00
Kay Denz	16/02/13	10030	Software	264.00	52.80
Charisma Design	16/02/13	10031	Hardware	320.00	64.00
				1,484.00	296.80

Task 4

You also on the same date have two credit notes to process. Enter the details shown below into the computer. Check your totals before saving and print out a Day Books: Customer Credits (Detailed) Report (12 to 13 Feb) to confirm the data that you have saved. Check your printout against the report on page 202.

Finally, print out a trial balance for February and check it against the the trial balance on page 202.

account	date	reference	details	net	VAT
Kay Denz	12/02/13	553	Hardware returned	16.00	3.20
Crowmatic Ltd	13/02/13	554	Hardware returned	20.00	4.00
				36.00	7.20

Reminder! Have you made a backup?

this chapter covers...

■ *This chapter should be read in conjunction with the last chapter 'Selling to customers on credit' as it represents 'the other side of the coin' – the invoice and the credit note as they are dealt with by the purchaser.*

■ *A business purchaser that buys on credit will receive an invoice for the goods or services supplied and will then have to pay at a later date.*

■ *Details of invoices and credit notes received are entered by the purchaser into the computer accounting records. In this way the total amount owing to the supplier is logged into the accounting system.*

■ *This chapter continues the Pronto Supplies Case Study and shows how details of invoices and credit notes received are entered into supplier accounts in the computer accounting records.*

INVOICES AND CREDIT NOTES

Make sure that you are familiar with the two types of financial document we will be dealing with – the invoice and the credit note. Read the descriptions below and remind yourself of the 'flow of documents' by studying the diagram on the opposite page.

invoice

The main document we will deal with in this chapter is the **invoice** which is sent by the seller to the buyer to state the amount that is owing and the date by which it has to be paid. See page 74 for an illustration.

credit note

The **credit note** is issued by the seller when some form of refund has to be given to the buyer of goods or services. As payment has not yet been made the credit note allows the buyer to deduct an amount from the invoice when settlement is finally made. See page 76 for an illustration.

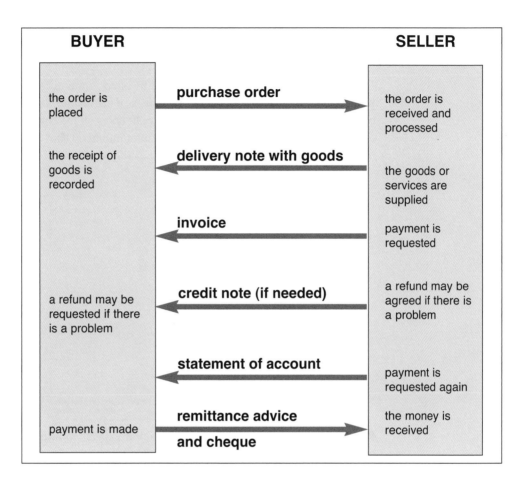

THE BOOKKEEPING BACKGROUND

Details of invoices and credit notes have to be entered into the accounting records of a business that buys on credit. They record the purchases made from supplier – the **payables** (**creditors**) of the business, known in Sage as 'Suppliers'.

The amounts from these documents combine to provide the total of the **Purchases Ledger**, which is the section of the accounting records which contains all the supplier accounts and their balances. The total of the **Purchases Ledger** (recorded in the **Creditors Control Account**) tells the business how much in total it owes to suppliers.

The documents received from the suppliers – invoices and credit notes – are recorded in the computer accounting system on the **batch** basis illustrated in the Case Study in the last chapter. Documents received from a seller should be checked carefully before input – is the buyer being overcharged, for example?

PURCHASES AND EXPENSES AND CAPITAL ITEMS

One point that is very important to bear in mind is the difference between **purchases** and **expenses** and **capital items**, as it affects the Nominal Account codes used when inputting invoices and credit notes on the computer. Look at the Pronto Supplies account list (with account numbers) shown below.

N/C	Name
0020	Plant and Machinery
0030	Office Equipment
0040	Furniture and Fixtures
1100	Debtors Control Account
1200	Bank Current Account
2100	Creditors Control Account
2200	Sales Tax Control Account
2201	Purchase Tax Control Account
2300	Loans
3000	Ordinary Shares
4000	Computer hardware sales
4001	Computer software sales
4002	Computer consultancy
5000	Materials Purchased
6201	Advertising
7000	Gross Wages
7100	Rent
7103	General Rates
7200	Electricity
7502	Office Stationery

Purchases are items a business buys which it expects to turn into a product or sell as part of its day-to-day business. For example:

- a business that makes cheese will buy milk to make the cheese
- a supermarket will buy food and consumer goods to sell to the public

All these items are bought because they will be sold or turned into a product that will be sold. In Sage these purchases will be recorded in a **purchases account**, normally 5000, or a number in that category. In the list shown above Pronto Supplies uses account 5000 for 'Materials Purchased'.

Expenses, on the other hand, are items which the business pays for which form part of the business running expenses (overheads), eg rent and electricity. They all have separate Nominal Account numbers.

Capital items are 'one off' items that the business buys and intends to keep for a number of years, for example office equipment and furniture. These categories of asset all also have separate Nominal Account numbers.

conclusion

The important point here is that all of these items may be bought on credit and will have to be entered into the computer accounting records, **with the correct Nominal Account number.**

Case Study	# PRONTO SUPPLIES LIMITED: PROCESSING PURCHASES INVOICES AND CREDIT NOTES

It is February 16 2013. Tom has a number of supplier invoices and supplier credit notes to enter into the computer accounting system.

He has the documents on file and has collected them in two batches.

PURCHASES INVOICES RECEIVED

invoice	name	date	details	net amount	VAT
11365	Delco PLC	9/02/13	Desktop computers	3,600.00	720.00
8576	Electron Supplies	9/02/13	Processors	2,000.00	400.00
2947	MacCity	12/02/13	MacroWorx software	3,680.00	736.00
Subtotals				9,280.00	1856.00
Batch total					11,136.00

CREDIT NOTES RECEIVED

credit note	name	date	details	net amount	VAT
7223	Delco PLC	6/02/13	1 x Computer	480.00	96.00
352	MacCity	8/02/13	1 x 10 optical mouse	38.00	7.60
Subtotals				518.00	103.60
Batch total					621.60

batch invoice entry

Tom will start by opening up the SUPPLIERS screen in Sage and clicking on the INVOICE icon. This will show the screen shown on the next page. He will then:

- identify the account references for each of the three suppliers
- enter each invoice on a new line
- take the data from the invoice: date, invoice no ('Ref'), product details and amounts
- ignore the Dept (0 by default), Project Ref and Cost Code columns
- enter the Materials Purchased account number 5000 under 'N/C'
- enter the T1 tax code for standard rate VAT and check that the VAT amount calculated on screen is the same as on the invoice. There could, for example, be a calculation mistake on the original invoice or a 'rounding' difference might occur.*

When the input is complete Tom should check his batch totals (Net, VAT and Total) against the computer totals. Once he is happy that his input is correct he should SAVE.

* Sometimes the VAT on the document will vary by a penny from the VAT on the screen. This is because Sage 'rounds' VAT up or down to the nearest penny, whereas the VAT authorities require that VAT is rounded down to the nearest penny. These one penny differences can be altered on the input screen to tally with the document VAT amount.

The batch suppliers' invoice screen will appear like this:

A/C	Date	Ref	Ex.Ref	N/C	Dept	Project Ref	Cost Code	Details	Net	T/C	VAT
DE001	09/02/2013	11365		5000	0			Desktop co...	3600.00	T1	720.00
EL001	09/02/2013	8576		5000	0			Processors	2000.00	T1	400.00
MA001	12/02/2013	2947		5000	0			Macroworx s...	3680.00	T1	736.00

A/C MacCity
N/C Materials Purchased

the batch total Tax Rate 20.00
Total 11136.00

the VAT total of the batch

the net total of the batch 9280.00 1856.00

Save Discard Calc. Net Memorise Recall Close

checking the invoices are on the system

As a further check Tom could print out a Day Book Report. This can be obtained through the REPORTS icon on the SUPPLIER menu bar. The title of the report is 'Day Books: Supplier Invoices (Detailed)'. The report appears as follows:

Pronto Supplies Limited
Day Books: Supplier Invoices (Detailed)

Date From:	09/02/2013	
Date To:	12/02/2013	

Supplier From:	
Supplier To:	ZZZZZZZZ

Transaction From:	1
Transaction To:	99,999,999

N/C From:	
N/C To:	99999999

Dept From:	0
Dept To:	999

Tran No.	Type	Date	A/C Ref	N/C	Inv Ref	Dept	Details	Net Amount	Tax Amount	T/C	Gross Amount	V	B
61	PI	09/02/2013	DE001	5000	11365	0	Desktop computers	3,600.00	720.00	T1	4,320.00	N	-
62	PI	09/02/2013	EL001	5000	8576	0	Processors	2,000.00	400.00	T1	2,400.00	N	-
63	PI	12/02/2013	MA001	5000	2947	0	Macroworx software	3,680.00	736.00	T1	4,416.00	N	-
							Totals	9,280.00	1,856.00		11,136.00		

batch credit note entry

Tom will input the details from the two credit notes in much the same way as he processed the invoices. He will open up the SUPPLIERS screen in Sage and click on the CREDIT icon. This will show the screen shown on the next page. He will then identify the account references for each of the two customers and input the credit note details as shown on the screen. He will use the Materials Purchased account number 5000. When the input is complete he should again check his original totals (Net, VAT and Batch total) against the computer totals. Once he is happy that his input is correct he should SAVE.

The batch suppliers' credit note screen will appear like this:

A/C MacCity							**Tax Rate**			20.00	
N/C Materials Purchased							**Total**			621.60	

A/C	Date	Credit No	Ex.Ref	N/C	Dept	Project Ref	Cost Code	Details	Net	T/C	VAT
DE001	06/02/2013	7223		5000	0			1 x computer	480.00	T1	96.00
MA001	08/02/2013	352		5000	0			1 x 10 Optic..	38.00	T1	7.60
									518.00		103.60

Save Discard Calc. Net Memorise Recall Close

checking the credit notes are on the system

As a further check Tom could print out a Day Book Report for Supplier Credit notes. This can be obtained through the REPORTS icon on the SUPPLIERS toolbar. The title of the report is 'Day Books: Supplier Credits (Detailed)'. The report appears as follows:

Pronto Supplies Limited

Day Books: Supplier Credits (Detailed)

Date From:	06/02/2013		**Supplier From:**	
Date To:	08/02/2013		**Supplier To:**	ZZZZZZZZ
Transaction From:	1		**N/C From:**	
Transaction To:	99,999,999		**N/C To:**	99999999
Dept From:	0			
Dept To:	999			

Tran No.	Type	Date	A/C Ref	N/C	Inv Ref	Dept	Details	Net Amount	Tax Amount	T/C	Gross Amount	V	B
64	PC	06/02/2013	DE001	5000	7223	0	1 x computer	480.00	96.00	T1	576.00	N	-
65	PC	08/02/2013	MA001	5000	352	0	1 x 10 Optical Mouse	38.00	7.60	T1	45.60	N	-
							Totals	518.00	103.60		621.60		

what next?

Tom has now entered into his computer:

• his company details and Nominal Accounts and balances

• customer and supplier details

• customer and supplier invoices

• customer and supplier credit notes

The next chapter shows how he enters details of payments made to suppliers and payments received from customers. The 'flow of documents' will be complete.

<table>
<tr><td>

Chapter Summary

</td><td>

- ■ When a business buys on credit it will receive invoices and possibly credit notes from its suppliers as part of the 'flow of documents'.

- ■ The details of invoices and credit notes must be entered into the accounting records of a business. If a computer program is used the details are normally input on screen on the batch basis.

- ■ In the case of supplier invoices and credit notes it is important that the correct Nominal Account number is used to describe whether the transaction relates to purchases, expenses or capital items.

- ■ It is essential to check the details of invoices and credit notes before input and the details of input by printing out, for example, a day book report.

</td></tr>
</table>

Key Terms		
	credit purchase	a purchase made where payment is due at a later date
	payables (creditors)	suppliers to whom the business owes money
	purchases ledger	the part of the accounting system where the suppliers' accounts are kept
	purchases	items bought which will be turned into a product or be sold as part of day-to-day-trading
	expenses	payments made which relate to the running of the business – also known as overheads
	capital items	items bought which the business intends to keep
	batch	a group of documents, eg invoices or credit notes

Activities

7.1   Define the term 'payables' (also known as 'creditors').

7.2   In what section of the accounting system are supplier balances kept? What information does this provide for the owner of the business?

7.3   What is the difference between purchases, expenses and capital items? Why is it important to identify these types of transaction before entering a supplier invoice on the computer?

7.4   Write a list of instructions for a person entering supplier invoices into a batch screen on a computer accounting program. Explain what data is entered in each of the columns and what checks should be made before and after input.

PRONTO SUPPLIES INPUTTING TASKS

Task 1

Set the program date to 16 February 2013. Enter the following invoice details into the computer. Check your totals before saving and print out a Day Books: Supplier Invoice (Detailed) Report. Check this against the report on page 90.

PURCHASES INVOICES RECEIVED					
invoice	**name**	**date**	**details**	**net amount**	**VAT**
11365	Delco PLC	9/02/13	Desktop computers	3,600.00	720.00
8576	Electron Supplies	9/02/13	Processors	2,000.00	400.00
2947	MacCity	12/02/13	MacroWorx software	3,680.00	736.00
Subtotals				9,280.00	1856.00
Batch total					11,136.00

Task 2

Enter the following credit note details into the computer. Check your totals before saving and print out a Day Books: Supplier Credits (Detailed) Report. Check this against the report on page 91.

CREDIT NOTES RECEIVED					
credit note	**name**	**date**	**details**	**net amount**	**VAT**
7223	Delco PLC	6/02/13	1 x Computer	480.00	96.00
352	MacCity	8/02/13	1 x 10 optical mouse	38.00	7.60
Subtotals				518.00	103.60
Batch total					621.60

Task 3

On the same day (16 February) Tom receives two further supplier invoices in the post. He wants them to be input straightaway while the computer is up and running. He checks all the documentation and finds that the invoices are both correct. You are to input them, taking care to use the correct Nominal Code (see the codes listed on page 88). The computer and printer purchased are not for resale to customers but are to be used permanently as office equipment at Pronto Supplies.

When the input is complete the totals should be checked and a Day Books: Supplier Invoices (Detailed) Report printed, showing just the last two invoices. Then print out a trial balance for February.

Check with the Day Book Report and trial balance shown on page 202.

invoice	name	date	details	net amount	VAT
11377	Delco PLC	14/02/13	Desktop computer	400.00	80.00
8603	Electron Supplies	14/02/13	Laser Printer	360.00	72.00
Subtotals				760.00	152.00
Batch total					912.00

Reminder! Have you made a back-up?

8 Customer and supplier payments

this chapter covers...

■ So far in this book we have set up accounts for customers and suppliers and entered details of financial documents. But we have not covered the way in which the accounting system records the payment of money by customers to the business or by the business to suppliers.

■ The bank account is central to any accounting system as the payment of money is vital to all business transactions.

■ The bank account will be used not only for payments by customers and to suppliers (credit transactions), but also for transactions for which settlement is made straightaway (cash transactions), for example payment of wages.

■ A computer accounting system may maintain more than one 'bank' account in its Nominal Ledger. For example, it may also keep a petty cash account for purchases made from the office petty cash tin.

■ This chapter concentrates on the use of the bank account for credit transactions, ie when a business receives payment of its customers' invoices and when it makes payments of its suppliers' invoices.

The 'cash' transactions mentioned above are covered in detail in the next two chapters.

THE BANK ACCOUNTS IN COMPUTER ACCOUNTING

The bank accounts and all the functions associated with them are found in Sage by clicking on the BANK button on the vertical toolbar.

The BANK screen then appears as shown below.

Study the screen below and read the notes that follow. The most important icons are explained by the text with the arrows.

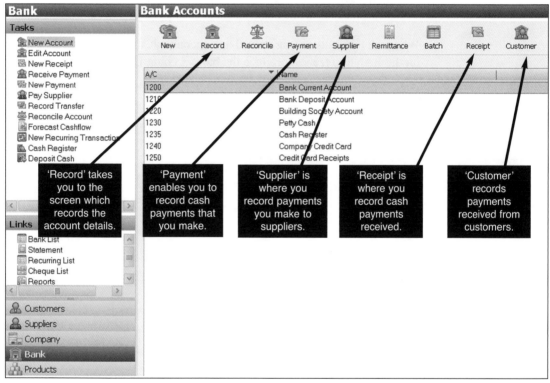

types of bank account

The accounts listed above come from the default list in the Chart of Accounts (see page 59 if you need reminding about this). The business does not have to adopt all the accounts listed here, but may use some of them if it needs them:

■ **bank current account** records all payments in and out of the bank 'cheque' account used for everyday purposes – it is the most commonly used account

■ **bank deposit account** and **Building Society account** can be used if the business maintains interest-paying accounts for savings and money that is not needed in the short term

- **petty cash account** can be used if the business keeps a petty cash tin in the office for small business purchases such as stationery and stamps

- **cash register** can be used to record takings in a retail business

- **company credit card account** can be used if the business issues credit cards to its employees to enable them to pay for expenses

- **credit card receipts account** can be used if the business receives a significant number of credit or debit card payments from its customers

When a business is setting up its bank accounts it should click on RECORD on the BANK screen to produce the bank account DETAILS screen . . .

This screen enables the business to input details of the account, the bank and bank contact and to see the activity on the account.

RECORDING PAYMENTS FROM CUSTOMERS

how do payments arrive?

When a payment arrives from a customer who has bought on credit it can arrive at the business in a variety of ways:

- A cheque and **remittance advice**. A remittance advice is a document stating what the payment relates to – eg which invoices and credit notes.
- A **BACS payment.** A BACS (Bankers Automated Clearing Services) payment is a payment sent directly between the banks' computers and does not involve a cheque. Information relating to the BACS payment may be received in the form of a BACS remittance advice or from the business bank statement.
- A **Cash payment.**

Examples of cheque and BACS remittance advices are shown below:

TO	REMITTANCE ADVICE	FROM
Pronto Supplies Ltd Unit 17 Severnvale Estate Broadwater Road Mereford MR1 6TF		**Compsync** **4 Friar Street** **Broadfield** **BR1 3RF** Tel 01908 761234 Fax 01908 761987 VAT REG GB 0745 8383 56

Account PS765   6 November 2013

date	your reference	our reference	payment amount
01 10 11	INVOICE 787923	47609	277.30
10 10 11	CREDIT NOTE 12157	47609	(27.73)
		CHEQUE TOTAL	249.57

BACS REMITTANCE ADVICE	FROM: Excelsior Services 17 Gatley Way Bristol BS1 9GH
TO Pronto Supplies Ltd Unit 17 Severnvale Estate, Broadwater Rd, Mereford MR1 6TF	06 12 13

Your ref	Our ref		Amount
13982	3323	BACS TRANSFER	465.00
		TOTAL	465.00

THIS HAS BEEN PAID BY BACS CREDIT TRANSFER DIRECTLY INTO YOUR BANK ACCOUNT AT ALBION BANK NO 11719881 SORT CODE 90 47 17

customer payments and the accounting system

An incoming payment from a customer settling one or more invoices (less any credit notes) needs to be recorded in the accounting system:

■ the balance in the bank account will increase (a debit in double-entry)

■ the balance in the customer's account (and the Debtors Control Account) will decrease because the customer will owe less (a credit in double-entry accounting)

In computer accounting the payment is input once and the two entries will be automatically made from the same screen.

the practicalities

The business will normally input a number of payments at one time on a regular basis, eg every week, using the remittance advice and/or the bank statement as the source document.

The appropriate bank account should first be selected on the BANK screen and then the CUSTOMER icon selected to access the Customer Receipt input screen:

processing the payments received

The procedure for recording the customer payment on this screen is to:

■ input the customer account reference – this will bring up on screen the account name and all the outstanding amounts due on invoices

- input a reference if required – for example you might type 'cheque' or 'BACS' or the numerical reference relating to the payment

- input the amount of the payment in the 'Amount' box

- click on the 'Receipt' box of the invoice that is being paid

- click on the 'Pay in Full' button at the bottom

- if cash/settlement discount has been deducted from the payment, enter the net amount received in the Receipt box and the discount taken in the 'Discount' box

- if there is more than one invoice being paid click on the items being paid as appropriate; the 'Analysis Total' box at the bottom will show a running total of the money allocated

- if there is a long list of invoices and a payment to cover them, click on 'Automatic' at the bottom and the computer will allocate the payment down the invoice list until it runs out

- if a credit note (code 'SC') has been taken account of in the net payment, this should be dealt with first – see the next section for a full explanation

- check that what you have done is correct and SAVE; details to check are:
  - customer, amount, invoices being paid and amount received
  - the amounts in the 'Amount' box and the 'Analysis Total' box should be the same (but see next point)

- if the amount received by way of payment is greater than the amount allocated to outstanding invoices the extra payment will show as a 'Payment on Account' after you have saved – see page 116

- if the amount received by way of payment is less than the amount of the invoice(s) it is settling, the amount received will be allocated to the appropriate invoice(s) and the unpaid amount will show as outstanding on the Customer's account – see page 116

- you should print out a Day Books: Customer Receipts (Summary) for these transactions from REPORTS in BANK to check that the total of the cheques (or BACS payments) received equals the total input

DEALING WITH CREDIT NOTES

When inputting payments from customers and to suppliers in a program like Sage, you may encounter the situation where the amount received (or paid out) is not the same as the amount of the invoice being settled.

For example, if a customer is issued with an invoice for £1,000 and then issued with a credit note for £100 because some of the goods are faulty, the customer will only owe – and pay – £900. The computer screen, however, will show this £900 as two separate lines: an invoice for £1,000 and a credit note for £100. If the £900 cheque received is allocated against the £1,000, the computer will think a balance of £100 still needs to be paid against this invoice, even though the account balance is nil.

the solution

The credit note needs to be allocated to the balance of the invoice. This is done by:

- clicking on the 'Receipt' box on the credit note line
- clicking on 'Pay in Full' so that the analysis total shows a minus amount
- clicking on the Receipt box on the invoice line and then 'Pay in Full' so that the analysis box shows the payment amount

This procedure can be carried out during or after the payments received routine. In the example below a credit note for £240 is being set off against an invoice for £3,400, the amount received being £3,160.

Note that the procedure for allocating supplier credit notes to supplier invoices works on exactly the same principle.

No.	Type	A/C	Date	Ref	Ex.Ref	Details	T/C	Amount £	Disputed?	Receipt £	Discount £
4	SI	DB001	10/01/2013	10016		Opening Bala...	n/a	3400.00		3400.00	0.00
52	SC	DB001	06/02/2013	551		Software retur...	n/a	540.00		540.00	0.00
55	SI	DB001	13/02/2013	10028		Hardware	n/a	720.00		0.00	0.00

DEALING WITH UNDERPAYMENTS AND OVERPAYMENTS

Sometimes a customer will send an amount which does not tally with the amount that appears on the customer's statement and the amount on the computer records. For example:

- the customer sends a part payment of an invoice because he or she is short of money, or thinks a credit note is due
- the customer sends too much money, ignoring a credit note that has been issued or paying the account twice

the solution – underpayment

The amount that has been received is allocated against the relevant invoice. The amount that is still owing will show on the computer records.

the solution – overpayment

The amount that has been received is allocated against all the relevant invoices. The extra amount that is received will show as a 'Payment on Account' which will be available to allocate against future invoices.

In the example below, D Boossey paid his account with a cheque for £4,120 at the end of the month. He unfortunately did not make an adjustment for a credit note for £540 he had received and so he overpaid by this amount. Note the 'Payment on Account' on the second screen which shows how his account appears following the payment.

the amount overpaid, now available to meet further invoices

RECORDING PAYMENTS TO SUPPLIERS

what documents are involved?

A business often pays its suppliers after it receives a **statement** setting out the amounts due from invoices and any deductions made following the issue of credit notes. This is not a hard and fast rule, however, and it is quite in order to pay individual invoices as and when they are received.

Payment may be made by cheque, although payments are increasingly processed electronically by BACS transfer between the banks' computers. Payment is normally made in full, but occasionally a part payment may be made. A typical payment cheque, together with a completed counterfoil (cheque stub) is shown opposite.

The business will send a **remittance advice** (see page 97) to the supplier with the cheque, or, if a BACS payment is being made, on its own.

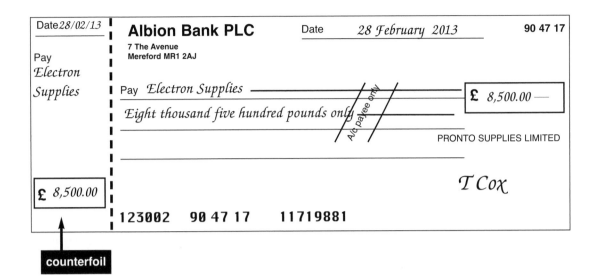

supplier payments and the accounting system

Payment to a supplier settling one or more invoices (less any credit notes) needs to be recorded in the accounting system:

■ the balance in the bank account will decrease (a credit in double-entry)

■ the balance in the supplier's account (and the Creditors Control Account) will decrease because the supplier will be owed less (a debit in double-entry accounting)

In computer accounting the payment is input once and the two entries will be automatically made from the same screen.

processing the payments

As with customer receipts, the business will normally input a number of payments at one time on a regular basis, for example just after the cheques have been written out, or the BACS payment instructions prepared.

The payments are input in Sage from the SUPPLIER icon on the BANK screen – after the appropriate bank account has been selected.

The procedure for recording the supplier payment is to:

■ input the supplier reference in the box next to the word 'Payee' on the 'cheque' – this will bring up on screen the account name and all the outstanding amounts due on invoices

■ input the cheque number on the cheque and alter the date if the cheque date is different

■ input the amount of the payment in the Amount box on the cheque; if it is a part payment the same procedure will be followed

- click on the 'Payment' box of the invoice that is being paid – here it is the first one – and click on the 'Pay in full' icon at the bottom; if there is more than one invoice being paid click on the items being paid as appropriate; any part payment will be allocated to the appropriate invoice(s) in the same way
- check that what you have done is correct (ie supplier, amount, invoices being paid) and SAVE (refer to page 105 if you wish to print out a remittance advice)
- print out a Day Books: Supplier Payments (Summary) from REPORTS in BANK to check that the total of the cheques (or BACS payments) issued equals the total input on the computer

Note that when processing supplier payments you may, as with customer payments, have to adjust for credit notes, overpayments and underpayments. These are covered in detail on pages 99-101.

A supplier payment screen is shown below.

Supplier Payment - Bank Current Account

| Bank A/C Ref | 1200 | Bank Current Account | | Date | 28/02/2013 | Cheque No. | BACS |

| Payee | EL001 | Electron Supplies |

Eight thousand, five hundred pounds £ 8500.00

Pronto Supplies Limited

Show All From 28/02/2013 To 28/02/2013

No.	Type	A/C	Date	Ref	Ex.Ref	Details	T/C	Amount £	Disputed?	Payment £	Discount £
8	PI	EL001	05/01/2013	8122		Opening Bala...	n/a	8500.00		8500.00	0.00
62	PI	EL001	09/02/2013	8576		Processors	n/a	2400.00		0.00	0.00
67	PI	EL001	14/02/2013	8603		Laser printer	n/a	432.00		0.00	0.00

| | Bank Balance | 29995.20 | Analysis Total | 8500.00 |

Save | Discard | Pay in Full | Wizard | Automatic | Dept. | Close

Print Bank Remittances

| Bank | 1200 | Bank Current Account |

Print

☐ Date Range From: / / To: / / Show printed items ☐

Details

Index No.	Date	Bank A/C	Cheque	Supplier A/C	Supplier Name	Amount £	Printed?	Items
0000001	28/02/2013	1200	BACS	DE001	Delco PLC	5174.00	N	2
0000002	28/02/2013	1200	BACS	EL001	Electron Supplies	8500.00	N	1
0000003	28/02/2013	1200	BACS	MA001	MacCity	4454.40	N	2

printing remittance advices and cheques

Remittance advices and cheques may be printed once a payment has been processed in Sage.

To print a remittance advice, click on REMITTANCE on the BANK toolbar. Select the transaction or transactions for which the remittance advice is required, click PRINT and then choose one of the remittance options and click RUN.

To print cheques (with remittance advice attached), click on CHEQUES on the BANK toolbar. Pre-printed cheques to use with Sage must be specially ordered.

An extract from the printed remittance advice is shown below.

Pronto Supplies Limited
Unit 17 Severnvale Estate
Broadwater Road
Mereford
Wyvern
MR1 6TF
Tel : 01908 748071
Email : mail@prontosupplies.co.uk
VAT Reg No. 404 7106 52

REMITTANCE ADVICE

Date	28/02/2013
Account Ref	EL001
Cheque No	BACS

Electron Supplies
17 Maxim Way

Manchester

M1 5TF

NOTE: All values are shown in Pound Sterling

Date	Ref	Details	Debit	Credit
05/01/2013	8122	Opening Balance		8,500.00

Case Study

PRONTO SUPPLIES LIMITED: PROCESSING PAYMENTS FROM CUSTOMERS AND TO SUPPLIERS

It is February 28 2013. Tom has received a number of payments (with remittance advices) from his customers in settlement of their accounts. Tom also has a list of supplier invoices to pay, the money being due at the end of the month.

receipts from customers

The list of payments received is shown below.

John Butler & Associates	£5,500.00	Cheque
Charisma Design	£2,419.20	Cheque
Crowmatic Limited	£3,234.00	BACS
David Boossey	£2,860.00	Cheque
Kay Denz	£6,500.00	BACS
L Garr & Co	£8,500.00	BACS
Total of payments received	£29,013.20	

Tom notes the following:

- The cheque from Charisma Design includes payment of an invoice for £19.20 issued on 6 February

- The cheque from David Boossey includes an adjustment made for a credit note issued on 6 February

These payments are entered into the computer accounting system under CUSTOMERS in the BANK section as shown on the screen below. This illustrates the John Butler & Associates cheque being input.

When entering the cheque received from David Boossey, Tom takes account of the credit note by clicking first in the 'Receipt' box on the credit note line and then 'Pay in Full', before allocating the amount to the line of the amount originally due.

Tom then prints out a report Day Books: Customer Receipts (Summary) which shows the transactions he has processed. This is shown on the next page. He checks the total on the report against the batch total of the payments (or remittance advices) he has received.

Customer Receipt - Bank Current Account

Bank Details

Account Ref	1200
Name	Bank Current Account
Balance	20156.00

Customer Details

Account	JB001
Name	John Butler & Associates

Receipt Details

Date	28/02/2013
Amount	5500.00
Reference	cheque

Show All   From 28/02/2013   To 28/02/2013

No.	Type	A/C	Date	Ref	Ex.Ref	Details	T/C	Amount £	Disputed?	Receipt £	Discount £
1	SI	JB001	05/01/2013	10013		Opening Bala...	n/a	5500.00		5500.00	0.00
48	SI	JB001	05/02/2013	10023		Hardware	n/a	480.00		0.00	0.00
54	SI	JB001	12/02/2013	10027		Consultancy	n/a	144.00		0.00	0.00

Analysis Total   5500.00

Save	Discard	Pay in Full	Wizard	Automatic	Dept.		Close

Pronto Supplies Limited

Day Books: Customer Receipts (Summary)

| Date From: | 28/02/2013 | | | Bank From: | 1200 |
| DateTo: | 28/02/2013 | | | Bank To: | 1200 |

| Transaction From: | 1 | | | Customer From : | |
| Transaction To: | 99,999,999 | | | Customer To: | ZZZZZZZZ |

| Bank | 1200 | | Currency | Pound Sterling | | | | | | | | |

No	Type	Date	Account	Ref	Details	Net £	Tax £	Gross £ B	Bank Rec. Date
68	SR	28/02/2013	JB001	cheque	Sales Receipt	5,500.00	0.00	5,500.00 N	
69	SR	28/02/2013	CH001	cheque	Sales Receipt	2,419.20	0.00	2,419.20 N	
70	SR	28/02/2013	CR001	BACS	Sales Receipt	3,234.00	0.00	3,234.00 N	
71	SR	28/02/2013	DB001	cheque	Sales Receipt	2,860.00	0.00	2,860.00 N	
72	SR	28/02/2013	KD001	BACS	Sales Receipt	6,500.00	0.00	6,500.00 N	
73	SR	28/02/2013	LG001	BACS	Sales Receipt	8,500.00	0.00	8,500.00 N	
					Totals £	29,013.20	0.00	29,013.20	

payments to suppliers

Tom has made a list of the amounts he owes to his suppliers for goods sent to Pronto Supplies Limited in January.

The documents he has for this are his original purchase orders, invoices received and any credit notes issued by his suppliers.

The data is now ready for input. The details are:

Delco PLC	£5,174.00	BACS
Electron Supplies	£8,500.00	BACS
MacCity	£4,454.40	BACS
Total of payments made	£18,128.40	

Tom notes that the payments from Delco PLC and MacCity include adjustments for credit notes issued.

These payments are entered into the computer accounting system under SUPPLIERS in the BANK section as shown below. Tom will also print out remittance advices to send out.

Tom then prints out a report Day Books: Supplier Payments (Summary) which shows the transactions he has processed. He checks the total on the report against the total of the payments he has issued.

Pronto Supplies Limited
Day Books: Supplier Payments (Summary)

Date From:	28/02/2013		Bank From:	1200
DateTo:	28/02/2013		Bank To:	1200
Transaction From:	1		Supplier From:	
Transaction To:	99,999,999		Supplier To:	ZZZZZZZZ

Bank 1200 Currency Pound Sterling

No	Type	Date	Supplier	Ref	Details	Net £	Tax £	Gross £	B	Bank R
74	PP	28/02/2013	DE001	BACS	Purchase Payment	5,174.00	0.00	5,174.00	N	
75	PP	28/02/2013	EL001	BACS	Purchase Payment	8,500.00	0.00	8,500.00	N	
76	PP	28/02/2013	MA001	BACS	Purchase Payment	4,454.40	0.00	4,454.40	N	
					Totals £	18,128.40	0.00	18,128.40		

Chapter Summary

- The bank account is a central account in the operation of any business as so many transactions pass through it.

- A business can set up not only the bank current account in the computer accounting system, but also a number of other 'money' accounts. These, which include petty cash account and credit card accounts, enable the business to keep track of the processing of money in a variety of forms.

- Payments received from customers who have bought on credit can be processed through the computer accounting system. The accounting system is adjusted in each case by an increase in the bank current account and a reduction of the customer's account balance in the Sales Ledger.

- Payments to suppliers from whom the business has bought on credit can also be processed on the computer and remittance advices printed if required. The accounting entries in this case are a decrease in the bank current account and a reduction in the supplier's account balance in the Purchases Ledger.

- The payment amount in each case (customer or supplier) will relate to invoices and any credit notes issued. Any overpayment or underpayment will be logged on the relevant Sage account.

- It is essential to check the input of payments from customers and to suppliers by obtaining a printout such as a Day Book Report from the computer.

Key Terms	current account	the 'everyday' bank account which handles routine receipts and payments
	cash payments	payments made straightaway
	credit payments	payments made at a later date following the issue of an invoice to a customer or by a supplier
	remittance advice	a document that tells a business that a payment is being made
	payments on account	an overpayment or amount that is not allocated to specific transactions

Activities

8.1 What do the icons Payment, Supplier, Receipt and Customer represent on a BANK menu bar?

8.2 Why is it helpful if a business receives a remittance advice when payment is made direct to its bank account from a customer settling an invoice or account?

8.3 What entries to the accounting system will be made when a business receives a payment from a credit customer and makes a payment to a supplier?

8.4 What printout from a computer accounting system lists payments made to suppliers on any particular day? Why is it important that a report like this is extracted?

PRONTO SUPPLIES INPUTTING TASKS

Task 1

Set the program date to 28 February 2013. Enter the following customer payments into BANK (CUSTOMERS). Check your total before saving and print out a Day Books: Customer Receipts (Summary) Report to confirm the accuracy of your input (see page 203).

Note:

■ the cheque from Charisma Design also includes payment of an invoice issued on 6 February

■ the cheque from David Boossey includes an adjustment made for a credit note, which will have to be allocated as described in the Case Study (see page 105)

John Butler & Associates	£5,500.00	Cheque
Charisma Design	£2,419.20	Cheque
Crowmatic Limited	£3,234.00	BACS
David Boossey	£2,860.00	Cheque
Kay Denz	£6,500.00	BACS
L Garr & Co	£8,500.00	BACS
Total of payments received	£29,013.20	

Task 2

Enter into the computer the three BACS payments listed below that Tom is paying to suppliers.

In the case of Delco PLC and MacCity, ensure that you adjust the account for credit notes issued.

Check your total before saving and print out a Day Books: Supplier Payments (Summary) Report to confirm the accuracy of your input (see page 203).

If you are able to, print out remittance advices.

Delco PLC	£5,174.00
Electron Supplies	£8,500.00
MacCity	£4,454.40
Total of payments made	£18,128.40

Task 3

Print out a trial balance for Pronto Supplies as at 28 February 2013 from the FINANCIALS module and check it against the trial balance on page 204.

Compare this new trial balance with the trial balance produced at the end of the last chapter.

Explain the changes you can see in the Bank Account balance, Debtors Control Account and Creditors Control Account. What has happened in the accounting system? Keep your printout with your answer.

Cash receipts and payments

this chapter covers...

■ The last chapter explained how payments settling invoices are recorded in a computer accounting system. These payments received from customers and made to suppliers settle up 'credit sales' where invoices are issued when the sale is made and payment is made later.

■ A business will also process a substantial number of varied 'cash payments' where the money is transferred at the same time as the transaction. Note that 'cash' does not just mean notes and coins in this context; it means immediate payment.

Example of these payments (and receipts) include:

- money received from sales – over the counter sales or online sales

- money spent on purchases – buying stock and material for use in the business

- running expenses paid – wages, power bills, rent

- items bought for permanent use in the business – fixed assets not bought on credit

- loans made to the business

- money (capital) put into the business by the owner(s)

■ A computer accounting system will record these 'cash' items in a different way from the 'credit' items seen in the last chapter. In a Sage system they are processed through the PAYMENT or RECEIPT icons on the BANK menu bar.

■ The transactions mentioned so far involve payments which are made straight through the bank current account. A business may also use other funds for making payments and receiving money. These are covered in the next chapter.

THE BANK ACCOUNTS

The last chapter started by looking at the different bank accounts that a Sage system will allow a business to set up. Whereas the last chapter concentrated on the use of the Bank Current Account for payments made on credit, this chapter examines the way in which cash payments (immediate payments) are recorded in the Bank Current Account of a computer accounting system.

The BANK screen shown below (the default accounts screen) explains the icons that you will be using in this chapter.

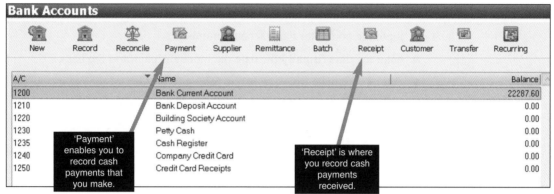

CASH RECEIPTS

Cash sales made by a business are usually sales made at a checkout or through an online shop. 'Cash' here means 'immediate payment.'

Receipts from cash sales can be made by cash, cheque, debit or credit card and BACS. The business should ensure the money is paid into the bank current account as soon as possible, so that it can be used to meet payments the business may have made or may have to make.

The input screen for cash sales is reached from the RECEIPT icon on the BANK menu bar. It looks like this:

Bank	Date	Ref	N/C	Dept	Project Ref	Details	Net	T/C	Tax
1200	09/02/2013	10736	4000	0		Hardware sal...	12500.00	T1	2500.00
1200	09/02/2013	10737	4001	0		Software sales	4680.00	T1	936.00
1200	16/02/2013	10738	4000	0		Hardware sal...	15840.00	T1	3168.00
1200	16/02/2013	10739	4001	0		Software sales	3680.00	T1	736.00
1200	23/02/2013	10740	4000	0		Hardware sal...	17800.00	T1	3560.00
1200	23/02/2013	10741	4001	0		Software sales	4800.00	T1	960.00

Bank: Bank Current Account
N/C: Computer software sales
Tax Rate: 20.00
Total: 71160.00

inputting bank receipts

Cash sales paid straight into the bank may be input from the bank paying-in slips recorded in the business cash book or from a sales listing sheet. These receipts are known in Sage as Bank Receipts and are input as follows:

■ input the computer bank account number

■ enter the date (usually the date the money is paid into the bank)

■ enter a reference (this can be the reference number of the paying-in slip)

■ input the appropriate nominal code (N/C) for the type of sales involved

■ enter a description of the payment (eg 'hardware sales') under 'Details'

■ enter the net amount of the sales (ie the sales amount excluding VAT) and then click on T1 if the goods are standard rated for VAT – the computer will then automatically calculate the VAT amount for you and show it in the right-hand column

■ check that the VAT amount shown agrees with your figure and change it on screen if it does not – there may be a rounding difference

■ check the input details and totals and then SAVE

a note on VAT

The rates of VAT (**tax codes**) that you are most likely to come across are:

T1	standard rate (20% at the time of writing)
T2	exempt from VAT – eg postage stamps, insurance
T0	zero-rated, ie VAT could be charged but it is zero at the moment – eg books, food and some children's clothes
T9	transactions not involving VAT

If you only have a VAT inclusive figure and do not know what the VAT amount is, enter the total figure in the 'Net' column and click on 'Calc.Net' at the bottom of the screen. The computer then automatically calculates and shows the Net amount and the VAT.

other cash receipts

You can also enter other cash (= not credit) receipts using the same Bank Receipts screen. Examples include:

■ money invested by the owner(s) of the business – capital (N/C 3000)

■ loans and grants from outside bodies (N/C 2300)

■ income from other sources such as rent received (N/C 4904), bank interest or commission received (N/C 4902)

This money is likely to be received in the form of a cheque or bank transfer and will need to be recorded as such.

CASH PAYMENTS

Most credit payments made by businesses, as we saw in the last chapter, are to suppliers for goods and services provided and paid for on invoice. But businesses also have to make payments on a day-to-day cash basis (immediate payment) for running costs and expenses such as wages, telephone bills, owner drawings and sundry (miscellaneous) expenses. Cash payments may also be made to suppliers where no credit terms have been agreed.

These payments are input from the screen reached by clicking on the PAYMENT icon on the BANK menu bar. See the example shown below.

Bank	Date	Ref	N/C	Dept	Project Ref	Cost Code	Details	Net	T/C	Tax
1200	12/02/2013	122992	5000	0			Cash purch...	15500.00	T1	3100.00
1200	14/02/2013	122993	6201	0			Advertising	10200.00	T1	2040.00
1200	15/02/2013	122994	0040	0			Furniture	5000.00	T1	1000.00
1200	23/02/2013	BACS	7200	0			Electricity	158.00	T1	31.60
1200	26/02/2013	BACS	7550	0			Telephone	310.00	T1	62.00
1200	28/02/2013	Debit ca...	7502	0			Stationery	340.00	T1	68.00
1200	28/02/2013	BACS	7000	0			Wages	16780.00	T9	0.00

Bank: Bank Current Account
N/C: Gross Wages
Tax Rate: 0.00
Total: 54589.60

48288.00   6301.60

Save | Discard | Calc. Net | Print Cheque | Memorise | Recall | Close

inputting cash payments

Cash payments can be input from the handwritten business **cash book** (if one is used), or from the cheques issued and bills being paid (which should show any VAT element). The procedure for inputting is:

- input the computer bank account number
- enter the date (the date the payment is made)
- enter a reference (normally the cheque number or 'BACS' if the payment is a BACS payment)
- input the appropriate nominal code (N/C) for the type of payment involved
- enter a brief description of the nature of the payment (eg 'Telephone') under 'Details'

■ enter the net amount of the payment (ie the amount excluding VAT) and then click on T1 if the product is standard rated for VAT – the computer will then automatically calculate the VAT amount for you and show it in the right-hand column

■ check that the VAT amount shown agrees with your figure and change it on screen if it does not – there may be a rounding difference

a note on VAT

The VAT rates used here are:

> T1 the telephone bill is standard rated
>
> T9 wages do not involve VAT

The code for a zero-rated item would have been T0. The code for a VAT exempt item would have been T2.

If you do not know what the VAT amount is included in a payment figure, enter the total figure in the 'Net' column and click on 'Calc.Net' at the bottom of the screen. The computer will then automatically calculate the VAT and adjust the Net figure accordingly.

checking the input data

It is important to check your input for each item against the source data for the input. You will see that the screen on the previous page has running total boxes below the Net and Tax columns. There is also a Total (Net plus Tax) box at the top. These boxes will all update as you enter the transactions.

If you are entering the data for a number of transactions you should add up the three 'batch' totals (Net, VAT and Total) and check them against the screen figures in the total boxes when you have finished your data entry.

As a final check you should print out a Day Book report (see extract below) from Reports in BANK and check the entries against your handwritten records (your cash book, for example).

Pronto Supplies Limited
Day Books: Bank Payments (Detailed)

								Net £	Tax £ T/C	Gross £ V B	Bank Date

Transaction From: 1   N/C From:
Transaction To: 99,999,999   N/C To: 99999999

Dept From: 0
Dept To: 999

Bank: 1200   Currency: Pound Sterling

No	Type	N/C	Date	Ref	Details	Dept	Net £	Tax £ T/C	Gross £ V B	Bank Date
83	BP	5000	12/02/2013	122992	Cash purchases	0	15,500.00	3,100.00 T1	18,600.00 N N	
84	BP	6201	14/02/2013	122993	Advertising	0	10,200.00	2,040.00 T1	12,240.00 N N	
85	BP	0040	15/02/2013	122994	Furniture	0	5,000.00	1,000.00 T1	6,000.00 N N	
86	BP	7200	23/02/2013	BACS	Electricity	0	158.00	31.60 T1	189.60 N N	
87	BP	7550	26/02/2013	BACS	Telephone	0	310.00	62.00 T1	372.00 N N	
88	BP	7502	28/02/2013	Debit card	Stationery	0	340.00	68.00 T1	408.00 N N	
89	BP	7000	28/02/2013	BACS	Wages	0	16,780.00	0.00 T9	16,780.00 - N	
						Totals £	48,288.00	6,301.60	54,589.60	

Case Study

PRONTO SUPPLIES LIMITED:
CASH RECEIPTS AND PAYMENTS

It is February 28 2013 and Tom has completed and checked his input of customer receipts and supplier payments (see pages 105-108).

He now has to input the various cash receipts and payments received and made during the month.

cash receipts

Pronto Supplies Limited paid takings of cash sales into the bank current account three times during the month. The amounts recorded in the cash book are shown below. The reference quoted is the paying-in slip reference.

Date	Details	Net amount (£)	VAT (£)	ref.
9 Feb 2013	Hardware sales	12,500.00	2500.00	10736
9 Feb 2013	Software sales	4,680.00	936.00	10737
16 Feb 2013	Hardware sales	15,840.00	3,168.00	10738
16 Feb 2013	Software sales	3,680.00	736.00	10739
23 Feb 2013	Hardware sales	17,800.00	3,560.00	10740
23 Feb 2013	Software sales	4,800.00	960.00	10741
	Totals	59,300.00	11,860.00	

These sales receipts are entered into the computer accounting system on the RECEIPTS screen reached from the BANK menu bar. Note that the Bank Current Account and the appropriate nominal sales code (N/C) are used each time.

Tom can use some helpful features when inputting. When in a line and wanting to copy the box above (eg the bank account number or the date) he presses F6; when wanting to raise the number in the box by one (eg reference number) he presses Shift F6.

Bank	Bank Current Account					Tax Rate		20.00
N/C	Computer software sales					Total		71160.00

Bank	Date	Ref	N/C	Dept	Project Ref	Details	Net	T/C	Tax
1200	09/02/2013	10736	4000	0		Hardware sal...	12500.00	T1	2500.00
1200	09/02/2013	10737	4001	0		Software sales	4680.00	T1	936.00
1200	16/02/2013	10738	4000	0		Hardware sal...	15840.00	T1	3168.00
1200	16/02/2013	10739	4001	0		Software sales	3680.00	T1	736.00
1200	23/02/2013	10740	4000	0		Hardware sal...	17800.00	T1	3560.00
120		10741				Software sales	4800.00	T1	960.00

Press F6 to copy the box above

Press Shift F6 to raise the number in the box above by 1

Tom then checks his listing totals against the on-screen totals for accuracy and clicks SAVE. He then prints out a Report Day Books: Bank Receipts (Detailed) as a paper-based record of the transactions he has processed. This is shown below. He again checks the totals on the report against the totals on his original listing.

Pronto Supplies Limited

Day Books: Bank Receipts (Detailed)

| Date From: | 09/02/2013 | | | | | | | | | | | | |
| DateTo: | 23/02/2013 | | | | | | | | | | | | |

| Transaction From: | 1 | | | | | | | N/C From: | | | | | |
| Transaction To: | 99,999,999 | | | | | | | N/C To: | | 99999999 | | | |

| Dept From: | 0 | | | | | | | | | | | | |
| Dept To: | 999 | | | | | | | | | | | | |

Bank: 1200   Currency: Pound Sterling

No	Type	N/C	Date	Ref	Details	Dept	Net £	Tax £ T/C	Gross £ V B
77	BR	4000	09/02/2013	10736	Hardware sales	0	12,500.00	2,500.00 T1	15,000.00 N N
78	BR	4001	09/02/2013	10737	Software sales	0	4,680.00	936.00 T1	5,616.00 N N
79	BR	4000	16/02/2013	10738	Hardware sales	0	15,840.00	3,168.00 T1	19,008.00 N N
80	BR	4001	16/02/2013	10739	Software sales	0	3,680.00	736.00 T1	4,416.00 N N
81	BR	4000	23/02/2013	10740	Hardware sales	0	17,800.00	3,560.00 T1	21,360.00 N N
82	BR	4001	23/02/2013	10741	Software sales	0	4,800.00	960.00 T1	5,760.00 N N
						Totals £	59,300.00	11,860.00	71,160.00

cash payments

Tom sees from the company cash book that Pronto Supplies Limited has made a number of cheque 'cash' payments during the month for a variety of purposes. They are listed below. They include:

- normal day-to-day running expenses paid by cheque, debit card and BACS on a cash basis
- the purchase of furniture for £5,000 (a fixed asset) on 15 February paid by cheque

Date	Details	Net amount (£)	VAT (£)	chq no
12 Feb 2013	Cash purchases	15,500.00	3,100.00	122992
14 Feb 2013	Advertising	10,200.00	2,040.00	122993
15 Feb 2013	Furniture	5,000.00	1,000.00	122994
23 Feb 2013	Electricity	158.00	31.60	BACS
26 Feb 2013	Telephone	310.00	62.00	BACS
26 Feb 2013	Stationery	340.00	68.00	D/CARD
28 Feb 2013	Wages	16,780.00	no VAT	BACS
	Totals	48,288.00	6,301.60	

These payments are entered into the computer accounting system on the PAYMENTS screen reached from the BANK menu bar. Note that the Bank Current Account and the appropriate nominal code (N/C) is used each time. The reference in each case is the relevant cheque number or payment method.

Bank	Date	Ref	N/C	Dept	Project Ref	Cost Code	Details	Net	T/C	Tax
1200	12/02/2013	122992	5000	0			Cash purch...	15500.00	T1	3100.00
1200	14/02/2013	122993	6201	0			Advertising	10200.00	T1	2040.00
1200	15/02/2013	122994	0040	0			Furniture	5000.00	T1	1000.00
1200	23/02/2013	BACS	7200	0			Electricity	158.00	T1	31.60
1200	26/02/2013	BACS	7550	0			Telephone	310.00	T1	62.00
1200	28/02/2013	Debit ca...	7502	0			Stationery	340.00	T1	68.00
1200	28/02/2013	BACS	7000	0			Wages	16780.00	T9	0.00

Bank: Bank Current Account
N/C: Gross Wages
Tax Rate: 0.00
Total: 54589.60

48288.00   6301.60

Save   Discard   Calc. Net   Print Cheque   Memorise   Recall   Close

If Tom wants to insert or delete lines when entering data, he can press F7 to insert a blank line between two lines already entered, or F8 to delete a line already entered.

Tom then checks his listing totals against the on-screen totals for accuracy and clicks SAVE. He prints out a Report Day Books: Bank Payments (Detailed) as a record of the transactions he has processed. This is shown below. He compares the totals on the report against the totals on his original listing as a final check of input accuracy.

Pronto Supplies Limited
Day Books: Bank Payments (Detailed)

Date From: 12/02/2013
DateTo: 28/02/2013

Transaction From: 1
Transaction To: 99,999,999

N/C From:
N/C To: 99999999

Dept From: 0
Dept To: 999

Bank: 1200   Currency: Pound Sterling

No	Type	N/C	Date	Ref	Details	Dept	Net £	Tax £	T/C	Gross £	V	B	Bank Date
83	BP	5000	12/02/2013	122992	Cash purchases	0	15,500.00	3,100.00	T1	18,600.00	N	N	
84	BP	6201	14/02/2013	122993	Advertising	0	10,200.00	2,040.00	T1	12,240.00	N	N	
85	BP	0040	15/02/2013	122994	Furniture	0	5,000.00	1,000.00	T1	6,000.00	N	N	
86	BP	7200	23/02/2013	BACS	Electricity	0	158.00	31.60	T1	189.60	N	N	
87	BP	7550	26/02/2013	BACS	Telephone	0	310.00	62.00	T1	372.00	N	N	
88	BP	7502	28/02/2013	Debit card	Stationery	0	340.00	68.00	T1	408.00	N	N	
89	BP	7000	28/02/2013	BACS	Wages	0	16,780.00	0.00	T9	16,780.00	-	N	
						Totals £	48,288.00	6,301.60		54,589.60			

RECEIPTS AND PAYMENTS AND THE ACCOUNTING SYSTEM

It is important to appreciate how the cash receipts and payments in this chapter relate to the accounting system of a business, particularly if you are also studying double-entry bookkeeping.

Remember that transactions involve debits and credits and that the debit amount always equals the credit amount. Because of the VAT included in many sales and purchases, these transactions may involve three entries:

■ the amount posted to the bank account (the full amount)

■ the 'net' amount (the amount before VAT is added on) posted to the sales account or purchases (or expense) account

■ any VAT involved in the transaction being posted to Sales or Purchases VAT account

The whole cash payment system is summarised in the linked diagram below. This shows how the money comes into and out of the bank account and illustrates how the double-entry bookkeeping works. If you are not studying double-entry, just concentrate on the types of receipts and payments and study how they are input.

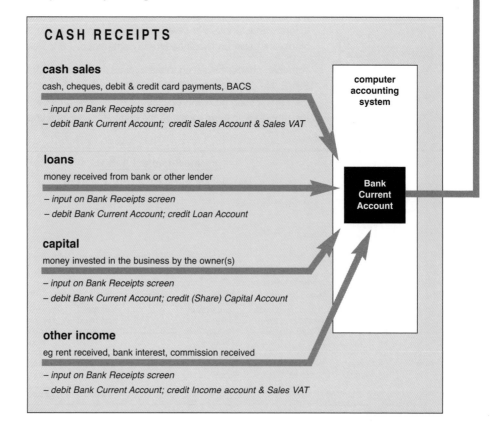

CASH RECEIPTS

cash sales
cash, cheques, debit & credit card payments, BACS

– *input on Bank Receipts screen*
– *debit Bank Current Account; credit Sales Account & Sales VAT*

loans
money received from bank or other lender

– *input on Bank Receipts screen*
– *debit Bank Current Account; credit Loan Account*

capital
money invested in the business by the owner(s)

– *input on Bank Receipts screen*
– *debit Bank Current Account; credit (Share) Capital Account*

other income
eg rent received, bank interest, commission received

– *input on Bank Receipts screen*
– *debit Bank Current Account; credit Income account & Sales VAT*

computer
accounting
system

Bank
Current
Account

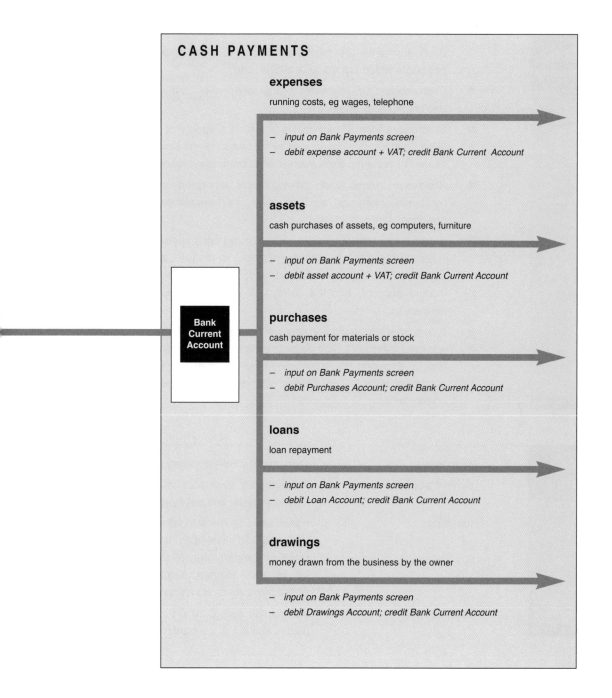

CASH PAYMENTS

expenses

running costs, eg wages, telephone

- *input on Bank Payments screen*
- *debit expense account + VAT; credit Bank Current Account*

assets

cash purchases of assets, eg computers, furniture

- *input on Bank Payments screen*
- *debit asset account + VAT; credit Bank Current Account*

Bank Current Account

purchases

cash payment for materials or stock

- *input on Bank Payments screen*
- *debit Purchases Account; credit Bank Current Account*

loans

loan repayment

- *input on Bank Payments screen*
- *debit Loan Account; credit Bank Current Account*

drawings

money drawn from the business by the owner

- *input on Bank Payments screen*
- *debit Drawings Account; credit Bank Current Account*

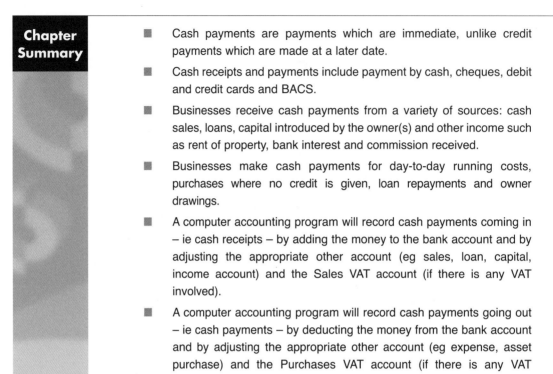

Chapter Summary

- Cash payments are payments which are immediate, unlike credit payments which are made at a later date.

- Cash receipts and payments include payment by cash, cheques, debit and credit cards and BACS.

- Businesses receive cash payments from a variety of sources: cash sales, loans, capital introduced by the owner(s) and other income such as rent of property, bank interest and commission received.

- Businesses make cash payments for day-to-day running costs, purchases where no credit is given, loan repayments and owner drawings.

- A computer accounting program will record cash payments coming in – ie cash receipts – by adding the money to the bank account and by adjusting the appropriate other account (eg sales, loan, capital, income account) and the Sales VAT account (if there is any VAT involved).

- A computer accounting program will record cash payments going out – ie cash payments – by deducting the money from the bank account and by adjusting the appropriate other account (eg expense, asset purchase) and the Purchases VAT account (if there is any VAT involved).

Key Terms

cash sales	sales made where payment is immediate
current account	the 'everyday' bank account which handles routine receipts and payments
tax codes	a term used by Sage to refer to the rate of VAT which is applied to transactions; T1 refers to standard rate, T0 to the zero rate, T2 to VAT exempt items and T9 to transactions which do not involve VAT
cash book	the manual record which records money paid in and out of the bank account

Activities

9.1   From which icon on the BANK menu bar will the screen needed for recording a cash sale from a customer be reached? RECEIPT or CUSTOMER?

9.2   From which icon on the BANK menu bar will the screen needed for recording a cash purchase from a supplier be reached? PAYMENT or SUPPLIER?

9.3   Complete the sentences below using the following computer account names:

   • Bank   • Purchases   • Sales   • Purchases VAT   • Sales VAT

(a)   A business makes a cash sale for £120.00, which is made up of £100 net and £20.00 VAT. The postings to the computer accounts will be:

£120.00 to .... account

£100.00 to .... account

£20.00 to .... account

(b)   A business makes a cash purchase for £960, which is made up of £800 net and £160 VAT. The postings to the computer accounts will be:

£160.00 to .... account

£960.00 to .... account

£800.00 to .... account

9.4   Businesses from time-to-time pay into the bank cash payments which are not received from cash sales. Give three examples of this type of cash receipt.

PRONTO SUPPLIES INPUTTING TASKS

Task 1

Set the program date to 28 February 2013. Enter the following bank receipts into the computer. Check your totals before saving and print out a Day Books: Bank Receipts (Detailed) Report (date range 9 Feb to 23 Feb) to confirm the accuracy of your input (see page 204).

Date	Details	Net amount (£)	VAT (£)	ref.
9 Feb 2013	Hardware sales	12,500.00	2500.00	10736
9 Feb 2013	Software sales	4,680.00	936.00	10737
16 Feb 2013	Hardware sales	15,840.00	3,168.00	10738
16 Feb 2013	Software sales	3,680.00	736.00	10739
23 Feb 2013	Hardware sales	17,800.00	3,560.00	10740
23 Feb 2013	Software sales	4,800.00	960.00	10741
	Totals	59,300.00	11,860.00	

Task 2

Keeping the program date as 28 February 2013, enter the following bank payments into the computer. Take care over the Nominal Accounts that you choose and the VAT Tax codes used. T1 is the standard rate code, T2 is for exempt items and T9 is the code for transactions which do not involve VAT.

Check your totals before saving and print out a Day Books: Bank Payments (Detailed) Report, using an appropriate date range to confirm the accuracy of your input (see page 205).

Date	Details	Net amount (£)	VAT (£)	chq no
12 Feb 2013	Cash purchases*	15,500.00	3,100.00	122992
14 Feb 2013	Advertising	10,200.00	2,040.00	122993
15 Feb 2013	Furniture	5,000.00	1,000.00	122994
23 Feb 2013	Electricity	158.00	31.60	BACS
26 Feb 2013	Telephone	310.00	62.00	BACS
26 Feb 2013	Stationery	340.00	68.00	Debit Card
28 Feb 2013	Wages	16,780.00	no VAT	BACS
	Totals	48,288.00	6,301.60	

*use 'Materials Purchased' account for this transaction, as the purchases are for stock

Task 3

Keep the program date as 28 February 2013.

Tom has won £5,000 on a Premium Bond. He decides to pay the cheque into the business as extra issued share capital under reference 10742, Code T9.

On 28 February he also spends £4,000 plus VAT on a new colour printer for his office, using cheque number 122995 for the cash purchase.

Make the necessary entries into the computer accounts (the Nominal Accounts used will be Ordinary Shares and Office Equipment).

Task 4

Print out a trial balance as at 28 February 2013 to check the accuracy of your input to date. Note particularly the increases in Share Capital and Office Equipment Accounts. Check with the trial balance on page 205.

10 Bank accounts, petty cash and recurring entries

this chapter covers...

■ The last chapter explained how cash payments made directly in and out of the bank current account are recorded in a computer accounting system. 'Cash payment' here means 'immediate payment'. It can involve cash, cheques, payments by debit and credit card and BACS.

■ The computer program also enables a business to set up accounts on the system which record funds of money held by the business. These funds are classified by Sage as 'Bank' accounts, but the money is not held at the bank – it is held by the business and managed by the business.

■ One example is the petty cash account – a cash fund held under lock and key in the office, used for making small purchases and payments. The money for this account will come from the bank current account and be recorded in Sage by a Bank Transfer.

■ If a business – a shop for example – receives cash payments and then holds them on the premises for a length of time before paying them into the bank, it may decide to use a Cash Account to record the takings.

When the money is eventually paid into the bank, the business will record a Bank Transfer from Cash Account in Sage to show the money being paid into the bank.

■ Businesses will from time-to-time need to record regular payments made in and out of the bank current account. Examples include standing orders and direct debits for outgoing payments of insurance premiums and business rates and incoming receipts of rent from tenants.

In Sage the Recurring Entries facility enables the business to set up the payments so that they can be recorded automatically each month in the accounts on the click of a button.

THE BANK ACCOUNTS IN COMPUTER ACCOUNTING

The bank accounts and all the functions associated with them are found in Sage by clicking on the BANK button in the vertical toolbar.

The accounts listed come from the default list in the chart of accounts. The business does not have to adopt all the accounts, but may use some of them if it needs them. It can also set up new accounts within the appropriate account number range by clicking on NEW on the menu bar and using the new account Wizard. A summary of the Sage bank accounts is on page 95.

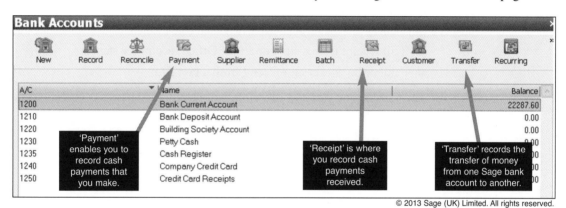

when is a bank account not a bank account?

The first three types of account shown on the above screen are actually maintained at the bank or building society. They are true 'bank' accounts. The last three accounts – petty cash and credit card payment and receipts accounts – are not kept at the bank but within the business. They are the accounts Sage uses to record money funds within the business which originally came from the bank or will be paid into the bank.

transfers between accounts

A TRANSFER facility on the BANK menu bar records movements between the 'bank' accounts. The screen below shows a transfer of £5,000 from the current account (1200) to the deposit account (1210).

OPENING UP A PETTY CASH ACCOUNT

what is a petty cash payment?

Petty cash is a float of cash – notes and coins – kept in an office, normally in a locked tin. It provides employees with the cash to make small purchases for the business, eg stationery, postage stamps and business taxi fares. The petty cash float is topped up with cash periodically.

The document used is the petty cash voucher (see below). When a payment is made, a petty cash voucher is completed and the appropriate evidence of payment is attached, for example:

- a till receipt from a shop or a Post Office receipt for stamps
- a rail or bus ticket or a receipt from a taxi firm

The cash can be paid out (or refunded) when the voucher is completed and authorised.

petty cash voucher		Number *807*	
	date	*15 May 2013*	
description			amount
		£	p
Envelopes		6	00
	VAT	*1*	20
Receipt obtained		7	20
signature	*T Harris*		
authorised	*R Patel*		

petty cash and the accounting system

Petty cash is a fund of money kept in the business in the same way as the bank current account is a fund of money kept in the bank. A 'bank' account will be set up for petty cash which will handle all the transactions:

- payments of cash into petty cash from the bank current account
- payments out of petty cash to pay for small expense items

payments into petty cash

The Sage computer system has a default Petty Cash Account which it classes as a bank account, although, of course, the money is not in the bank. The computer sees it as a 'money fund'.

When cash is needed to top up the petty cash a reimbursement request document may be raised. The business will then cash a cheque at the bank and then put the money in the cash tin. The computer program requires the business to input the transaction as a TRANSFER from the BANK menu bar. In the screen below, the business has cashed a £100 cheque at the bank (using cheque 122991) to provide the cash.

Bank Transfer		
From	1200 Bank Current Account	Amount 100.00
To	1230 Petty Cash	
Date	01/02/2013 Reference 122991	
Description	From bank to petty cash	
Department	0	

payments out of petty cash

Payments out of Petty Cash Account are handled in exactly the same way on the computer as payments out of Bank Current Account. The PAYMENTS screen is reached through the BANK menu bar. The details are then input from the petty cash vouchers or the petty cash book in which they are recorded.

The screen below shows the input of the petty cash voucher for stationery shown on the opposite page.

Bank	Date	Ref	N/C	Dept	Project Ref	Cost Code	Details	Net	T/C	Tax
1230	15/05/2013	807	7502	0			Stationery	6.00	T1	1.20

Bank: Petty Cash
N/C: Office Stationery
Tax Rate: 20.00
Total: 7.20

Total: 6.00 / 1.20

Points to remember are:

- the bank account number used is the Petty Cash Account number
- the reference is the petty cash voucher number
- petty cash vouchers and their receipts will not always show the VAT amount – the VAT and net amount can be calculated on the computer by inputting the full amount under 'Net' and then clicking on 'Calc.Net' at the bottom of the screen (using T1 code to denote standard rate VAT)
- when the details have been checked you should SAVE
- the details can also be checked against a Cash Payments Day Book printout if required (accessed through REPORTS in BANK)

<table>
<tr><td>**Case Study**</td><td>

PRONTO SUPPLIES LIMITED: SETTING UP THE PETTY CASH SYSTEM

</td></tr>
</table>

At the beginning of February Tom Cox set up a petty cash system at Pronto Supplies Limited. The situation at 28 February is as follows:

- Tom notes that he cashed cheque no 122991 for £100 at the bank on 1 February.
- The £100 cash was transferred to the petty cash tin on 1 February.
- The tin contains three vouchers for payments made during the month – these are shown below and on the next page. They are ready for entry in the petty cash book as part of the month-end routine.

Voucher PC101 shows the VAT included in the total (standard rate: T1)

Voucher PC102 does not have any VAT in it (postage stamps are exempt: T2)

Voucher PC103 does not show the VAT included in the total (standard rate: T1) because it was not shown on the original receipt.

petty cash voucher		Number *PC101*
	date	*7 Feb 2013*

description		amount	
		£	p
A4 paper		36	00
	VAT	7	20
Receipt obtained		43	20

signature *Nick Vellope*

authorised *Tom Cox*

petty cash voucher

Number *PC102*

date *14 Feb 2013*

description		amount	
		£	p
Postage stamps		25	00
	VAT		
Receipt obtained		25	00

signature *R Patel*

authorised *Tom Cox*

petty cash voucher

Number *PC103*

date *20 Feb 2013*

description		amount	
		£	p
Envelopes			
Receipt obtained (VAT included but not VAT *shown separately)*		19	20

signature *B Radish*

authorised *Tom Cox*

the transfer to petty cash

Tom Cox first inputs the £100 transfer from the Bank Current Account to the Petty Cash Account. The screen is illustrated below. Note the use of the cheque number as the reference.

Bank Transfer					X
From	1200 Bank Current Account		Amount	100.00	
To	1230 Petty Cash				
Date	01/02/2013	Reference	122991		
Description	From bank to petty cash				
Department	0				
Save	Discard				Close

inputting the vouchers

The petty cash payments are entered into the computer accounting system on the PAYMENTS screen reached from the BANK menu bar.

Note that the bank Petty Cash Account number and the appropriate nominal code (N/C) is used each time.

The postage stamps nominal code was taken from the default nominal list.

The reference in each case is the relevant petty cash voucher number.

Postage stamps are VAT exempt. The VAT on the third petty cash voucher was not on the receipt but has been calculated on-screen by inputting the total amount of £19.20 in the 'Net' column and clicking on 'Calc.Net' at the bottom of the screen:

Bank	Date	Ref	N/C	Dept	Project Ref	Cost Code	Details	Net	T/C	Tax
1230	07/02/2013	PC101	7502	0			Copy paper	36.00	T1	7.20
1230	14/02/2013	PC102	7501	0			Postage sta...	25.00	T2	0.00
1230	20/02/2013	PC103	7502	0			Envelopes	16.00	T1	3.20

Bank: Petty Cash
N/C: Office Stationery
Tax Rate: 20.00
Total: 87.40

Net total: 77.00   Tax total: 10.40

Buttons: Save | Discard | Calc. Net | Print Cheque | Memorise | Recall | Close

Tom then checks the batch total with the total of the vouchers and when he is happy that all the details are correct he will SAVE. The Day Book Report will now show the petty cash payments. Note that the transaction code is 'CP' (second column from the left). This stands for 'Cash Payment'. This distinguishes the petty cash payments from payments from the bank current account (input through the same screen). These payments have the code 'BP' which stands for 'Bank Payment'.

Pronto Supplies Limited
Day Books: Cash Payments (Detailed)

| Date From: | 07/02/2013 | | | | | | | | | | Bank From: | 1230 |
| DateTo: | 20/02/2013 | | | | | | | | | | Bank To: | 1230 |

| Transaction From: | 1 | | | | | | | | | | N/C From: | |
| Transaction To: | 99,999,999 | | | | | | | | | | N/C To: | 99999999 |

| Dept From: | 0 |
| Dept To: | 999 |

| Bank: | 1230 | | Currency: | Pound Sterling | | | | | | | | | Bank |
No	Type	N/C	Date	Ref	Details	Dept	Net £	Tax	£ T/C	Gross £	V	B	Date
93	CP	7502	07/02/2013	PC101	Copy paper	0	36.00	7.20	T1	43.20	N	-	
94	CP	7501	14/02/2013	PC102	Postage stamps	0	25.00	0.00	T2	25.00	N	-	
95	CP	7502	20/02/2013	PC103	Envelopes	0	16.00	3.20	T1	19.20	N	-	
						Totals £	77.00	10.40		87.40			

CARD ACCOUNTS

use of company credit cards

Credit cards are often issued by an employer for use by their employees when they are out on business – for example a sales representative who needs to buy fuel for the company car and to take a client out to lunch. All expenses are billed to the company on the credit card statement and are checked by the management to make sure that the expenses are valid claims.

company credit card payments in the accounts

The business with a computer accounting system can make use of the Credit Card Account in the BANK function. This will be used to record all payments in Sage using the BANK PAYMENT screen seen earlier in this chapter, but inputting the payments to the Company Credit Card Account.

When the business pays the credit card bill the total amount will be input on the TRANSFER screen in the same way as the petty cash can be topped up (see page 127).

credit/debit card receipt accounts

A business using computer accounting might also open up an account in BANK to record credit and debit card receipts. Totals will then be transferred to the current account in Sage (1200). Alternatively, these receipts can be entered directly into the current account. Totals should be reconciled with the advices from the card merchant.

USING A CASH RECEIPTS ACCOUNT

We have seen so far that cash receipts – for example the cash and cheque takings from a shop – are best paid into the bank current account as soon as possible. This reduces the risk of theft and means that the business has the use of the money earlier rather than later.

There may be a case, however, where a business keeps its cash takings on the premises for some time before paying in. This could happen when a week's takings of a shop, for example, are paid in the following Monday. The business here could use the Cash Register Account in BANK to record the money fund kept on the premises. The procedure would be:

- select the Cash Register Account in BANK

- enter the totals of daily takings in RECEIPT from the BANK menu – the totals could be taken from the various till listings or a summary

- using TRANSFER from the BANK menu, record the amounts as and when they are paid into the bank current account – the source document is the paying-in slip and the transfer is made from Cash Register Account to Bank Current Account

The RECEIPT and TRANSFER screens are shown below and on the next page.

Bank	Date	Ref	N/C	Dept	Project Ref	Details	Net	T/C	Tax
1235	04/11/2013	12343	4000	0		Cash sales	4332.67	T1	866.53
1235	05/11/2013	12344	4000	0		Cash sales	6532.50	T1	1306.50
1235	06/11/2013	12345	4000	0		Cash sales	2345.45	T1	469.09
1235	07/11/2013	12346	4000	0		Cash sales	3452.56	T1	690.51
1235	08/11/2013	12347	4000	0		Cash sales	2653.94	T1	530.79
1235	09/11/2013	12348	4000	0		Cash sales	6754.35	T1	1350.87
							26071.47		5214.29

Bank: Cash Register — Tax Rate 20.00 — Total 31285.76

Save | Discard | Calc. Net | Memorise | Recall | Close

Here the takings for a week's trading (Monday to Saturday) by a shop are recorded on the BANK RECEIPTS screen. The money will be paid in on the following Monday and is held securely on the shop premises.

Here the shop takings for the week are being paid into the bank on a paying-in slip on Monday. The amount is transferred from Cash Register Account to Bank Current Account. The balance on the Cash Register Account should then revert to nil as all the money will have left the premises.

RECURRING PAYMENTS AND RECEIPTS

Recurring entries are payments or transfers which are made monthly or weekly or at other intervals. Businesses, for example

- *receive* recurring payments, for example rent from an office owned

- *make* recurring payments, for example loan repayments, insurance premiums, rent and rates paid

These payments are often made direct from the bank account of the payer to the bank account of the recipient ('beneficiary') by direct debit or standing order using the computer transfer BACS system.

Payments due are often recorded on a document called a 'Standing order/Direct debit schedule'. If a business operates a manual accounting system these payments will be written individually in the cash book each time they are made or received – a laborious and time-consuming process. A business using a computer accounting system such as Sage can automate this procedure.

setting up recurring entries in Sage

The RECURRING ENTRIES routine is reached from the RECURRING icon on the BANK menu bar.

The RECURRING ENTRIES screen shows any existing entries already set up. If there are none, the screen will be blank.

To add a recurring entry, the 'Add' button at the bottom of the screen should be clicked.

Now study the Case Study on the next two pages.

PRONTO SUPPLIES LIMITED:
SETTING UP RECURRING ENTRIES

setting up a recurring payment

Tom has set up a maintenance contract for his Xerax 566 colour printer/copier. He has to pay £19.80 plus VAT every month for the next 12 months and has completed a direct debit form so that the money can be taken directly from Pronto's bank current account.

The RECURRING ENTRIES routine is reached from the RECURRING icon on the BANK menu bar.

The RECURRING ENTRIES screen is blank because there are no existing recurring entries.To add a recurring entry, Tom clicks the Add button at the bottom of the screen and then inputs the details as follows:

Note the following:

- Tom indicates that the entry is a Bank/Cash/Credit Card Payment

- he inputs the bank account and nominal account to be used (which is already set up on the Chart of Accounts)

- the Transaction Reference entered is 'DD' (which stands for Direct Debit)

- the Transaction Details explain what the payment is for

- the Posting Frequency is every 15th of the month

- the number of Total Required Postings is 12

- the Net Amount and VAT (tax) code T1 are entered to generate the VAT amount

setting up a recurring receipt

Pronto Supplies receives from the tenant of a small office at 10A High Street regular monthly rent payments of £456. Tom charges VAT on these payments. The payment is made by standing order to the bank current account.

Tom clicks the 'Add' button at the bottom of RECURRING ENTRIES and then inputs the details as follows:

Add / Edit Recurring Entry				
Recurring Entry From / To				
Bank A/C To	1200		Bank Current Account	
Nominal Code	4904		Rent Income	
Recurring Entry Details				
Transaction Type	Bank/Cash/Credit Card Receipt			
Transaction Ref	STO			
Transaction Details	Rent 10A High Street			
Department	0			
Posting Frequency				
Every	1	Month(s)	Total Required Postings	6
Start Date	15/02/2013		Finish Date	15/07/2013
Next Posting Date	15/02/2013		Suspend Posting ?	☐
Last Posted				
Posting Amounts				
Net Amount	456.00	Tax Code T1 20.00	VAT	91.20
			OK	Cancel

Note the following:

- Tom indicates that the entry is a Bank/Cash/Credit Card Receipt
- he inputs the bank account and nominal account to be used (which is already set up on the Chart of Accounts)
- the Transaction Reference is 'STO' (which stands for Standing Order)
- the Transaction Details explain what the payment is for
- the Posting Frequency is every 15th of the month and the number of postings is 6
- the Net Amount and VAT (tax) code T1 are entered to generate the VAT amount

Tom returns to the RECURRING ENTRIES screen, which shows the two payments:

Type	Ref	Details	Amount	Posting Frequency	Next Posting	Postings Made	Postings Remaining	Posted Value	Remaining Value
BP	DD	Xerox 566 maintenance	23.76	1 Month(s)	15/02/2013	0	12	0.00	285.12
BR	STO	Rent 10A High Street	547.20	1 Month(s)	15/02/2013	0	6	0.00	3283.20

Tom can process all the payments up to the current date by clicking on the 'Process' button. The program will only allow him to process each payment and receipt once in each month.

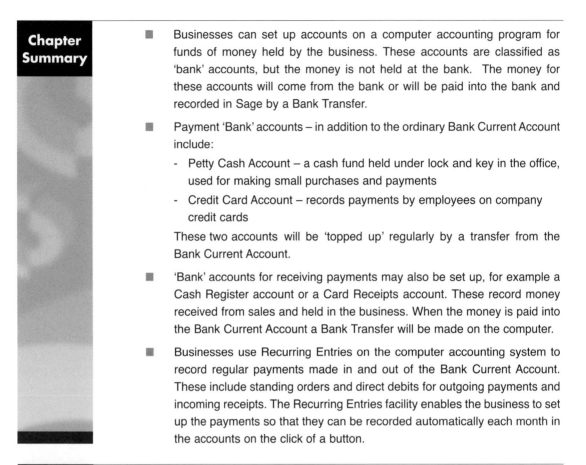

Chapter Summary

- Businesses can set up accounts on a computer accounting program for funds of money held by the business. These accounts are classified as 'bank' accounts, but the money is not held at the bank. The money for these accounts will come from the bank or will be paid into the bank and recorded in Sage by a Bank Transfer.

- Payment 'Bank' accounts – in addition to the ordinary Bank Current Account include:
  - Petty Cash Account – a cash fund held under lock and key in the office, used for making small purchases and payments
  - Credit Card Account – records payments by employees on company credit cards

  These two accounts will be 'topped up' regularly by a transfer from the Bank Current Account.

- 'Bank' accounts for receiving payments may also be set up, for example a Cash Register account or a Card Receipts account. These record money received from sales and held in the business. When the money is paid into the Bank Current Account a Bank Transfer will be made on the computer.

- Businesses use Recurring Entries on the computer accounting system to record regular payments made in and out of the Bank Current Account. These include standing orders and direct debits for outgoing payments and incoming receipts. The Recurring Entries facility enables the business to set up the payments so that they can be recorded automatically each month in the accounts on the click of a button.

Key Terms

petty cash	a float of cash kept in the office for making small purchases
petty cash account	an account used to record payments of small cash purchases from the office petty cash fund
petty cash voucher	the document which records and authorises a payment out of petty cash
company credit card account	an account used to record payments made on credit cards issued to employees to cover business expenses
cash receipts account	an account used to record cash receipts made by a business where the money is kept for a time by the business before it is paid into the bank
recurring entry	a bank payment or receipt which occurs on a regular basis and which is automated within the computer accounting program
Standing order/Direct debit schedule	a document which lists recurring payments and receipts with their due dates

Activities

10.1 What entries to the computer accounts are made when the Petty Cash system is operated? State which screens are used:

(a) for payments into Petty Cash

(b) for payments out of Petty Cash

10.2 You are getting some petty cash vouchers ready for input and notice some points which you think might cause problems:

(a) A petty cash voucher for postage stamps does not have any VAT shown on it.

(b) A petty cash voucher for stationery does not have any VAT shown on it.

(c) A petty cash voucher does not have an authorisation signature on it.

Write down what you think should be done in these three situations.

10.3 If a shop kept the cash and cheques taken from sales on the premises and only paid into the bank at the end of every week, it might use the Cash Register Account on the computer.

(a) Describe the entries the business would make on the Cash Register Account.

(b) Write down two disadvantages to the business of keeping money on the premises.

10.4 Describe the circumstances in which a business might set up Recurring Entries on the computer.

PRONTO SUPPLIES INPUTTING TASKS

Task 1

Set the program date as 28 February 2013.

On 1 February Tom cashed cheque 122991 for £100 at his bank to set up a petty cash system.

Carry out a bank transfer from Bank Current Account to Petty Cash Account for this amount.

Task 2

Keep the program date as 28 February 2013.

Tom has just authorised two more petty cash vouchers (shown below). Input these together with the three petty cash vouchers on pages 130 to 131 into Bank Payments, taking particular care with the VAT element on each one (postages are VAT exempt and packaging – nominal code 5003 – is standard-rated). Print out a Day Books: Cash Payments (Detailed) Report to confirm the accuracy of your input of the five vouchers (see p206). Hint: remember to select the Petty Cash Bank account on screen before running the report.

petty cash voucher

Number *PC104*

date   *28 Feb 2013*

description		amount	
		£	p
Postage stamps		5	00
	VAT		
Receipt obtained		5	00

signature   *R Cook*

authorised   *Tom Cox*

petty cash voucher

Number *PC105*

date   *28 Feb 2013*

description		amount	
		£	p
Packing tape		4	00
	VAT		80
Receipt obtained		4	80

signature   *R Patel*

authorised   *Tom Cox*

Task 3

Keep the program date as 28 February 2013.

Tom sees that he has three days' of cash takings in the office safe and so decides to enter these in the Cash Register Account. Take care over selecting the correct Sales Account number. The details are:

Date	Details	Net amount (£)	VAT (£)	ref.
26 Feb 2013	Hardware sales	5,000.00	1,000.00	10743
26 Feb 2013	Software sales	480.00	96.00	10743
27 Feb 2013	Hardware sales	1,200.00	240.00	10744
27 Feb 2013	Software sales	890.00	178.00	10744
28 Feb 2013	Hardware sales	600.00	120.00	10745
28 Feb 2013	Software sales	120.00	24.00	10745
	Totals	8,290.00	1,658,00	

Enter these transactions, check the totals, SAVE and print out a Bank Receipts (Detailed) Day Book Report. Check with the printout on page 206.

Task 4

Keep the program date as 28 February 2013.

Create recurring entries for the payments and receipts on the schedule below.

You will need to ensure that your Nominal List includes the following accounts:

7701 Office Machine Maintenance; 4904 Rent Income; 7100 Rent (paid out); 7103 General Rates

When the recurring entries have been set up, process them for February.

Pronto Supplies Standing Order and Direct Debit Schedule						
Start date	Type	To/from	Details	Value	Frequency	Total payments
15 02 13	DD payment	Xerax Machines	Maintenance	£19.80 plus VAT	Monthly	12
15 02 13	STO receipt	F Morton	Rent 10A High St	£456.00 plus VAT	Monthly	6
16 02 13	DD payment	Broadwater Properties	Rent paid	£4500.00 plus VAT	Monthly	10
19 02 13	STO payment	Wyvern DC	Rates	£350.00 (VAT exempt)	Monthly	2

Task 5

Keep the program date as 28 February 2013. Print out a trial balance as at 28 February 2013 (this can be checked against the trial balance on page 207)

Reminder! Have you made a back-up?

11 Reports and routines

this chapter covers...

- One of the major advantages of running a computer accounting system is that it will provide the business manager and administrative staff with a wide range of reports – on demand.

- These reports are produced regularly – sometimes at the end of the month – to enable the business to check the accuracy of its records and to ensure that customer and supplier payments are being made on time.

- The reports that can be produced to help with checking the accuracy of the records include:
  - the trial balance – a full list of the Nominal Account balances
  - the audit trail – a full numbered list of the transactions input on the computer in order of input.

- The reports that can be produced to help with dealing with customers and suppliers include:
  - 'aged' analyses – separate lists of customers and suppliers which show what payments are due and when
  - activity reports – lists of transactions on individual accounts
  - account lists – lists of customers and suppliers with telephone numbers
  - label lists – names and addresses of customers and suppliers – suitable for mailing labels
  - customer statements – sent to each sales ledger customer, listing transactions and telling the customer the amount that is due.

- A further regular checking routine is the bank reconciliation statement which agrees the bank statement with the accounting records of the business.

- The end of the month is also a good time to process recurring entries and other regular account transfers.

- The business in the Case Study – Pronto Supplies Limited – has reached the end of February and so will be used in this chapter to illustrate the various reports and routines and their uses.

THE IMPORTANCE OF INFORMATION

information for management

The accounting system of any business – whether hand-written or computer-based – contains important information for management and provides an accurate basis for decision-making. The advantage of using a computer accounting system is that this information is available instantly.

The **trial balance** is a list of the Nominal Account balances at a set date – which is often the last day of the month. The figures are set out in balancing debit and credit columns to prove the accuracy of the bookkeeping entries. If the column totals are not the same in a manual system, there are likely to be errors in the double-entry bookkeeping. Computerised trial balances will normally balance.

The trial balance figures show how much money there is in the bank and provides management with details about sales and expense accounts.

Activity on individual Nominal Accounts, eg sales, can be printed using a **nominal activity** report.

information for finance and administrative staff

The computer accounting program also enables finance and administrative staff to extract useful information, for example:

- The **audit trail** is a full list of the transactions input into the computer, presented in order of input. Accounts staff will use the audit trail to check the accuracy of the input and trace any discrepancies and errors.
- The analysis of customer accounts (the **aged debtor analysis**) tells credit control staff which customers need chasing for payment and which debts may need writing off. The computer can also print letters to customers chasing overdue accounts.
- The analysis of supplier accounts (the **aged creditor analysis**) tells accounts staff which bills and invoices need paying and when.
- The computer will also produce **activity reports** on individual customer and supplier accounts; these list all the transactions on each individual account and are useful to bring up on screen when a customer telephones in with a query.
- Computer-produced **account lists** set out the names, account codes and telephone numbers of customers and suppliers. These are useful to sales and accounts staff when contacting customers and suppliers and when coding invoices and credit notes.
- The computer will also produce the names and addresses of customers and suppliers on **labels**, which is useful when doing a promotional mailing or a change of address notification.

We will now illustrate these procedures with a continuation of the Case Study.

PRONTO SUPPLIES LIMITED: END-OF-MONTH REPORTS

It is 28 February 2013. Tom Cox has completed the input into his computer accounting system during the course of the month. Looking back he can see that he has:

*   set up the company details and the Nominal Ledger balances

*   entered customer and supplier records and balances

*   input customer and supplier invoices and credit notes processed during February

*   input payments received from customers and sent to suppliers during February

*   input cash receipts and payments for February

*   set up a petty cash system and recurring entries for standing orders and direct debits

trial balance

Tom first extracts his trial balance as at the end of February. He does this by clicking on TRIAL on the FINANCIALS menu bar. His printout is shown below.

Pronto Supplies Limited
Period Trial Balance

To Period: Month 2, February 2013

N/C	Name	Debit	Credit
0020	Plant and Machinery	35,000.00	
0030	Office Equipment	19,760.00	
0040	Furniture and Fixtures	30,000.00	
1100	Debtors Control Account	2,853.60	
1200	Bank Current Account	36,984.64	
1230	Petty Cash	2.80	
1235	Cash Register	9,948.00	
2100	Creditors Control Account		12,048.00
2200	Sales Tax Control Account		31,918.00
2201	Purchase Tax Control Account	36,521.16	
2300	Loans		35,000.00
3000	Ordinary Shares		80,000.00
4000	Computer hardware sales		139,380.00
4001	Computer software sales		29,914.00
4002	Computer consultancy		2,640.00
4904	Rent Income		456.00
5000	Materials Purchased	93,362.00	
5003	Packaging	4.00	
6201	Advertising	22,600.00	
7000	Gross Wages	33,010.00	
7100	Rent	9,000.00	
7103	General Rates	800.00	
7200	Electricity	308.00	
7501	Postage and Carriage	30.00	
7502	Office Stationery	567.00	
7550	Telephone and Fax	585.00	
7701	Office Machine Maintenance	19.80	
	Totals:	331,356.00	331,356.00

The trial balance shows the balances of the Nominal Accounts. The debit column on the left equals the credit column on the right because in double entry bookkeeping the total of debit entries should always equal the total of credit entries.

If in a manual accounting system the two columns totals were not the same, there could be one or more errors in the bookkeeping entries. In a computer-based system the totals should always be the same because the computer generates equal debits and credits from every entry. If Tom's column totals were not the same it would mean that the computer data had become corrupted, which could be a major problem.

audit trail

Tom regularly prints an audit trail as a further check (and also to satisfy his accountants). This shows each transaction entered into the computer in order of input. It is done from the AUDIT icon on the FINANCIALS menu bar. An extract from a Detailed Audit Trail is shown below.

Pronto Supplies Limited
Audit Trail (Detailed)

| | | | | | | | Customer From: | |
| | | | | | | | Customer To: ZZZZZZZZ | |

| Transaction From: | 1 | | | | Supplier From: | |
| Transaction To: | 99,999,999 | | | | Supplier To: ZZZZZZZZ | |

Exclude Deleted Tran: No

No	Type	A/C	N/C	Dept	Details	Date	Ref	Net	Tax	T/C	Pd	Paid	V	B	Bank Rec. Date
68	SR	JB001				28/02/2013	cheque	5,500.00	0.00		Y	5,500.00	N		
		68	1200	0	Sales Receipt			5,500.00	0.00	T9		5,500.00	-		
					5500.00 to SI 1	28/02/2013	10013					5,500.00			
69	SR	CH001				28/02/2013	cheque	2,419.20	0.00		Y	2,419.20	N		
		69	1200	0	Sales Receipt			2,419.20	0.00	T9		2,419.20	-		
					2400.00 to SI 2	28/02/2013	10014					2,400.00			
					19.20 to SI 49	28/02/2013	10024					19.20			
70	SR	CR001				28/02/2013	BACS	3,234.00	0.00		Y	3,234.00	R	28/02/2013	
		70	1200	0	Sales Receipt			3,234.00	0.00	T9		3,234.00	-		
					3234.00 to SI 3	28/02/2013	10015					3,234.00			
71	SR	DB001				28/02/2013	cheque	2,860.00	0.00		Y	2,860.00	N		
		71	1200	0	Sales Receipt			2,860.00	0.00	T9		2,860.00	-		
					2860.00 to SI 4	28/02/2013	10016					2,860.00			
72	SR	KD001				28/02/2013	BACS	6,500.00	0.00		Y	6,500.00	R	28/02/2013	
		72	1200	0	Sales Receipt			6,500.00	0.00	T9		6,500.00	-		
					6500.00 to SI 5	28/02/2013	10017					6,500.00			
73	SR	LG001				28/02/2013	BACS	8,500.00	0.00		Y	8,500.00	R	28/02/2013	
		73	1200	0	Sales Receipt			8,500.00	0.00	T9		8,500.00	-		
					8500.00 to SI 6	28/02/2013	10019					8,500.00			
74	PP	DE001				28/02/2013	BACS	5,174.00	0.00		Y	5,174.00	R	28/02/2013	
		74	1200	0	Purchase Payment			5,174.00	0.00	T9		5,174.00	-		
					5174.00 to PI 7	28/02/2013	4563					5,174.00			
75	PP	EL001				28/02/2013	BACS	8,500.00	0.00		Y	8,500.00	R	28/02/2013	
		75	1200	0	Purchase Payment			8,500.00	0.00	T9		8,500.00	-		
					8500.00 to PI 8	28/02/2013	8122					8,500.00			

Every transaction input into the computer (within the time period stipulated) is shown on the audit trail. The columns of the audit trail show, from the left . . .

1   the unique number allocated by the computer to the transaction

2   the type of transaction, for example SI = sales invoice, PI = purchase invoice

3   the account into which the item is entered

4   the Nominal Account code relating to the transaction

5   the Department reference, normally only used in larger organisations

6   the description of the transaction. In the case of a sales receipt (SR) the allocation of the amount to specific transactions is shown

7   the date of the transaction (which is not necessarily the date of input)

8   the transaction reference (eg invoice or cheque number) input at the time

9   the net amount

10   any VAT

11   VAT tax code

12   whether paid

13   the gross ('paid') amount

14   whether the item is VAT reconciled

15   whether the item is bank reconciled (with the date)

Tom will need to keep the audit trail for future reference in case any errors or discrepancies come to light. His accountants may also need to see it if they have to verify his accounts.

nominal activity

Tom can check his monthly sales for each sales code. He selects code 4000 (Computer hardware sales) in the Nominal Ledger screen and then clicks on REPORTS. In Nominal Activity Reports he chooses Nominal Activity and enters the date range of 1-28 February. The report, shown below, shows total computer hardware sales of £54,380 for the month.

Pronto Supplies Limited
Nominal Activity

Date From: 01/02/2013		**N/C From:** 4000
Date To: 28/02/2013		**N/C To:** 4000
Transaction From: 1		
Transaction To: 99,999,999		

N/C: 4000   **Name:** Computer hardware sales   **Account Balance:** 139,380.00 CR

No	Type	Date	Account	Ref	Details	Dept	T/C	Value	Debit	Credit	V	B
48	SI	05/02/2013	JB001	10023	Hardware	0	T1	400.00		400.00	N	-
49	SI	06/02/2013	CH001	10024	Hardware	0	T1	16.00		16.00	N	-
53	SC	06/02/2013	LG001	552	Hardware returned	0	T1	40.00	40.00		N	-
55	SI	13/02/2013	DB001	10028	Hardware	0	T1	600.00		600.00	N	-
56	SI	16/02/2013	LG001	10029	Hardware	0	T1	180.00		180.00	N	-
58	SI	16/02/2013	CH001	10031	Hardware	0	T1	320.00		320.00	N	-
59	SC	12/02/2013	KD001	553	Hardware returned	0	T1	16.00	16.00		N	-
60	SC	13/02/2013	CR001	554	Hardware returned	0	T1	20.00	20.00		N	-
77	BR	09/02/2013	1200	10736	Hardware sales	0	T1	12,500.00		12,500.00	N	N
79	BR	16/02/2013	1200	10738	Hardware sales	0	T1	15,840.00		15,840.00	N	N
81	BR	23/02/2013	1200	10740	Hardware sales	0	T1	17,800.00		17,800.00	N	N
99	BR	26/02/2013	1235	10743	Hardware sales	0	T1	5,000.00		5,000.00	N	-
101	BR	27/02/2013	1235	10744	Hardware sales	0	T1	1,200.00		1,200.00	N	-
103	BR	28/02/2013	1235	10745	Hardware sales	0	T1	600.00		600.00	N	-

Totals:	76.00	54,456.00
History Balance:		54,380.00

aged debtors analysis

It is important to Tom that he knows that his customers who buy on credit pay up on time. The credit period is indicated to them on the bottom of each invoice. Tom allows his customers 30 days from the date of the invoice in which to pay.

An Aged Debtors Analysis shows the amount owing by each customer and splits it up according to the length of time it has been outstanding. The Aged Debtors Analysis can be printed from the REPORTS icon on the CUSTOMERS menu bar. Alternatively an aged balance list can be produced from the AGED icon on CUSTOMERS.

Tom's Aged Debtors Analysis Report as at 28 February 2013 is shown below:

Pronto Supplies Limited
Aged Debtors Analysis (Summary)

Report Date:	28/02/2013				Customer From:			
Include future transactions:	No				Customer To:	ZZZZZZZ		
Exclude later payments:	No							

** NOTE: All report values are shown in Base Currency, unless otherwise indicated **

A/C	Name	Credit Limit	Turnover	Balance	Future	Current	Period 1	Period 2	Period 3	Older
CH001	Charisma Design	£ 5,000.00	2,736.00	384.00	0.00	384.00	0.00	0.00	0.00	0.00
CR001	Crowmatic Ltd	£ 5,000.00	3,664.00	516.00	0.00	516.00	0.00	0.00	0.00	0.00
DB001	David Boossey	£ 5,000.00	3,550.00	720.00	0.00	720.00	0.00	0.00	0.00	0.00
JB001	John Butler & Associates	£ 15,000.00	6,020.00	624.00	0.00	624.00	0.00	0.00	0.00	0.00
KD001	Kay Denz	£ 10,000.00	6,868.00	441.60	0.00	441.60	0.00	0.00	0.00	0.00
LG001	L Garr & Co	£ 15,000.00	8,640.00	168.00	0.00	168.00	0.00	0.00	0.00	0.00
	Totals:		31,478.00	2,853.60	0.00	2,853.60	0.00	0.00	0.00	0.00

The columns show (from left to right)

- the customer account number and name
- the credit limit (the maximum amount of credit Tom will allow on the account)
- the turnover (total net sales for each customer in the current financial year)
- the balance (the total balance on the customer's account)
- any transactions due in future months
- 'current' invoices are February invoices, period 1 is January, and so on

Note that the Report can be dated at any date required. Here it is dated 28 February.

The Report shows the following:

- All the accounts are trading within their credit limits (ie the figure in the 'Balance' column is less than the 'Credit Limit' column) – this is a good sign.
- The total of the Balance column shows that Pronto Supplies Limited is owed a total of £2,433.60 on 28 February. As a further check this figure could be agreed with the balance of Debtors Control Account on the trial balance (see page 144).

aged creditors analysis

Tom also needs to check on the amounts that Pronto Supplies Limited owes its Suppliers (creditors) for goods purchased, and to make sure that there are no amounts outstanding for longer than they should be. The Aged Creditors Analysis enables him to do this. It can be printed from REPORTS on the SUPPLIERS menu bar. The layout of the columns works on the same principles as the Aged Debtors Analysis (see previous page). Alternatively the AGED icon on SUPPLIERS can also be used to produce a list of amounts due to suppliers.

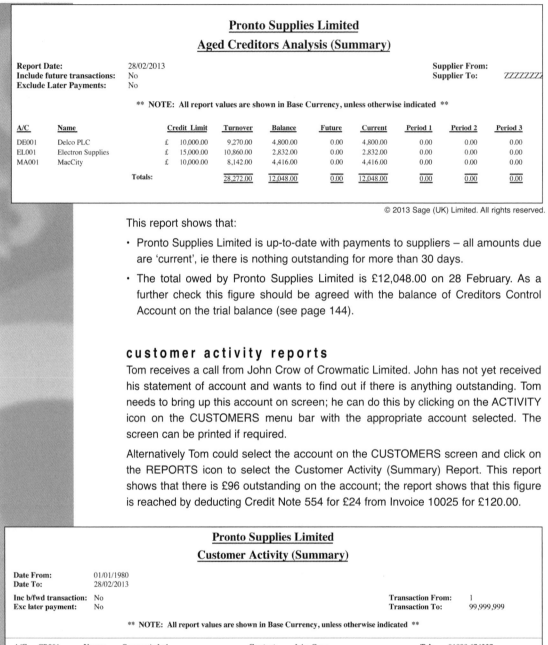

Pronto Supplies Limited

Aged Creditors Analysis (Summary)

Report Date:	28/02/2013						Supplier From:			
Include future transactions:	No						Supplier To:	ZZZZZZZ		
Exclude Later Payments:	No									

** NOTE: All report values are shown in Base Currency, unless otherwise indicated **

A/C	Name		Credit Limit	Turnover	Balance	Future	Current	Period 1	Period 2	Period 3
DE001	Delco PLC	£	10,000.00	9,270.00	4,800.00	0.00	4,800.00	0.00	0.00	0.00
EL001	Electron Supplies	£	15,000.00	10,860.00	2,832.00	0.00	2,832.00	0.00	0.00	0.00
MA001	MacCity	£	10,000.00	8,142.00	4,416.00	0.00	4,416.00	0.00	0.00	0.00
		Totals:		28,272.00	12,048.00	0.00	12,048.00	0.00	0.00	0.00

This report shows that:

- Pronto Supplies Limited is up-to-date with payments to suppliers – all amounts due are 'current', ie there is nothing outstanding for more than 30 days.

- The total owed by Pronto Supplies Limited is £12,048.00 on 28 February. As a further check this figure should be agreed with the balance of Creditors Control Account on the trial balance (see page 144).

customer activity reports

Tom receives a call from John Crow of Crowmatic Limited. John has not yet received his statement of account and wants to find out if there is anything outstanding. Tom needs to bring up this account on screen; he can do this by clicking on the ACTIVITY icon on the CUSTOMERS menu bar with the appropriate account selected. The screen can be printed if required.

Alternatively Tom could select the account on the CUSTOMERS screen and click on the REPORTS icon to select the Customer Activity (Summary) Report. This report shows that there is £96 outstanding on the account; the report shows that this figure is reached by deducting Credit Note 554 for £24 from Invoice 10025 for £120.00.

Pronto Supplies Limited

Customer Activity (Summary)

Date From:	01/01/1980								
Date To:	28/02/2013								
Inc b/fwd transaction:	No						Transaction From:	1	
Exc later payment:	No						Transaction To:	99,999,999	

** NOTE: All report values are shown in Base Currency, unless otherwise indicated **

| A/C: CR001 | | Name: | Crowmatic Ltd | | Contact: | John Crow | | Tel: | 01908 674237 |

No	Items	Type	Date	Ref	Details	Value	O/S	Debit	Credit
3	1	SI	09/01/2013	10015	Opening Balance	3,234.00	0.00	3,234.00	
50	1	SI	06/02/2013	10025	Software	540.00 *	540.00	540.00	
60	1	SC	13/02/2013	554	Hardware returned	24.00 *	-24.00		24.00
70	1	SR	28/02/2013	BACS	Sales Receipt	3,234.00	0.00		3,234.00
						516.00	516.00	3,774.00	3,258.00

Amount Outstanding	516.00
Amount Paid this period	3,234.00
Credit Limit £	5,000.00

other useful reports

Tom has also printed a Customer List from his computer; this is an alphabetically sorted account list of customers, together with their contact numbers. A similar report – Customer Address List – produces customer addresses. These reports can be accessed from REPORTS in CUSTOMERS.

Pronto Supplies Limited
Customer List

Customer From:
Customer To: ZZZZZZZZ

A/C	Name	Contact Name	Telephone	Fax
CH001	Charisma Design	Lindsay Foster	01908 345287	01908 345983
CR001	Crowmatic Ltd	John Crow	01908 674237	01908 674345
DB001	David Boossey	David Boossey	01908 333981	01908 333761
JB001	John Butler & Associates	John Butler	01908 824342	01908 824295
KD001	Kay Denz	Kay Denz	01908 624945	01908 624945
LG001	L Garr & Co	Win Norberry	01621 333691	01621 333982

The same exercise can be carried out from the SUPPLIERS menu bar to produce a list of Suppliers with contact numbers.

The computer will also enable Tom to print out name and address labels for Customers and Suppliers. This could be very useful when marketing products to Customers – sending out a catalogue, for example. The labels can be printed by clicking on the LABELS icon on the CUSTOMERS or SUPPLIERS menu bar and selecting an appropriate label format. The labels shown below are extracted from Tom's Customer details printed as Laser Sales Labels (A4).

Lindsay Foster	John Crow	David Boossey
Charisma Design	Crowmatic Ltd	David Boossey
36 Dingle Road	Unit 12 Severnside Estate	17 Harebell Road
Mereford	Mereford	Mereford Green
MR2 8GF	MR3 6FD	MR6 4NB

---

customer statements

At the end of each month Tom will print out statements and send them to his Customers. This can be done in Sage from the STATEMENT icon on the CUSTOMER menu bar. A suitable format can then be chosen from the list shown on the screen. At this point Tom could choose to email statements to his customers using the Email option in the Preview screen. The statements set out the transactions on the Customer account and state the amount owing. Statements are important documents because many customers will pay from the monthly statement rather than the invoice.

An extract from the statement for Crowmatic Limited is shown on the next page.

Pronto Supplies Limited
Unit 17 Severnvale Estate
Broadwater Road
Mereford
Wyvern
MR1 6TF

Crowmatic Ltd
Unit 12 Severnside Estate
Mereford
MR3 6FD

CR001

28/02/2013

1

NOTE All values are shown in Pound Sterling

09/01/13	10015	Opening Balance	3,234.00	
06/02/13	10025	Software	540.00*	
13/02/13	554	Hardware returned	*	24.00
28/02/13	BACS	Sales Receipt		3,234.00

Pronto Supplies Limited
Unit 17 Severnvale Estate
Broadwater Road
Mereford
Wyvern
MR1 6TF

Crowmatic Ltd
Unit 12 Severnside Estate
Mereford
MR3 6FD

CR001

28/02/2013

1

NOTE All values are shown in **Pound Sterling**

09/01/13	10015	Opening Balance	3,234.00	
06/02/13	10025	Software	540.00	
13/02/13	554	Hardware returned		24.00
28/02/13	BACS	Sales Receipt		3,234.00

BANK RECONCILIATION ON THE COMPUTER

the reasons for bank reconciliation

A further routine carried out on a regular basis, with the help of the computer accounting system, is the task of comparing and agreeing the entries in the Sage bank account for a set period of time, eg a month, and the entries on the actual bank statement for the same period. This process is known as **bank reconciliation**. It reconciles:

■ the bank statement – what the bank states the balance actually is

with . . .

■ the bank account of a business – the balance representing what the accounting records of the business states it has in the bank

It is quite common that **differences** will arise and that the two amounts will not be the same.

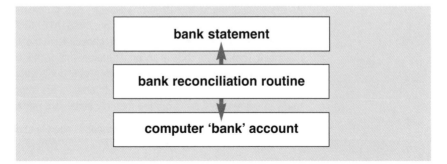

timing differences

These variations can arise from **timing differences**.

For example, a cheque that is issued by the business and sent off to a supplier will be input into the computer accounting records of the business when it is issued, but will not yet have been paid in at the bank by the supplier. Consequently the bank balance on the computer of the business writing the cheque will differ by this amount from the bank balance of the business shown on the bank statement - until, of course, the cheque is paid in and eventually deducted from the bank account. This is a 'timing difference'.

Another timing difference will occur when cheques received from customers of a business have been entered into the bank account on the computer but are still waiting to be paid into the bank on a paying-in slip. The accounting records of the business will show that the money has gone into the bank account, but the actual bank statement will only show the increase after the cheques have been paid into the bank, possibly a day or two later.

Also, there may be items on the bank statement which the business will not immediately know about and will need to enter into the accounting records **after** it has received the bank statement. Examples are bank charges, bank interest paid and bank interest received.

bank reconciliation in Sage

As seen on the previous page, bank reconciliation forms a link between the balances shown in the bank statement and in the accounting records of the business. All the reconciliation is doing in effect is explaining what items make up the difference between the bank statement and the bank account in the accounting records of the business.

The Bank Reconciliation screen, accessed through RECONCILE in BANK, is illustrated in the Case Study which follows. The procedure is as follows:

1. In the statement summary screen enter a statement reference (optional), the closing balance on the bank statement and the bank statement date. Any interest earned or bank charges can be added at this point. Click OK to move to the main Bank Reconciliation screen.

2. Check that the Matched Balance box at the bottom agrees to the opening balance on the bank statement.

3. Compare the items in the upper window on the screen with the bank statement. Click to select any items that appear on both, then click the Match button to transfer the matched item/s to the lower window. Alternatively double-click the matched items individually to transfer them.

4. Update the computer with any items appearing on the bank statement but not in Sage by inputting them using the 'Adjust' button.

5. When you have transferred all the matched items to the lower screen and made any adjustments, check that the Statement Balance equals the bank statement closing balance and the Difference box shows zero.

6. Click 'Reconcile'.

Now read the Case Study which follows.

Case Study

PRONTO SUPPLIES LIMITED:
BANK RECONCILIATION ROUTINE

It is 28 February 2013. Tom Cox has just printed out an online bank statement for Pronto Supplies Limited. He has access to this facility from the Albion Bank website.

The bank statement is shown below.

Tom wants to carry out a reconciliation routine and so clicks RECONCILE in BANK. This is shown on the opposite page.

ALBION BANK PLC

Online statement of account as at: 28 02 2013 15.54

Account 90 47 17 11719881 Pronto Supplies Limited

		Paid out	Paid in	Balance
31/01/2013	Balance b/f			14,656.00
01/02/2013	Cheque 122991	100.00		14,556.00
09/02/2013	Credit 10736		15,000.00	29,556.00
09/02/2013	Credit 10737		5,616.00	35,172.00
12/02/2013	Cheque 122992	18,600.00		16,572.00
15/02/2013	DD Xerox	23.76		-1,691.76
15/02/2013	STO F Morton		547.20	-1,144.56
16/02/2013	Credit 10738		19,008.00	17,863.44
16/02/2013	Credit 10739		4,416.00	22,279.44
16/02/2013	DD Broadwater Properties	5,400.00		16,879.44
19/02/2013	STO Wyvern DC	350.00		16,529.44
19/02/2013	Cheque 122993	12,240.00		4,332.00
19/02/2013	Cheque 122994	6,000.00		-1,668.00
23/02/2013	Credit 10740		21,360.00	37,889.44
23/02/2013	Credit 10741		5,760.00	43,649.44
27/02/2013	Cheque 122995	189.60		43,459.84
28/02/2013	Cheque 122996	372.00		43,087.84
28/02/2013	BACS		3,234.00	46,321.84
28/02/2013	BACS (multiple beneficiary)	18,128.40		28,193.44
28/02/2013	BACS	16,780.00		11,413.44
28/02/2013	122998	4,800.00		6,613.44
28/02/2013	BACS		6,500.00	13,113.44
28/02/2013	BACS		8,500.00	21,613.44
28/02/2013	Bank charges	50.00		21,563.44

Note that the BACS supplier payments to Delco, Electron and MacCity (see page 108) on 28 February are shown as one total (£18,128.40)

Tom compares the bank statement with the computer screen.

- He completes the Statement Summary screen with a Statement Reference (he uses the date), the bank statement end balance (£6,563.44) and the statement date (28 February 2013). He clicks OK to move to the main reconciliation screen.

Statement Summary				✕
Bank:	1200	Bank Current Account		
Statement Reference:		28 02 13		
Ending Balance:	21563.44	**Statement Date:**	28/02/2013	
Interest Earned:				
Amount:	0.00	Date: 28/02/2013	NC:	TC: T2 -0.00
Account Charges:				
Amount:	0.00	Date: 28/02/2013	NC:	TC: T2 -0.00
			OK	Cancel

- He checks that the opening balance on the bank statement is the same as the Matched Balance on the screen (it is £14,656.00)
- He selects the items in the upper window that are also on the bank statement. He can use the scroll bar to move up and down or he can change the size of the upper and lower windows by dragging on the horizontal bar between them.

Bank Reconciliation - 1200 - Bank Current Account

Stmt. Reference 28 02 13   Edit...   End Date 28/02/2013   End Balance 21563.44

Date	No.	Reference	Details	Payments	Receipts	
23/02/2013	86	BACS	Electricity	189.60		Find...
26/02/2013	87	BACS	Telephone	372.00		Swap
28/02/2013	68	cheque	Sales Receipt		5500.00	Clear
28/02/2013	69	cheque	Sales Receipt		2419.20	
28/02/2013	70	BACS	Sales Receipt		3234.00	
28/02/2013	71	cheque	Sales Receipt		2860.00	
28/02/2013	72	BACS	Sales Receipt		6500.00	
28/02/2013	73	BACS	Sales Receipt		8500.00	
28/02/2013	74	BACS	Purchase Payment	5174.00		
28/02/2013	75	BACS	Purchase Payment	8500.00		
28/02/2013	76	BACS	Purchase Payment	4454.40		
28/02/2013	88	Debit card	Stationery	408.00		
28/02/2013	89	BACS	Wages	16780.00		
28/02/2013	90	10742	Share capital		5000.00	
28/02/2013	91	122995	Colour printer	4800.00		6957.44

Match >>

Date	No.	Reference	Details	Payments	Receipts	Balance	
	O/Bal		Last reconciled balance			14656.00	

<< Unmatch   0.00

↑ ↓

Swap
Clear
Adjust...

	Totals				
Book Balance	Payments	Receipts	Matched Balance	~ Statement Balance	= Difference
36984.64	0.00	0.00	14656.00	21563.44	-6907.44

Reconcile   Save   Print...   Send to Excel...   View History   Report   Close

- Now he clicks the Match button to transfer the matched transactions to the lower window.

Bank Reconciliation - 1200 - Bank Current Account

Date	No.	Reference	Details	Payments	Receipts
28/02/2013	68	cheque	Sales Receipt		5500.00
28/02/2013	69	cheque	Sales Receipt		2419.20
28/02/2013	71	cheque	Sales Receipt		2860.00
28/02/2013	88	Debit card	Stationery	408.00	
28/02/2013	90	10742	Share capital		5000.00

Stmt. Reference: 28 02 13 End Date: 28/02/2013 End Balance: 21563.44

Date	No.	Reference	Details	Payments	Receipts	Balance
26/02/2013	87	BACS	Telephone	372.00		43087.84
28/02/2013	70	BACS	Sales Receipt		3234.00	46321.84
28/02/2013	72	BACS	Sales Receipt		6500.00	52821.84
28/02/2013	73	BACS	Sales Receipt		8500.00	61321.84
28/02/2013	74	BACS	Purchase Payment	5174.00		56147.84
28/02/2013	75	BACS	Purchase Payment	8500.00		47647.84
28/02/2013	76	BACS	Purchase Payment	4454.40		43193.44
28/02/2013	89	BACS	Wages	16780.00		26413.44
28/02/2013	91	122995	Colour printer	4800.00		21613.44

Book Balance: 36984.64

Totals — Payments: 82983.76 Receipts: 89941.20

Matched Balance: 21613.44 − Statement Balance: 21563.44 = Difference: 50.00

- There is a figure of £50 in the Difference box. This is the Bank charges which have not yet been entered. Tom clicks on the 'Adjust' button and then chooses Bank Payment. He now enters a payment for the charges in the normal way. The nominal code is 7901 and the VAT code is T2. He then clicks 'Save'.

Bank Payments

Bank: Bank Current Account   Tax Rate: 0.00
N/C: Bank Charges   Total: 50.00

Bank	Date	Ref	N/C	Dept	Project Ref	Cost Code	Details	Net	T/C	Tax
1200	28/02/2013	BANK	7901	0			Bank charg...	50.00	T2	0.00

	50.00	0.00

- Finally Tom is returned to the Bank Reconciliation screen where he checks that the Difference box is now showing zero.

All the unselected (ie 'unreconciled') items on the screen will appear next time the routine is carried out – normally when the next bank statement is received.

By carrying out this routine Tom can make sure that he has entered all his bank transactions correctly, and equally importantly, that the bank has not made any errors.

Tom clicks the 'Report' button to print a Bank Reconciliation report.

| Date: 22/03/2013 | | Pronto Supplies Limited | | | Page: 1 |
| Time: 12:51:43 | | Bank Reconciliation | | | |

Bank Ref:	1200		Date To:	28/02/2013
Bank Name:	Bank Current Account		Statement	28 02 13
Currency:	Pound Sterling			

Balance as per cash book at 28/02/2013:   36,934.64

Add: Unpresented Payments

Tran No	Date	Ref	Details	£
88	28/02/2013	Debit	Stationery	408.00

                                                                            408.00

Less: Outstanding Receipts

Tran No	Date	Ref	Details	£
68	28/02/2013	cheque	Sales Receipt	5,500.00
69	28/02/2013	cheque	Sales Receipt	2,419.20
71	28/02/2013	cheque	Sales Receipt	2,860.00
90	28/02/2013	10742	Share capital	5,000.00

                                                                          (15,779.20)

Reconciled balance :   21,563.44

Balance as per statement :   21,563.44

Difference :   0.00

Now he can click 'Reconcile' to complete the task.

OTHER MONTH-END ROUTINES

It is important for a business with a computer accounting system to establish an end-of-month routine which will include the production of the reports illustrated in the Case Studies in this chapter. Examples of other month-end routines involving the computer accounting system are explained below.

checking that all transactions have been input

The business must check that all the necessary transactions – sales and purchases transactions, payments made and received – have been input into the computer before extracting the reports.

recurring entries

Recurring entries – standing orders and direct debits – may be processed monthly, and it should become part of the month-end routine to ensure that this is done. Sage helps by displaying a warning message on the screen when you open the program up, letting you know if there are outstanding recurring entries. Recurring entries are dealt with in detail on pages 135 to 137.

SCREENSHOTS

An image of the screen can be 'exported' to another program using the 'Print Scr' button on the keyboard. The image is held in the computer's memory until it is pasted into another program, eg Word or Paint. It can then be saved and given a suitable filename.

Such images are useful for demonstration purposes (they have been used extensively in this publication) and in a training environment where the student needs to show, or print a copy of, something that appeared on screen.

**Chapter
Summary**

■ A computer accounting system has the advantage that it can provide a wide range of useful printed reports quickly and accurately. These are useful both for the management of the business and also for accounts assistants.

■ Reports can be produced to help with checking the accuracy of the records. These are often produced at the end of each month and include:

- the trial balance – a full list of the Nominal Account balances
- the audit trail – a numbered list of transactions set out in order of input on the computer.

■ Reports can be produced to help with day-to-day dealings with customers and suppliers. Month-end reports include:

- 'aged' analyses – separate lists of customers and suppliers which show when payments are due and if any payments are overdue
- activity reports – lists of transactions on individual accounts which need to be looked into
- customer statements of account

Other day-to-day useful printouts include customer and supplier account lists and label lists – useful for mailing purposes.

■ Another regular routine is the bank reconciliation, which agrees the entries on the actual bank statement with those in the bank account records of the organisation.

■ The end-of-month is the time to process recurring entries and other regular account transfers.

Key Terms	**trial balance**	a list of Nominal Account balances set out in debit and credit columns, the totals of which should be the same
	audit trail	a numbered list of transactions on the computer produced in order of input
	aged debtor analysis	a list of customer balances which are split up according to the length of time they have been outstanding
	aged creditor analysis	a list of supplier balances which are split up according to the length of time they have been outstanding
	activity report	a list of transactions on individual Nominal, Customer and Supplier accounts
	bank reconciliation	the process of checking the bank statement entries against the accounting records of an organisation and identifying the differences that exist between the two documents

Activities

11.1 What is the purpose of a trial balance in a manual accounting system?

11.2 Why should the debit and credit columns in a trial balance add up to the same total when a computer accounting system is used?

11.3 What else does a trial balance tell the owner of a business?

11.4 An audit trail is a numbered list of transactions input into a computer accounting system. How is it set out – in date order or in order of input?

11.5 What is the main purpose of

(a) an Aged Debtors Analysis?

(b) an Aged Creditors Analysis?

11.6 The Aged Debtors Analysis of Pronto Supplies Limited as at 28 February 2013 is shown below. Pronto Supplies allows customers to pay up to 30 days from the date of the invoice.

(a) What is the total amount owed by the customers of Pronto Supplies Limited?

(b) Against which figure in the trial balance (see next page) should this total in (a) be checked?

(c) Suppose that in two months time the balance of D Boossey's account still stood at £720 and this figure appeared in the 'Period 2' column. What does this tell Tom about the account? What other document could Tom print out to give him – and the customer – more information?

Pronto Supplies Limited   Page:

Aged Debtors Analysis (Summary)

Report Date:	28/02/2013						Customer From:			
Include future transactions:	No						Customer To:		ZZZZZZZZ	
Exclude later payments:	No									

** NOTE: All report values are shown in Base Currency, unless otherwise indicated **

A/C	Name	Credit Limit	Turnover	Balance	Future	Current	Period 1	Period 2	Period 3	Older
CH001	Charisma Design	£ 5,000.00	2,736.00	384.00	0.00	384.00	0.00	0.00	0.00	0.00
CR001	Crowmatic Ltd	£ 5,000.00	3,664.00	516.00	0.00	516.00	0.00	0.00	0.00	0.00
DB001	David Boossey	£ 5,000.00	3,550.00	720.00	0.00	720.00	0.00	0.00	0.00	0.00
JB001	John Butler & Associates	£ 15,000.00	6,020.00	624.00	0.00	624.00	0.00	0.00	0.00	0.00
KD001	Kay Denz	£ 10,000.00	6,868.00	441.60	0.00	441.60	0.00	0.00	0.00	0.00
LG001	L Garr & Co	£ 15,000.00	8,640.00	168.00	0.00	168.00	0.00	0.00	0.00	0.00
	Totals:		31,478.00	2,853.60	0.00	2,853.60	0.00	0.00	0.00	0.00

11.7 The trial balance (extract) of Pronto Supplies Limited at the close of business on 28 February 2013 is shown below. Study the figures and answer the questions that follow.

Pronto Supplies Limited
Period Trial Balance

To Period: Month 2, February 2013

N/C	Name	Debit	Credit
0020	Plant and Machinery	35,000.00	
0030	Office Equipment	19,760.00	
0040	Furniture and Fixtures	30,000.00	
1100	Debtors Control Account	2,853.60	
1200	Bank Current Account	36,934.64	
1230	Petty Cash	2.80	
1235	Cash Register	9,948.00	
2100	Creditors Control Account		12,048.00
2200	Sales Tax Control Account		31,918.00
2201	Purchase Tax Control Account	36,521.16	
2300	Loans		35,000.00
3000	Ordinary Shares		80,000.00
4000	Computer hardware sales		139,380.00
4001	Computer software sales		29,914.00
4002	Computer consultancy		2,640.00
4904	Rent Income		456.00
5000	Materials Purchased	93,362.00	
5003	Packaging	4.00	
6201	Advertising	22,600.00	
7000	Gross Wages	33,010.00	
7100	Rent	9,000.00	
7103	General Rates	800.00	
7200	Electricity	308.00	
7501	Postage and Carriage	30.00	
7502	Office Stationery	567.00	
7550	Telephone and Fax	585.00	
7701	Office Machine Maintenance	19.80	
7901	Bank Charges	50.00	
	Totals:	331,356.00	331,356.00

(a) How much money has the company got in the bank?

(b) How much money has the company got stored on the premises?

(c) What is the company's total sales income (excluding rent) for the period up to 28 February?

11.8 The Administration Supervisor of Pronto Supplies asks for a list of customers together with their contact telephone numbers. Print out the report the supervisor needs.

PRONTO SUPPLIES INPUTTING TASKS

Set the program date to 28 February 2013.

1   Print a Nominal Activity report for account number 4000 for the month of February. Check it against the one on page 208.

2   Following the instructions on pages 152 to 155, carry out a bank reconciliation from RECONCILE in BANK.

     Check that the opening balance is the same on both the bank statement and the 'reconcile' screen.

     Remember to click on the screen only the items which appear in the bank statement.

     Carry out any 'adjustments' that need to be done (ie inputting any items on the bank statement which have not yet been input into the computer accounting system).

     Check that the Matched Balance is the same as the Statement Balance, ie that the difference is zero. Print a Bank Reconciliation Report before proceeding to Reconcile. Check the report against the one in the Case Study on page 155.

3   Print an Audit Trail (Detailed) for all transactions dated 28 Feb. Check it against the one on page 209.

4   Back up your data and take a screenshot of the completed back-up screen. Check it against the one on page 210.

12 Corrections and adjustments

this chapter covers...

■ *When you are operating a computer accounting program it is inevitable that errors will be made. These might be your own input errors or they might be errors on the part of a customer or a supplier. Whatever the source of the error might be, it will have to be put right.*

■ *The CORRECTIONS function contained in Sage will enable you to change most details on invoices, credit notes and payments. It is most commonly used for internal corrections – before any documents are sent out of the business.*

■ *The JOURNAL function contained in Sage is used for transferring amounts from one Nominal Account to another. One of its uses is therefore for correcting mistakes where the wrong Nominal Account number has been used. A knowledge of the use of debits and credits is needed for the JOURNAL.*

■ *The computer also allows you to make adjustments to the records, for example:*

- *you may need to 'write off' a customer account because you consider you will never get the money – the customer may have become bankrupt, for example*

■ *A customer cheque may be returned unpaid by the customer's bank.*

THE CORRECTIONS FUNCTION

You will be able to correct most input errors within Sage using the CORRECTIONS function which is part of MAINTENANCE reached through FILE on the main menu bar.

This leads to a screen which lists all the transactions which have passed through the computer accounting system and are available for correction.

You highlight the transaction which needs correcting (see screen below) and click on 'Edit Item' to bring up the screen shown at the bottom of the page. The correction has already been made on this screen.

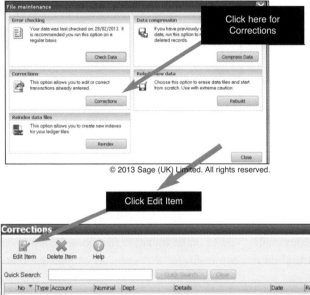

Number 66, Purchase Invoice

Purchase Invoice Details

N/C	0030	Nominal code can be changed
Details	Desktop computer
Date	14/02/2013
Department	0
Ex.Ref	
Project Ref		Cost Code	
Net	400.00	T/C	T1 20.00
Tax	80.00	Paid	0.00
Paid in full	☐	Disputed	☐

Payment Allocations

| Type | Date | Payment Ref | Details | Amount |

Edit

The last screen on the previous page allows correction of:

- the account to which the invoice is posted
- the product description
- the reference and date

Further amendments can be made to an individual item highlighted in the bottom box by clicking 'Edit'. These include:

- the nominal code
- details
- the amounts charged
- the VAT rate and VAT amount

JOURNAL ENTRIES

Journal entries enable you to make transfers from one Nominal Account to another. Journal entries are used, for example, when you are completing a VAT return and need to transfer VAT amounts from one VAT account to another. They are another way of putting things right when you have input the wrong Nominal Account.

Journals can also be used to enter opening balances and advanced accounting adjustments such as depreciation of fixed assets.

journals and double entry

You need to be confident about **double-entry** bookkeeping and using debits and credits when doing journal entries. You will have to decide which accounts have debit entries and which accounts have credit entries. The rule is that for every transaction there are balancing debit and credit entries:

debits	=	money paid into the bank
		purchases and expenses
		an increase in an asset
credits	=	payments out of the bank
		sales and income
		an increase in a liability

If you are still in any doubt about debits and credits, use CORRECTIONS wherever possible to adjust account entries.

example

Suppose you were inputting a batch of Bank Payments which included a number of bills that had to be paid. You have written out a cheque for £96 to RPower for a gas bill, but when inputting it you thought it was for electricity and so posted it to electricity (nominal account 7200) instead of gas (7201).

the solution

You could either use CORRECTIONS, but as you are a double-entry expert you choose to correct your mistake using a journal entry. You bring up the screen by clicking on the JOURNALS icon on the NOMINAL menu bar:

N/C	Name	Dept	Details	T/C	Debit	Credit
7201	Gas	0	Correction of misposting	T1	80.00	0.00
7200	Electricity	0	Correction of misposting	T1	0.00	80.00

Reference: 6436   Posting Date: 28/02/2011   Balance: 0.00

Nominal Ledger Journals

The procedure is:

■ enter your reference (this could be the transaction number you can find by opening up the FINANCIALS module and locating the transaction)

■ enter the nominal code of the account to which you are going to post the debit; here it is Gas Account because you are recording an expense

■ enter the reason for the transaction – here you are adjusting a misposting

■ enter the VAT tax code input on the original (wrong) entry

■ enter the net amount in the debit column (ie the amount before VAT has been added on) – here the net amount is £80 and VAT (assumed here at standard rate) is £16 and the total is £96; note that neither the VAT nor the total appear on the screen because you are not adjusting the VAT; *only the net amount* has gone to the wrong account

then on the next line . . .

■ enter the nominal code of the account to which you are going to post the credit; here it is Electricity Account because you are effectively refunding the amount to the account – it is an income item and so a credit

■ enter the remaining data as you did for the debit, but enter the net amount in the right-hand credit column

■ make sure the Balance box reads zero – meaning that the debit equals the credit – and SAVE

ADJUSTMENTS TO THE ACCOUNTS

A business may from time-to-time need to make adjustments to the data which has already been input into the computer accounting system. Situations where this happens include:

■ A credit customer is going or has gone 'bust' (bankrupt) and cannot pay invoices – the account will need to be 'written off' as a bad debt

■ a cheque paid to the business by a credit customer has 'bounced' – it has been returned by the bank after it has been paid in and the money is taken off the account of the business by the bank

We will look at each of the procedures in turn.

write offs

All businesses from time-to-time will encounter bad debts. A **bad debt** is a credit customer who does not pay. It may be that the customer has gone 'bust' or that the cost of continuing to send statements, reminders and demands is too high in relation to the amount owing. A business will decide in these circumstances to **write off** the debt in the accounts. This involves:

■ debiting 'Bad Debts Account' set up in NOMINAL

■ crediting the customer with the amount due – wiping it off the account

In Sage this transfer is carried out through the WRITE OFF/REFUND option on the vertical toolbar when the Customers module is open. This brings up the Write Off, Refund and Returns wizard which gives a choice of accounting adjustments ...

Screens then follow which allow the business to select the outstanding invoices to write off (all of them as the whole account is being written off) and then to date and confirm the details.

After this procedure the customer account will show as a nil balance and a corresponding Bad Debts Account in NOMINAL will show the write off amount as an expense to the business. The Debtors Control Account value will also be decreased by the amount of the write off. Eventually a write off – like any expense – will reduce the business profits.

adjusting for returned cheques

A **returned cheque** is a cheque which has been received by a business and paid in but returned by the cheque issuer's bank for a variety of reasons: there may be a lack of funds, or the cheque may have been stopped, or it may be technically incorrect (eg unsigned by the customer).

The appropriate computer accounting entries in Sage will be made through the Write off, Refunds and Returns Wizard under 'Customer Cheque Returns'. The cheque screen is shown below.

Here a cheque for £5,500 received from John Butler and Associates has been returned from their bank, marked 'Refer to Drawer'.

PRONTO SUPPLIES LIMITED: CORRECTIONS AND ADJUSTMENTS

It is 28 February 2013. Tom is still finalising his accounts. He encounters a number of situations which require him to carry out corrections and adjustments straightaway.

incorrect invoice description

Tom realises that a purchase invoice number was entered incorrectly in February.

Invoice 11377 from Delco dated 14 February 2013 should be 11737.

Tom identifies the invoice from the audit trail he has printed out. It is transaction 66.

Tom goes into CORRECTIONS from FILE MAINTENANCE and selects transaction 66. He amends the invoice number in the 'Reference' field.

He clicks SAVE and YES when asked 'Do you wish to post these changes?'

Number 66, Purchase Invoice ✕

You can change details of all grouped items at once by using the fields below, or select individual transactions in the list to amend a specific item.

Purchase Invoice Details

Account	DE001	Due on	16/03/2013
Reference	11737		
Description	Desktop computer	Posted by	MANAGER
Created on	14/02/2013		
Posted on	12/03/2013	VAT Rec. Date	/ /
Net	400.00	Paid	0.00
Tax	80.00		
Currency	1 Pound Sterling	Foreign gross	480.00
Exchange rate	1.000000		

☐ Paid in full ☐ Finance charge ☐ Disputed ☐ Printed
☐ Opening balance ☐ CIS reconciled ☐ Revaluation

Item Line Details

No	N/C	Details	Net	T/C	Tax
66	0030	Desktop computer	400.00	T1	80.00

journal entries

On checking the paperwork relating to the accounts for the month Tom spots that a bill from RPower has been paid but the expense has been posted by mistake to Electricity Account instead of Gas account.

The bill was for £158 plus VAT.

Tom decides to carry out journal entries to switch the expense from one account to the other. In double-entry bookkeeping terms this means:

debit   Gas Account (code 7201) £158 – recording an expense

credit   Electricity Account (code 7200) £158 – recording a refund

Tom accesses the Journal through the JOURNALS icon on the NOMINAL menu bar. The journal screen after input appears as follows:

Nominal Ledger Journals

Reference	Posting Date						Balance	
86	28/02/2013							0.00

N/C	Name	Ex.Ref	Dept	Details	T/C	Debit	Credit
7201	Gas		0	86 posting error	T9	158.00	0.00
7200	Electricity		0	86 posting error	T9	0.00	158.00

Note that:

- no VAT is involved here because it is only the net amount (amount before VAT is added on) that has gone to the wrong account

- the reference used is the audit trail number of the original transaction

- the Balance box shows as zero because the debit entry equals the credit entry – as you would expect (the Balance is the difference between the entries)

Tom can keep a printed record of his journals by going to Reports in the Nominal module and printing Day Books: Nominal Ledger.

Pronto Supplies Limited

Day Books: Nominal Ledger

Date From:	28/02/2013		N/C From:	
Date To:	28/02/2013		N/C To:	99999999

Transaction From:	1		Dept From:	0
Transaction To:	99,999,999		Dept To:	999

No	Type	N/C	Date	Ref	Ex.Ref	Details	Dept	T/C	Debit	Credit	V	B
110	JD	7201	28/02/2013	86		86 posting error	0	T9	158.00			
111	JC	7200	28/02/2013	86		86 posting error	0	T9		158.00	-	-
								Totals:	158.00	158.00		

checking corrections and adjustments

Sage does not automatically generate a report as a result of corrections to transaction data, so to confirm that the adjustments have been made, the audit trail should be checked.

The way in which a correction is reported depends on how important the change is in accounting terms. Some changes result in a simple substitution, such as a change to Details or Reference (as in the change of reference number in the Case Study). Some result in the original transaction being amended and an additional entry being inserted on the audit trail showing what has been deleted, eg where a major alteration like a change to the nominal code has been made. For example, in the audit trail extract below, transactions 63 and 64 show the deleted transactions while 61 and 62 show the corrected transactions.

Pronto Supplies Limited
Audit Trail (Summary)

Date From:	01/01/1980	
Date To:	31/12/2019	
Transaction From:	61	
Transaction To:	64	
Dept From:	0	
Dept To:	999	
Exclude Deleted Tran:	No	

Customer From:	
Customer To:	ZZZZZZZ
Supplier From:	
Supplier To:	ZZZZZZZZ
N/C From:	
N/C To:	99999999

No	Type	Date	A/C	N/C	Dept	Ref	Details	Net	Tax	T/C	Pd	Paid	V	B	Bank Rec. Date
61	PI	14/02/2013	DE001	0030	0	11737	Desktop computer	400.00	80.00	T1	N	0.00	N	-	
62	PI	14/02/2013	EL001	0030	0	8603	Laser printer	360.00	72.00	T1	N	0.00	N	-	
63	PI	14/02/2013	DE001	5000	0	11737	Deleted - see tran 61	400.00	80.00	T1	N	0.00	-	-	
64	PI	14/02/2013	EL001	5000	0	8603	Deleted - see tran 62	360.00	72.00	T1	N	0.00	-	-	

Changes to amounts of Journals transactions require a different treatment as they cannot be changed in CORRECTIONS. The way to do this is to choose the 'Reversals' option from the NOMINAL toolbar. This will enable you to reverse (cancel out) the original transaction and to then enter the correct journal debit and credit entries.

Chapter Summary

- Errors inevitably occur when processing accounts on the computer. Errors can involve incorrect references or descriptions, incorrect prices, wrong VAT codes and wrong accounts used.

- Most errors within Sage can be corrected using the CORRECTIONS routine within MAINTENANCE. This will enable corrections to be made to invoices, credit notes and payments.

- Adjustments to Nominal Accounts can also be carried out by transfers through the JOURNALS function within Sage. This process requires a knowledge of double-entry bookkeeping.

- The computer accounting records may also be adjusted for situations such as account writeoffs and returned customer cheques.

Key Terms

journal	the part of the accounting system which enables you to make transfers from one Nominal Account to another, and to enter new balances
double-entry	the system of bookkeeping which involves each transaction having two entries made – a debit and a credit; computer accounting programs (which are largely single entry systems) deal with the double entry automatically
write off	the removal of a Customer (or Supplier) account balance from the accounting records
bad debt	a debt that is never likely to be paid and so will need to be written off
returned cheque	a cheque that has been paid into a bank account but has been returned unpaid by the bank either because of lack of funds, or because of some technical irregularity on the cheque

Activities

12.1 What method of adjustment in a computer accounting program would you use if . . .

(a) A customer's cheque which you have paid in is returned to you marked 'cheque stopped by order of drawer'.

(b) You discover that a payment for advertising has been input in error to the stationery account.

(c) You are told that a credit customer who owes you money has been declared bankrupt. The debt will not be paid.

PRONTO SUPPLIES INPUTTING TASKS

Ensure the program date is set at 28 February 2013.

Task 1

Correct the Delco Supplier invoice reference number in the Case Study on page 168 using CORRECTIONS.

Task 2

Carry out the Journal entries for the misposting in the Case Study on page 169. Use Ref 86.

Task 3

When you have completed your corrections, print out a trial balance. Check the figures on the trial balance with the figures on page 211. Then explain the changes in the trial balance to:

(a) Bank Current Account

(b) Electricity Account

These changes can be seen by comparing the two trial balances on pages 207 and 211.

Extended exercise

Interlingo
Translation
Services

Extended exercise: Interlingo Translation Services

This is a 'standalone' extended exercise which puts into practice all the computer accounting skills you will have developed while working through this book.

It features a small company run by Jo Lane who has set up a translation bureau 'Interlingo' which sells language books and CDs as a sideline. Jo has been operating for a month using a manual bookkeeping system and has then decided to set up the accounting records in a Sage system in the second month.

The activities to be covered are:

1   *Setting up the business in Sage.*

2   *Setting up Customers and Supplier records and inputting opening balances.*

3   *Setting up the Nominal Ledger in Sage and inputting opening balances from the trial balance produced at the end of the first month of trading.*

4   *Processing sales invoices and credit notes.*

5   *Processing purchase invoices and credit notes.*

6   *Processing payments received – including payments from credit customers, cash payments from small translation jobs, and books and CDs over the counter.*

7   *Processing payments made to suppliers and for running expenses.*

8   *Setting up a Petty Cash Account and processing Petty Cash Payments.*

9   *Setting up recurring receipts and payments through the Bank Current Account.*

10 *Printing month-end reports and extracting information from the computer accounting records for use in the business.*

11 *Dealing with security aspects – formulating a back up policy, setting passwords and access rights.*

ACTIVITY 1 – SETTING UP THE BUSINESS IN SAGE

introduction

Interlingo Translation Services Limited is a small company business run by Jo Lane, a linguist who has worked as a translator with the European Commission in Brussels and has now settled back in her home town of Mereford. Jo rents a small office in the town.

Interlingo Translation Services provides translation services and also sells books and CDs.

translation services

Larger clients, for example importers and exporters who need documents translated into English and sales literature translated into foreign languages, are supplied by Jo on credit terms (ie they are invoiced and pay later).

Small, local 'private' translating jobs which come about from local adverts are normally paid for on a cash basis (ie cash or cheque) and are not invoiced.

language books and CDs

Jo has found that selling language books and CDs is a useful sideline. They are all sold for cash, but are bought on credit from the publishers.

the accounting system

Interlingo Translation Services was set up on 2 July 2013. The business is registered for VAT and after a month of using a manual accounting system Jo has decided to transfer her accounts to Sage 50 software and sign up for a year's telephone technical support. Her main problem, common to so many small businesses, is that of time – finding time to process her accounts and to see how she is getting on in financial terms.

Jo has chosen Sage 50 because it will enable her to:

• process the invoices issued to business customers who are supplied on credit

• record the cash sales of books and CDs and small translation jobs

• pay the publishers of the books and CDs on the due date

• keep a record of money received and paid out

• print out reports which will tell her who has not paid on time

• print out reports which will tell her what she is spending

In short Jo hopes that Sage will help her save time (and money) in running her accounting system.

backups

Remember to back-up your data after each inputting Task, just as Jo would.

task 1

Ensure that the computer is set up correctly. You should adopt the 'Limited Company: Standard Accounts' as the Business Type to be used.

The financial year should be set to start in July 2013.

task 2

Set up the details of the business in Sage. Company Preferences in SETTINGS can be used if you are not using the ActiveSetup Wizard.

- Enter the address details: Interlingo Translation Services
14 Privet Road
Mereford
MR5 1HP

Tel: 01908 335876

Fax: 01908 335899

Email: mail@interlingo.co.uk

www.interlingo.co.uk

VAT Reg: 416 1385 51

- Ensure that the non-VAT code in Parameters in Company Preferences (SETTINGS) is set at T9. Also check that the VAT Cash Accounting box is blank.

- Set the program date to 31 July 2013 (SETTINGS).

ACTIVITY 2 – SETTING UP THE CUSTOMER AND SUPPLIER RECORDS

introduction

Interlingo Translation sells on credit to five businesses that use its translation services on a regular basis. Jo will have to set up the details of these customers on the computer.

The business also buys its books and CDs from two wholesale companies. Delivery services are provided by a carrier. These suppliers will also have to be input onto the computer.

task 1

The defaults for the customers, reached through SETTINGS, should be set up as follows:

Configuration Editor (Terms):

Payment due days	30 days
Terms	Payment 30 days of invoice

Customer Defaults:

VAT rate	20% standard rate (code T1)
Default nominal code	4000

task 2

Input the details and opening balance for each of the five customers through RECORD in CUSTOMERS. The opening balance in each case is the total of the invoice already issued and is a gross amount. You do not need to deal with VAT at this stage. Do <u>not</u> post these invoices as a separate batch.

The credit limits and 'Terms Agreed' will also need to be entered (in the Credit Control tab).

Account name	**RS Export Agency**
Account reference	RS001
Address	46 Chancery Street Mereford MR1 9FD
Contact name	Raspal Singh

Telephone 01908 564187, Fax 01908 564911
Email rsingh@zipnet.co.uk

Credit limit £1,000

Invoice reference 10010 for £850.00 issued on 06 07 13.

Account name	**Playgames PLC**
Account reference	PL001
Address	Consul House
	Viney Street
	Mereford
	MR2 6PL
Contact name	Jacquie Mills

Telephone 01908 749724, Fax 01908 749355
Email mail@playgames.com
www.playgames.com

Credit limit £1,000

Invoice reference 10011 for £795.00 issued on 12 07 13

Account name	**Rotherway Limited**
Account reference	RT001
Address	78 Sparkhouse Street
	Millway
	MY5 8HG
Contact name	Darsha Patel

Telephone 01987 875241, Fax 01987 875267
Email mail@rotherway.co.uk
www.rotherway.co.uk

Credit limit £2,000

Invoice reference 10012 for £1,210.00 issued on 17 07 13

Account name	**Hill & Dale & Co, Solicitors**
Account reference	HD001
Address	17 Berkeley Chambers
	Penrose Street
	Mereford
	MR2 6GF
Contact name	Helen Lexington

Telephone 01908 875432, Fax 01908 875444
Email hlex@hilldale.co.uk

Credit limit £1,000

Invoice reference 10013 for £345.00 issued on 19 07 13

Account name	**Schafeld Ltd**
Account reference	SC001
Address	86 Tanners Lane
	Millway
	MY7 5VB
Contact name	Hans Rautmann

Telephone 01987 619086, Fax 01987 619097
Email hrautmann@schafeld.com
www.schafeld.com
Credit limit £1,000

Invoice reference 10014 for £800.00 issued on 20 07 13

task 3

Print out a Day Books: Customer Invoices (Detailed) Report and check your printout against the printout on page 212. The batch total should be £4,000.

task 4

The SUPPLIER defaults (reached through SETTINGS) should be set up as follows:

VAT rate	20% standard rate (code T1)
Default nominal code	5000

task 5

Input the details and opening balance for the two suppliers of books and CDs through RECORD in SUPPLIERS. The credit limits and payment terms agreed will also need to be entered on the Credit Control screen. The 'Terms Agreed' box will also need to be ticked.

Account name	**TDI Wholesalers**
Account reference	TD001
Address	Markway Estate
	Nottingham
	NG1 7GH
Contact name	Ron Beasley

Telephone 0115 295992, Fax 0115 295976, Email sales@tdi.co.uk
www.tdi.co.uk

Credit limit granted £5,000, payment terms 30 days of invoice date

Invoice reference 2347 for £780.00 issued on 07 07 13.

TDI Wholesalers supply Jo with language CDs, which are standard-rated for VAT.

Account name	**Bardners Books**
Account reference	BB001
Address	Purbeck House
	College Street
	Cambridge
	CB3 8HP
Contact name	Sarah Rooney

Telephone 01223 400652, Fax 01223 400648
Email sales@bardners.co.uk
www.bardners.co.uk

Credit limit granted £2,000, payment terms 30 days of invoice date

Invoice reference 9422 for £420.00 issued on 08 07 13.

Bardners Books supply Jo with language books, which are zero-rated for VAT. This supplier account may therefore be set up with a default tax code of T0.

Account name	**A2B Carriers**
Account reference	AB001
Address	Beech Drive
	Mereford
	MR6 3AD
Contact name	Jake Johns

Telephone 01908 364201, Fax 01908 364770
Email info@a2bcarriers.com
www.a2b.com

Credit limit granted £2,500, payment terms monthly

No opening balance

A2B provide delivery services which are standard-rated for VAT. The default nominal code is 5100 carriage.

task 6

Print out a Day Books: Supplier Invoices (Detailed) Report and check your printout against the printout on page 212. The batch total should be £1,200.

task 7

Print out a Trial Balance Report from FINANCIALS to check the total of the Debtors Control Account (the total of the Customer invoices) and the Creditors Control Account (the total of the Supplier invoices). The report should appear as follows:

Interlingo Translation Services
Period Trial Balance

To Period: Month 1, July 2013

N/C	Name	Debit	Credit
1100	Debtors Control Account	4,000.00	
2100	Creditors Control Account		1,200.00
9998	Suspense Account		2,800.00
	Totals:	4,000.00	4,000.00

ACTIVITY 3 – SETTING UP THE NOMINAL LEDGER

introduction

Interlingo Translation Services has been set up in Sage with a default Chart of Accounts (Nominal Accounts list) which can be used as a structure for the Nominal Account balances which were outstanding at the end of July.

Jo has already set up a trial balance on a spreadsheet. The figures are shown below. The right-hand column shows the Nominal Account number which Jo has allocated to each account from the list of Nominal Accounts. The grey backgrounds show where the default account name needs changing.

	Dr	Cr	Account
	£	£	
Office computers	5000		0020
Office equipment	2500		0030
Furniture and fixtures	3000		0040
Debtors control account	4000		1100
Bank current account	7085		1200
Creditors control account		1200	2100
Sales tax control account		814	2200
Purchase tax control account	623		2201
Loans		5000	2300
Ordinary Shares		15000	3000
Translation services income		3660	4000
Sales of language books		456	4001
Sales of language CDs		950	4002
Purchases of books	300		5000
Purchases of CDs	750		5001
Advertising	550		6201
Gross wages	2000		7000
Rent	250		7100
General rates	129		7103
Electricity	61		7200
Postage & Carriage	86		7501
Office Stationery	471		7502
Telephone	275		7550
	27,080	27,080	

Note: Earlier versions of Sage used account numbers 7502 and 7504 respectively for Telephone and Office Stationery

task 1

Ensure the program date is set at 31 July 2013.

Select the accounts that you wish to enter in the records from the NOMINAL opening screen. Use the account numbers in the right-hand column. Do not worry if the account names are different - they will be amended in Task 3. But do not select the Debtors Control Account or the Creditors Control Account as they should already show their balances.

Select RECORD from NOMINAL and enter the balance of each account from the trial balance, using the 31 July date. You may need to click on the Balance field or the O/B button to bring up the balance entry screen. Ensure that the amount is recorded in the correct debit or credit box.

task 2

Print out a trial balance as at 1 August 2013 from FINANCIALS.

task 3

Now change the account names that need changing (see the accounts with grey backgrounds on page 182) in RECORD in NOMINAL. Print out a further trial balance to check your corrections. The print out should appear as shown below. Check your input against this Report.

Interlingo Translation Services
Period Trial Balance

To Period: Month 2, August 2013

N/C	Name	Debit	Credit
0020	Office computers	5,000.00	
0030	Office Equipment	2,500.00	
0040	Furniture and Fixtures	3,000.00	
1100	Debtors Control Account	4,000.00	
1200	Bank Current Account	7,085.00	
2100	Creditors Control Account		1,200.00
2200	Sales Tax Control Account		814.00
2201	Purchase Tax Control Account	623.00	
2300	Loans		5,000.00
3000	Ordinary Shares		15,000.00
4000	Translation services income		3,660.00
4001	Sales of language books		456.00
4002	Sales of language CDs		950.00
5000	Purchases of books	300.00	
5001	Purchases of CDs	750.00	
6201	Advertising	550.00	
7000	Gross Wages	2,000.00	
7100	Rent	250.00	
7103	General Rates	129.00	
7200	Electricity	61.00	
7501	Postage and Carriage	86.00	
7502	Office Stationery	471.00	
7550	Telephone and Fax	275.00	
	Totals:	27,080.00	27,080.00

ACTIVITY 4 - ISSUING INVOICES AND CREDIT NOTES FOR TRANSLATIONS

introduction

It is 31 August and Jo has to process customer invoices and a credit note for work done during the month. She uses batch entry to enter the details into Sage 50.

task 1

Set the program date to 31 August 2013. Input the following invoices using the batch entry system.

invoice	account	date	net(£)	VAT(£)	description
10015	HD001	10 08 2013	520.00	104.00	Translation of sales contracts
10016	PL001	16 08 2013	120.00	24.00	Translation of sales literature
10017	RS001	20 08 2013	100.00	20.00	Translation of shipping docs
10018	RT001	20 08 2013	320.00	64.00	Translation of sales contracts
10019	SC001	22 08 2013	160.00	32.00	Translation of sales contracts

task 2

Hill & Dale & Co, who have passed substantial work to Interlingo, have written formally to ask for a 10% discount backdated to the beginning of the month.

Enter the following credit note to Hill & Dale & Co:

ref	account	date	net(£)	VAT(£)	description
501	HD001	31 08 2013	52.00	10.40	Refund of 10% discount, invoice 10015

task 3

Print out detailed Day Books Reports for the customer invoices and credit note entered. Check them against the those on page 214.

Reminder! Have you made a back-up?

ACTIVITY 5 – PROCESSING PURCHASE INVOICES AND CREDIT NOTES

introduction

Jo's purchases on credit are for supplies of language CDs and books and delivery services. During August she received three invoices in total.

task 1

Set the program date to 31 August 2013.

Input the two invoices below and on the next page as a batch into Invoices in SUPPLIERS.

Note that the Nominal code for CDs is 5001 and for books is 5000.

task 2

A supplier invoice has been received from A2B Carriers as follows:

invoice	date	net(£)	VAT(£)	description
72/554	15 08 2013	100.00	20.00	Miscellaneous deliveries

Enter the invoice details in Sage using Nominal code 5100.

task 3

Print out a Day Books: Supplier Invoices (Detailed) Report and check your printout against the printout on page 215.

INVOICE

TDI Wholesalers

Markway Estate, Nottingham, NG1 7GH
Tel 0115 295992 Fax 0115 295976 www.TDI.co.uk

invoice to

Interlingo Translation Services
14 Privet Road
Mereford
MR5 1HP

invoice no	2561
account	3023
your reference	984
date/tax point	15 08 13

product code	description	quantity	price	unit	total	VAT	total
2421	Beginners French CDs	100	5.00	set	500.00	100.00	600.00
2634	Advanced Italian CDs	50	6.00	set	300.00	60.00	360.00

goods total	800.00
VAT	160.00
TOTAL	960.00

INVOICE

BARDNERS BOOKS

Purbeck House, College Street, Cambridge CB3 8HP
Tel 01223 400652 Fax 01223 400648 www.Bardners.co.uk

invoice to

Interlingo Translation Services
14 Privet Road
Mereford
MR5 1HP

invoice no	11231
account	IL9987
your reference	985
date/tax point	20 08 13

product code	description	quantity	price	unit	total	VAT zero-rate	total
G778	German First Course	60	4.95	each	297.00	00.00	297.00
2634	French Second Course	45	5.95	each	267.75	00.00	267.75
					goods total		564.75
					VAT		00.00
					TOTAL		564.75

task 4

Jo discovers that ten of the sets of Beginners French CDs are faulty. She sends them back and asks for a credit note. This arrives on 31 August. Input the document (see below) into Credit in SUPPLIERS (Nominal Code 5001) and print out a Day Books: Suppliers Credits (Detailed) Report. Check your printout against the printout on page 215.

credit note from TDI Wholesalers (extract)

Interlingo Translation Services
14 Privet Road
Mereford
MR5 1HP

credit note no	1919
account	3023
your reference	984
date/tax point	28 08 13

product code	description	quantity	price	unit	total	VAT	total
2421	Beginners French CDs	10	5.00	set	50.00	10.00	60.00
					goods total		50.00
					VAT		10.00
					TOTAL		60.00

REASON FOR CREDIT
Faulty CDs returned

Reminder! Have you made a back-up?

ACTIVITY 6 – PROCESSING PAYMENTS RECEIVED

introduction

Jo has received payments from a number of different sources during August:

- payments from customers who have bought on credit during July

- cash payments for small translation jobs

- cash payments for books and CDs

They all have to be input into the computer accounting system.

task 1

Ensure the program date is set at 31 August 2013.

Input in BANK (Customer) the following payments received during August and paid into the Bank Current Account on the dates indicated. The reference number is the paying-in slip number.

account	date	customer	amount (£)	reference
HD001	10 08 2013	Hill & Dale & Co	345.00	100110
PL001	17 08 2013	Playgames PLC	795.00	100112
RS001	24 08 2013	RS Export Agency	850.00	100114
RT001	24 08 2013	Rotherway Limited	1,210.00	100114
SC001	31 08 2013	Schafeld Ltd	800.00	100116
		Total	4,000.00	

task 2

Print out a Day Books: Customer Receipts (Summary) Report for the month from BANK and check your printout against the printout on page 216.

task 3

Jo has also paid the takings from cash sales (ie from small translation jobs, books and CDs) into the Bank Current Account each week. She has totalled up each week's takings from these three sources and paid them in on one paying-in slip each Friday (the reference is shown in the right-hand column). The manual records she has kept show the cash receipts as follows:

date paid in	description	net (£)	VAT (£)	gross (£)	reference
10 08 2013	Translations	96.00	19.20	115.20	100111
	CDs	240.00	48.00	288.00	
	Books	160.00	T0 code	160.00	
	Paying-in slip total			563.20	

date paid in	description	net (£)	VAT (£)	gross (£)	reference
17 08 2013	Translations	116.00	23.20	139.20	100113
	CDs	180.00	36.00	216.00	
	Books	107.00	T0 code	107.00	
	Paying-in slip total			462.20	
24 08 2013	Translations	104.00	20.80	124.80	100115
	CDs	220.00	44.00	264.00	
	Books	84.00	T0 code	84.00	
	Paying-in slip total			472.80	
31 08 2013	Translations	82.00	16.40	98.40	100117
	CDs	190.00	38.00	228.00	
	Books	113.00	T0 code	113.00	
	Paying-in slip total			439.40	
BATCH TOTALS		1,692.00	245.60	1,937.60	

Input each of these cash receipts in BANK as BANK RECEIPTS. Remember to use the correct nominal codes for each type of sale: 4000 for translations, 4001 for books, 4002 for CDs. The reference in the right-hand column is the paying-in slip reference and should be used for each line of input.

task 4

Print out a Day Books: Bank Receipts (Detailed) Report for the month from BANK and check your printout against the printout on page 216.

ACTIVITY 7 – PAYING SUPPLIERS AND EXPENSES

introduction

During August Jo has had to pay her suppliers (of books and CDs) who have invoiced her in July on 30 days terms. She has also had to pay a number of expenses.

task 1

Ensure the program date is set at 31 August 2013.

Input in BANK (Supplier) these two outstanding items which were paid on 6 August:

TDI Wholesalers	Invoice 2347	£780.00	Due 07 08 2013	Cheque 120006
Bardners Books	Invoice 9422	£420.00	Due 08 08 2013	Cheque 120007

If possible, print out remittance advices from the computer to accompany the cheques.

task 2

Print out a Day Books: Supplier Payments (Summary) Report for 6 August from BANK and check your printout against the printout on page 217.

task 3

Input the following expense payments through PAYMENT in BANK.

In most cases you will need to work out the nominal codes from the trial balance on page 183.

The cheque number should be used as the reference.

The tax code is T1 unless indicated otherwise.

date	cheque	details	net(£)	VAT(£)
07 08 2013	120009	Office furniture	140.00	28.00
08 08 2013	120010	Advertising	600.00	120.00
15 08 2013	120011	Rent	250.00	50.00
17 08 2013	120012	Stationery	126.00	25.20
20 08 2013	120013	Rates	129.00	T2
22 08 2013	120014	Telephone	186.00	37.20
24 08 2013	120015	Electricity	84.00	16.80
30 08 2013	120016	Postages	45.60	T2
31 08 2013	BACS	Wages	2,240.00	T9
		Totals	3,800.60	277.20
				4,077.80

task 4

Print out a Day Books: Bank Payments (Detailed) Report for 7 – 31 August from BANK and check your printout against the printout on page 217.

Reminder! Have you made a back-up?

ACTIVITY 8 – SETTING UP A PETTY CASH SYSTEM

introduction

Jo finds that her temporary office assistant, Ella, often needs to make small payments in cash for items such as postage stamps and stationery for the office. She therefore decides to set up a petty cash system and cashes a cheque for £80 on 6 August to provide the funds.

task 1

Set the program date to 31 August 2013.

Process a Transfer in BANK for the £80 cheque (No. 120008) cashed on 6 August 2013. The accounts involved are Bank Current Account 1200 and Petty Cash Account 1230.

task 2

Input into BANK (Payments) Petty Cash Account the transactions represented by the four petty cash vouchers shown below and opposite.

Note that on one of them you will have to calculate the VAT on screen.

Postage stamps are VAT exempt (Tax code T2)

task 3

Print out a Day Books: Cash Payments (Detailed) Report from BANK and check your printout against the printout on page 218. Remember to select Petty Cash Account on the Bank opening screen first.

The net total should be £72.00 and the VAT total £7.20.

petty cash voucher		Number *0001*	
	date	*7 Aug 2013*	
description			amount
		£	p
A4 paper		*16*	*00*
		16	*00*
	VAT	*3*	*20*
VAT receipt obtained		*19*	*20*
signature *Ella Smith*			
authorised *Jo Lane*			

petty cash voucher   Number *0002*

                              date   *7 Aug 2013*

description		amount	
		£	p
Postage stamps		24	00
VAT			
		24	00

signature   *Ella Smith*

authorised   *Jo Lane*

---

petty cash voucher   Number *0003*

                              date   *15 Aug 2013*

description		amount	
		£	p
Box files		24	00
VAT			
Receipt obtained (VAT not shown)		24	00

signature   *Ella Smith*

authorised   *Jo Lane*

note that the receipt in this case does not show the VAT that has been charged – it will have to be worked out on input

---

petty cash voucher   Number *0004*

                              date   *22 Aug 2013*

description		amount	
		£	p
Postage stamps		12	00
VAT			
		12	00

signature   *Ella Smith*

authorised   *Jo Lane*

Reminder! Have you made a back-up?

ACTIVITY 9 – SETTING UP RECURRING PAYMENTS IN BANK

introduction

Jo has set up standing order and direct debit payments and receipts through the Bank Current Account. She can process these in Sage by setting up Recurring Payments in RECURRING in BANK. Click on the ADD button at the bottom of the screen to bring up the necessary window.

task 1

Set up a Recurring Payment for the following:

Bank Account   1200

Payment type   Direct Debit (Transaction ref: DD)

Payee   Suresafe Insurance (premises insurance)

Nominal code   7104

Tax code   T2

Amount   £98.50 per month

Frequency   12 monthly payments, starting 10 August 2013

Take a screenshot of the set up screen and check it against the image on page 218.

task 2

Set up a Recurring Payment for the following:

Bank Account   1200

Payment type   Standing order (Transaction ref: STO)

Payee   Albion Bank (standing charge)

Nominal code   7901

Tax code   T2

Amount   £15.00 per month

Frequency   5 monthly payments starting 25 August 2013

task 3

Set up a Recurring Receipt for the following:

Bank Account   1200

Payment type   Standing order (Transaction ref: STO)

Payee   Worldwide Translations (referrals)

Nominal code   4902

Tax code   T1

Amount   £12.00 per week (plus VAT)

Frequency   13 weekly payments starting 4 August 2013

task 4

Set the program date to 31 August 2013 and process the Recurring Payments for August in BANK.

task 5

Print out a trial balance of the business as at 31 August 2013. It should agree with the trial balance shown below.

Interlingo Translation Services

Period Trial Balance

To Period: Month 2, August 2013

N/C	Name	Debit	Credit
0020	Office computers	5,000.00	
0030	Office Equipment	2,500.00	
0040	Furniture and Fixtures	3,140.00	
1100	Debtors Control Account	1,401.60	
1200	Bank Current Account	7,608.90	
1230	Petty Cash	0.80	
2100	Creditors Control Account		1,584.75
2200	Sales Tax Control Account		1,302.80
2201	Purchase Tax Control Account	1,077.40	
2300	Loans		5,000.00
3000	Ordinary Shares		15,000.00
4000	Translation services income		5,226.00
4001	Sales of language books		920.00
4002	Sales of language CDs		1,780.00
4902	Commissions Received		48.00
5000	Purchases of books	864.75	
5001	Purchases of CDs	1,500.00	
5100	Carriage	100.00	
6201	Advertising	1,150.00	
7000	Gross Wages	4,240.00	
7100	Rent	500.00	
7103	General Rates	258.00	
7104	Premises Insurance	98.50	
7200	Electricity	145.00	
7501	Postage and Carriage	167.60	
7502	Office Stationery	633.00	
7550	Telephone and Fax	461.00	
7901	Bank Charges	15.00	
	Totals:	30,861.55	30,861.55

Trial balance of Interlingo Translation Services as at 31 August 2013

Reminder! Have you made a back-up?

ACTIVITY 10 – END-OF-MONTH PROCEDURES

introduction

At the end of August Jo is ready to carry out her end-of-month procedures.

task 1

Jo has printed a bank statement online, shown below. Carry out a bank reconciliation as at 31 August. Print a Bank Reconciliation Report and check it against the one on page 219.

	ALBION BANK PLC			
	Online statement of account as at: 31 08 2013			
	Account 90 47 17 11894422 Interlingo Translation Services Ltd			
		Paid out	Paid in	Balance
31/07/2013	Balance b/f			7085.00
04/08/2013	DD Worldwide Trans		14.40	7099.40
06/08/2013	120008	80.00		7019.40
09/08/2013	120006	780.00		6239.40
10/08/2013	120007	420.00		5819.40
10/08/2013	Credit 100111		563.20	6382.60
10/08/2013	120009	168.00		6214.60
10/08/2013	Credit 100110		345.00	6559.60
10/08/2013	DD Suresafe	98.50		6461.10
10/08/2013	120010	720.00		5741.10
11/08/2013	DD Worldwide Trans		14.40	5755.50
17/08/2013	Credit 100112		795.00	6550.50
17/08/2013	Credit 100113		462.20	7012.70
17/08/2013	120011	300.00		6712.70
18/08/2013	DD Worldwide Trans		14.40	6727.10
20/08/2013	120012	151.20		6575.90
22/08/2013	120013	129.00		6446.90
24/08/2013	Credit 100114		2060.00	8506.90
24/08/2013	Credit 100115		472.80	8979.70
24/08/2013	120014	223.20		8756.50
25/08/2013	DD Worldwide Trans		14.40	8770.90
25/08/2013	SO Albion Bank	15.00		8755.90
31/08/2013	Credit 100116		800.00	9555.90
31/08/2013	Credit 100117		439.40	9995.30
31/08/2013	BACS Wages	2240.00		7755.30

task 2

Print out the following reports:

- the month-end trial balance (note that this is the trial balance printed in Activity 9, Task 5).

- customer statements of account from STATEMENT in CUSTOMERS

- an Aged Debtors Analysis from Reports in CUSTOMERS (see page 220)

- a Detailed Audit Trail for the period 25-31 August from Reports in FINANCIALS (see page 220)

task 3

Obtain a Customer Activity (Detailed) Report (see page 221) for Hill & Dale & Co and examine the Customer Record. Describe what has happened on the account and advise Jo how much is owed.

task 4

Print out a Supplier Activity (Detailed) Report for TDI Wholesalers (see page 221) and examine the Supplier Record. Describe what has happened on the account during the month and advise Jo what the amount of her next payment should be.

task 5

Jim Draxman, a friend of Jo, who is helping her with her marketing, asks her for a list of the names and addresses of her customers.

Produce a suitable list, either from Labels or from a Customer Address List Report (both accessible in CUSTOMERS). (See page 222.)

ACTIVITY 11 – DEALING WITH SECURITY

introduction

At the end of August Jo is concerned that the security of her computer and the data kept on it is not as good as it could be. She takes measures to improve the safety of her machines and data.

task 1

Jo sometimes gets in a muddle over her data back-up disks for her computer accounting program and has on one occasion had to reinput data.

Recommend to Jo a back up system which will prevent this happening in the future.

task 2

Jo is concerned about unauthorised members of staff accessing data on Sage. How can she control this?

Sage printout checklist

The Sage printouts that follow are provided so that tutors and students carrying out the processing exercises and extended activities can periodically check their progress.

The page numbers for the relevant printouts can be found by referring to the index below.

Please note that all these printouts are © 2013 Sage (UK) Limited. All rights reserved.

Chapter 4

Task 3

Pronto Supplies Limited

Day Books: Customer Invoices (Summary)

| Date From: | 01/01/1980 | | | | | Customer From: | | |
| Date To: | 31/12/2019 | | | | | Customer To: | ZZZZZZZZ | |

Transaction From: 1
Transaction To: 99,999,999

Tran No.	Items	Tp	Date	A/C Ref	Inv Ref	Details	Net Amount	Tax Amount	Gross Amount
1	1	SI	05/01/2013	JB001	10013	Opening Balance	5,500.00	0.00	5,500.00
2	1	SI	05/01/2013	CH001	10014	Opening Balance	2,400.00	0.00	2,400.00
3	1	SI	09/01/2013	CR001	10015	Opening Balance	3,234.00	0.00	3,234.00
4	1	SI	10/01/2013	DB001	10016	Opening Balance	3,400.00	0.00	3,400.00
5	1	SI	10/01/2013	KD001	10017	Opening Balance	6,500.00	0.00	6,500.00
6	1	SI	17/01/2013	LG001	10019	Opening Balance	8,500.00	0.00	8,500.00
						Totals:	29,534.00	0.00	29,534.00

Task 4

Pronto Supplies Limited

Day Books: Supplier Invoices (Summary)

| Date From: | 01/01/1980 | | | | | Supplier From: | | |
| Date To: | 31/12/2019 | | | | | Supplier To: | ZZZZZZZZ | |

Transaction From: 1
Transaction To: 99,999,999

Tran No.	Item	Type	Date	A/C Ref	Inv Ref	Details	Net Amount	Tax Amount	Gross Amount
7	1	PI	04/01/2013	DE001	4563	Opening Balance	5,750.00	0.00	5,750.00
8	1	PI	05/01/2013	EL001	8122	Opening Balance	8,500.00	0.00	8,500.00
9	1	PI	09/01/2013	MA001	9252	Opening Balance	4,500.00	0.00	4,500.00
						Totals	18,750.00	0.00	18,750.00

Task 5

Pronto Supplies Limited

Period Trial Balance

To Period: Month 1, January 2013

N/C	Name	Debit	Credit
1100	Debtors Control Account	29,534.00	
2100	Creditors Control Account		18,750.00
9998	Suspense Account		10,784.00
	Totals:	29,534.00	29,534.00

Chapter 5

Task 3

Pronto Supplies Limited

Period Trial Balance

To Period: Month 1, January 2013

N/C	Name	Debit	Credit
0020	Plant and Machinery	35,000.00	
0030	Office Equipment	15,000.00	
0040	Furniture and Fixtures	25,000.00	
1100	Debtors Control Account	29,534.00	
1200	Bank Current Account	14,656.00	
2100	Creditors Control Account		18,750.00
2200	Sales Tax Control Account		17,920.00
2201	Purchase Tax Control Account	26,600.00	
2300	Loans		35,000.00
3000	Ordinary Shares		75,000.00
4000	Sales Type A		85,000.00
4001	Sales Type B		15,000.00
4002	Sales Type C		2,400.00
5000	Materials Purchased	69,100.00	
6201	Advertising	12,400.00	
7000	Gross Wages	16,230.00	
7100	Rent	4,500.00	
7103	General Rates	450.00	
7200	Electricity	150.00	
7502	Office Stationery	175.00	
7550	Telephone and Fax	275.00	
	Totals:	249,070.00	249,070.00

Chapter 6

Task 3

Pronto Supplies Limited

Day Books: Customer Invoices (Detailed)

Date From:	12/02/2013	
Date To:	16/02/2013	

Customer From:	
Customer To:	ZZZZZZZZ

Transaction From:	1
Transaction To:	99,999,999

N/C From:	
N/C To:	99999999

Dept From:	0
Dept To:	999

Tran No.	Type	Date	A/C Ref	N/C	Inv Ref	Dept.	Details	Net Amount	Tax Amount	T/C	Gross Amount	V	B
54	SI	12/02/2013	JB001	4002	10027	0	Consultancy	120.00	24.00	T1	144.00	N	-
55	SI	13/02/2013	DB001	4000	10028	0	Hardware	600.00	120.00	T1	720.00	N	-
56	SI	16/02/2013	LG001	4000	10029	0	Hardware	180.00	36.00	T1	216.00	N	-
57	SI	16/02/2013	KD001	4001	10030	0	Software	264.00	52.80	T1	316.80	N	-
58	SI	16/02/2013	CH001	4000	10031	0	Hardware	320.00	64.00	T1	384.00	N	-
							Totals:	1,484.00	296.80		1,780.80		

Task 4

Pronto Supplies Limited

Day Books: Customer Credits (Detailed)

Date From:	12/02/2013								**Customer From:**			
Date To:	13/02/2013								**Customer To:**	ZZZZZZZZ		
Transaction From:	1								**N/C From:**			
Transaction To:	99,999,999								**N/C To:**	99999999		
Dept From:	0											
Dept To:	999											

Tran No.	Type	Date	A/C Ref	N/C	Inv Ref	Dept.	Details	Net Amount	Tax Amount	T/C	Gross Amount	V	B
59	SC	12/02/2013	KD001	4000	553	0	Hardware returned	16.00	3.20	T1	19.20	N	-
60	SC	13/02/2013	CR001	4000	554	0	Hardware returned	20.00	4.00	T1	24.00	N	-
							Totals:	36.00	7.20		43.20		

Task 4

Pronto Supplies Limited

Period Trial Balance

To Period: Month 2, February 2013

N/C	Name	Debit	Credit
0020	Plant and Machinery	35,000.00	
0030	Office Equipment	15,000.00	
0040	Furniture and Fixtures	25,000.00	
1100	Debtors Control Account	31,866.80	
1200	Bank Current Account	14,656.00	
2100	Creditors Control Account		18,750.00
2200	Sales Tax Control Account		18,308.80
2201	Purchase Tax Control Account	26,600.00	
2300	Loans		35,000.00
3000	Ordinary Shares		75,000.00
4000	Computer hardware sales		86,440.00
4001	Computer software sales		15,264.00
4002	Computer consultancy		2,640.00
5000	Materials Purchased	69,100.00	
6201	Advertising	12,400.00	
7000	Gross Wages	16,230.00	
7100	Rent	4,500.00	
7103	General Rates	450.00	
7200	Electricity	150.00	
7502	Office Stationery	175.00	
7550	Telephone and Fax	275.00	
	Totals:	251,402.80	251,402.80

Chapter 7

Task 3

Pronto Supplies Limited

Day Books: Supplier Invoices (Detailed)

Date From:	14/02/2013	
Date To:	14/02/2013	

Supplier From:	
Supplier To:	ZZZZZZZ

Transaction From:	1
Transaction To:	99,999,999

N/C From:	
N/C To:	99999999

Dept From:	0
Dept To:	999

Tran No.	Type	Date	A/C Ref	N/C	Inv Ref	Dept	Details	Net Amount	Tax Amount	T/C	Gross Amount	V	B
66	PI	14/02/2013	DE001	0030	11377	0	Desktop computer	400.00	80.00	T1	480.00	N	-
67	PI	14/02/2013	EL001	0030	8603	0	Laser printer	360.00	72.00	T1	432.00	N	-
							Totals	760.00	152.00		912.00		

Pronto Supplies Limited

Period Trial Balance

To Period: Month 2, February 2013

N/C	Name	Debit	Credit
0020	Plant and Machinery	35,000.00	
0030	Office Equipment	15,760.00	
0040	Furniture and Fixtures	25,000.00	
1100	Debtors Control Account	31,866.80	
1200	Bank Current Account	14,656.00	
2100	Creditors Control Account		30,176.40
2200	Sales Tax Control Account		18,308.80
2201	Purchase Tax Control Account	28,504.40	
2300	Loans		35,000.00
3000	Ordinary Shares		75,000.00
4000	Computer hardware sales		86,440.00
4001	Computer software sales		15,264.00
4002	Computer consultancy		2,640.00
5000	Materials Purchased	77,862.00	
6201	Advertising	12,400.00	
7000	Gross Wages	16,230.00	
7100	Rent	4,500.00	
7103	General Rates	450.00	
7200	Electricity	150.00	
7502	Office Stationery	175.00	
7550	Telephone and Fax	275.00	
	Totals:	262,829.20	262,829.20

Chapter 8

Task 1

Pronto Supplies Limited
Day Books: Customer Receipts (Summary)

Date From: 28/02/2013		**Bank From:** 1200
DateTo: 28/02/2013		**Bank To:** 1200
Transaction From: 1		Customer From :
Transaction To: 99,999,999		Customer To: ZZZZZZZ

Bank 1200   **Currency** Pound Sterling

No	Type	Date	Account	Ref	Details	Net £	Tax £	Gross £ B	Bank Rec. Date
68	SR	28/02/2013	JB001	cheque	Sales Receipt	5,500.00	0.00	5,500.00 N	
69	SR	28/02/2013	CH001	cheque	Sales Receipt	2,419.20	0.00	2,419.20 N	
70	SR	28/02/2013	CR001	BACS	Sales Receipt	3,234.00	0.00	3,234.00 N	
71	SR	28/02/2013	DB001	cheque	Sales Receipt	2,860.00	0.00	2,860.00 N	
72	SR	28/02/2013	KD001	BACS	Sales Receipt	6,500.00	0.00	6,500.00 N	
73	SR	28/02/2013	LG001	BACS	Sales Receipt	8,500.00	0.00	8,500.00 N	
					Totals £	29,013.20	0.00	29,013.20	

Task 2

Pronto Supplies Limited
Day Books: Supplier Payments (Summary)

Date From: 28/02/2013		**Bank From:** 1200
DateTo: 28/02/2013		**Bank To:** 1200
Transaction From: 1		Supplier From:
Transaction To: 99,999,999		Supplier To: ZZZZZZZZ

Bank 1200   **Currency** Pound Sterling

No	Type	Date	Supplier	Ref	Details	Net £	Tax £	Gross £ B	Bank Rec. Date
74	PP	28/02/2013	DE001	BACS	Purchase Payment	5,174.00	0.00	5,174.00 N	
75	PP	28/02/2013	EL001	BACS	Purchase Payment	8,500.00	0.00	8,500.00 N	
76	PP	28/02/2013	MA001	BACS	Purchase Payment	4,454.40	0.00	4,454.40 N	
					Totals £	18,128.40	0.00	18,128.40	

Task 3

Pronto Supplies Limited

Period Trial Balance

To Period: Month 2, February 2013

N/C	Name	Debit	Credit
0020	Plant and Machinery	35,000.00	
0030	Office Equipment	15,760.00	
0040	Furniture and Fixtures	25,000.00	
1100	Debtors Control Account	2,853.60	
1200	Bank Current Account	25,540.80	
2100	Creditors Control Account		12,048.00
2200	Sales Tax Control Account		18,308.80
2201	Purchase Tax Control Account	28,504.40	
2300	Loans		35,000.00
3000	Ordinary Shares		75,000.00
4000	Computer hardware sales		86,440.00
4001	Computer software sales		15,264.00
4002	Computer consultancy		2,640.00
5000	Materials Purchased	77,862.00	
6201	Advertising	12,400.00	
7000	Gross Wages	16,230.00	
7100	Rent	4,500.00	
7103	General Rates	450.00	
7200	Electricity	150.00	
7502	Office Stationery	175.00	
7550	Telephone and Fax	275.00	
	Totals:	244,700.80	244,700.80

Chapter 9

Task 1

Pronto Supplies Limited

Day Books: Bank Receipts (Detailed)

Date From:	09/02/2013		Bank From:	1200
DateTo:	23/02/2013		Bank To:	1200
Transaction From:	1		N/C From:	
Transaction To:	99,999,999		N/C To:	99999999
Dept From:	0			
Dept To:	999			

Bank: 1200   **Currency:** Pound Sterling

No	Type	N/C	Date	Ref	Details	Dept	Net £	Tax £ T/C	Gross £ V	B	Bank Rec. Date
77	BR	4000	09/02/2013	10736	Hardware sales	0	12,500.00	2,500.00 T1	15,000.00 N	N	
78	BR	4001	09/02/2013	10737	Software sales	0	4,680.00	936.00 T1	5,616.00 N	N	
79	BR	4000	16/02/2013	10738	Hardware sales	0	15,840.00	3,168.00 T1	19,008.00 N	N	
80	BR	4001	16/02/2013	10739	Software sales	0	3,680.00	736.00 T1	4,416.00 N	N	
81	BR	4000	23/02/2013	10740	Hardware sales	0	17,800.00	3,560.00 T1	21,360.00 N	N	
82	BR	4001	23/02/2013	10741	Software sales	0	4,800.00	960.00 T1	5,760.00 N	N	
						Totals £	59,300.00	11,860.00	71,160.00		

Task 2

Pronto Supplies Limited

Day Books: Bank Payments (Detailed)

Date From:		12/02/2013								**Bank From:**		1200	
DateTo:		28/02/2013								**Bank To:**		1200	
Transaction From:		1								**N/C From:**			
Transaction To:		99,999,999								**N/C To:**		99999999	
Dept From:		0											
Dept To:		999											

Bank:	1200		**Currency:**	Pound Sterling										
No	**Type**	**N/C**	**Date**	**Ref**	**Details**	**Dept**	**Net £**	**Tax £ T/C**	**Gross £ V**	**B**	**Bank Date**
83	BP	5000	12/02/2013	122992	Cash purchases	0	15,500.00	3,100.00 T1	18,600.00 N	N	
84	BP	6201	14/02/2013	122993	Advertising	0	10,200.00	2,040.00 T1	12,240.00 N	N	
85	BP	0040	15/02/2013	122994	Furniture	0	5,000.00	1,000.00 T1	6,000.00 N	N	
86	BP	7200	23/02/2013	BACS	Electricity	0	158.00	31.60 T1	189.60 N	N	
87	BP	7550	26/02/2013	BACS	Telephone	0	310.00	62.00 T1	372.00 N	N	
88	BP	7502	28/02/2013	Debit card	Stationery	0	340.00	68.00 T1	408.00 N	N	
89	BP	7000	28/02/2013	BACS	Wages	0	16,780.00	0.00 T9	16,780.00 -	N	
						Totals £	48,288.00	6,301.60	54,589.60		

Task 4

Pronto Supplies Limited

Period Trial Balance

To Period: Month 2, February 2013

N/C	Name	Debit	Credit
0020	Plant and Machinery	35,000.00	
0030	Office Equipment	19,760.00	
0040	Furniture and Fixtures	30,000.00	
1100	Debtors Control Account	2,853.60	
1200	Bank Current Account	42,311.20	
2100	Creditors Control Account		12,048.00
2200	Sales Tax Control Account		30,168.80
2201	Purchase Tax Control Account	35,606.00	
2300	Loans		35,000.00
3000	Ordinary Shares		80,000.00
4000	Computer hardware sales		132,580.00
4001	Computer software sales		28,424.00
4002	Computer consultancy		2,640.00
5000	Materials Purchased	93,362.00	
6201	Advertising	22,600.00	
7000	Gross Wages	33,010.00	
7100	Rent	4,500.00	
7103	General Rates	450.00	
7200	Electricity	308.00	
7502	Office Stationery	515.00	
7550	Telephone and Fax	585.00	
	Totals:	320,860.80	320,860.80

Chapter 10

Task 2

Pronto Supplies Limited

Day Books: Cash Payments (Detailed)

Date From:		01/02/2013								**Bank From:**	1230
DateTo:		28/02/2013								**Bank To:**	1230
Transaction From:		1								**N/C From:**	
Transaction To:		99,999,999								**N/C To:**	99999999
Dept From:		0									
Dept To:		999									

Bank: 1230   **Currency:** Pound Sterling

No	Type	N/C	Date	Ref	Details	Dept	Net £	Tax £ T/C	Gross £ V B
94	CP	7502	07/02/2013	PC101	A4 paper	0	36.00	7.20 T1	43.20 N -
95	CP	7501	14/02/2013	PC102	Postage stamps	0	25.00	0.00 T2	25.00 N -
96	CP	7502	20/02/2013	PC103	Envelopes	0	16.00	3.20 T1	19.20 N -
97	CP	7501	28/02/2013	PC104	Postage stamps	0	5.00	0.00 T2	5.00 N -
98	CP	5003	28/02/2013	PC105	Packing tape	0	4.00	0.80 T1	4.80 N -
						Totals £	86.00	11.20	97.20

Task 3

Pronto Supplies Limited

Day Books: Bank Receipts (Detailed)

Date From:		01/01/1980								**Bank From:**	1235
DateTo:		31/12/2019								**Bank To:**	1235
Transaction From:		1								**N/C From:**	
Transaction To:		99,999,999								**N/C To:**	99999999
Dept From:		0									
Dept To:		999									

Bank: 1235   **Currency:** Pound Sterling

No	Type	N/C	Date	Ref	Details	Dept	Net £	Tax £ T/C	Gross £ V B
99	BR	4000	26/02/2013	10743	Hardware sales	0	5,000.00	1,000.00 T1	6,000.00 N -
100	BR	4001	26/02/2013	10743	Software sales	0	480.00	96.00 T1	576.00 N -
101	BR	4000	27/02/2013	10744	Hardware sales	0	1,200.00	240.00 T1	1,440.00 N -
102	BR	4001	27/02/2013	10744	Software sales	0	890.00	178.00 T1	1,068.00 N -
103	BR	4000	28/02/2013	10745	Hardware sales	0	600.00	120.00 T1	720.00 N -
104	BR	4001	28/02/2013	10745	Software sales	0	120.00	24.00 T1	144.00 N -
						Totals £	8,290.00	1,658.00	9,948.00

Task 5

Pronto Supplies Limited

Period Trial Balance

To Period: Month 2, February 2013

N/C	Name	Debit	Credit
0020	Plant and Machinery	35,000.00	
0030	Office Equipment	19,760.00	
0040	Furniture and Fixtures	30,000.00	
1100	Debtors Control Account	2,853.60	
1200	Bank Current Account	36,984.64	
1230	Petty Cash	2.80	
1235	Cash Register	9,948.00	
2100	Creditors Control Account		12,048.00
2200	Sales Tax Control Account		31,918.00
2201	Purchase Tax Control Account	36,521.16	
2300	Loans		35,000.00
3000	Ordinary Shares		80,000.00
4000	Computer hardware sales		139,380.00
4001	Computer software sales		29,914.00
4002	Computer consultancy		2,640.00
4904	Rent Income		456.00
5000	Materials Purchased	93,362.00	
5003	Packaging	4.00	
6201	Advertising	22,600.00	
7000	Gross Wages	33,010.00	
7100	Rent	9,000.00	
7103	General Rates	800.00	
7200	Electricity	308.00	
7501	Postage and Carriage	30.00	
7502	Office Stationery	567.00	
7550	Telephone and Fax	585.00	
7701	Office Machine Maintenance	19.80	
	Totals:	331,356.00	331,356.00

Chapter 11

Task 1

Pronto Supplies Limited

Nominal Activity

Date From:	01/02/2013			**N/C From:**	4000
Date To:	28/02/2013			**N/C To:**	4000
Transaction From:	1				
Transaction To:	99,999,999				

N/C:	4000	**Name:**	Computer hardware sales	**Account Balance:**	139,380.00 CR

No	Type	Date	Account	Ref	Details	Dept	T/C	Value	Debit	Credit	V	B
48	SI	05/02/2013	JB001	10023	Hardware	0	T1	400.00		400.00	N	-
49	SI	06/02/2013	CH001	10024	Hardware	0	T1	16.00		16.00	N	-
53	SC	06/02/2013	LG001	552	Hardware returned	0	T1	40.00	40.00		N	-
55	SI	13/02/2013	DB001	10028	Hardware	0	T1	600.00		600.00	N	-
56	SI	16/02/2013	LG001	10029	Hardware	0	T1	180.00		180.00	N	-
58	SI	16/02/2013	CH001	10031	Hardware	0	T1	320.00		320.00	N	-
59	SC	12/02/2013	KD001	553	Hardware returned	0	T1	16.00	16.00		N	-
60	SC	13/02/2013	CR001	554	Hardware returned	0	T1	20.00	20.00		N	-
77	BR	09/02/2013	1200	10736	Hardware sales	0	T1	12,500.00		12,500.00	N	N
79	BR	16/02/2013	1200	10738	Hardware sales	0	T1	15,840.00		15,840.00	N	N
81	BR	23/02/2013	1200	10740	Hardware sales	0	T1	17,800.00		17,800.00	N	N
99	BR	26/02/2013	1235	10743	Hardware sales	0	T1	5,000.00		5,000.00	N	-
101	BR	27/02/2013	1235	10744	Hardware sales	0	T1	1,200.00		1,200.00	N	-
103	BR	28/02/2013	1235	10745	Hardware sales	0	T1	600.00		600.00	N	-
							Totals:		76.00	54,456.00		
							History Balance:			54,380.00		

Task 3

Pronto Supplies Limited

Audit Trail (Detailed)

Date From:	28/02/2013			Customer From:	
Date To:	28/02/2013			Customer To:	ZZZZZZZ
Transaction From:	1			Supplier From:	
Transaction To:	99,999,999			Supplier To:	ZZZZZZZ
Exclude Deleted Tran:	No				

No	Type	A/C	N/C	Dept	Details	Date	Ref	Net	Tax	T/C	Pd	Paid	V	B	Bank Rec. D
68	SR	JB001				28/02/2013	cheque	5,500.00	0.00		Y	5,500.00	N		
		68	1200	0	Sales Receipt			5,500.00	0.00	T9		5,500.00 -			
					5500.00 to SI 1	28/02/2013	10013					5,500.00			
69	SR	CH001				28/02/2013	cheque	2,419.20	0.00		Y	2,419.20	N		
		69	1200	0	Sales Receipt			2,419.20	0.00	T9		2,419.20 -			
					2400.00 to SI 2	28/02/2013	10014					2,400.00			
					19.20 to SI 49	28/02/2013	10024					19.20			
70	SR	CR001				28/02/2013	BACS	3,234.00	0.00		Y	3,234.00	R		28/02/2013
		70	1200	0	Sales Receipt			3,234.00	0.00	T9		3,234.00 -			
					3234.00 to SI 3	28/02/2013	10015					3,234.00			
71	SR	DB001				28/02/2013	cheque	2,860.00	0.00		Y	2,860.00	N		
		71	1200	0	Sales Receipt			2,860.00	0.00	T9		2,860.00 -			
					2860.00 to SI 4	28/02/2013	10016					2,860.00			
72	SR	KD001				28/02/2013	BACS	6,500.00	0.00		Y	6,500.00	R		28/02/2013
		72	1200	0	Sales Receipt			6,500.00	0.00	T9		6,500.00 -			
					6500.00 to SI 5	28/02/2013	10017					6,500.00			
73	SR	LG001				28/02/2013	BACS	8,500.00	0.00		Y	8,500.00	R		28/02/2013
		73	1200	0	Sales Receipt			8,500.00	0.00	T9		8,500.00 -			
					8500.00 to SI 6	28/02/2013	10019					8,500.00			
74	PP	DE001				28/02/2013	BACS	5,174.00	0.00		Y	5,174.00	R		28/02/2013
		74	1200	0	Purchase Payment			5,174.00	0.00	T9		5,174.00 -			
					5174.00 to PI 7	28/02/2013	4563					5,174.00			
75	PP	EL001				28/02/2013	BACS	8,500.00	0.00		Y	8,500.00	R		28/02/2013
		75	1200	0	Purchase Payment			8,500.00	0.00	T9		8,500.00 -			
					8500.00 to PI 8	28/02/2013	8122					8,500.00			
76	PP	MA001				28/02/2013	BACS	4,454.40	0.00		Y	4,454.40	R		28/02/2013
		76	1200	0	Purchase Payment			4,454.40	0.00	T9		4,454.40 -			
					4454.40 to PI 9	28/02/2013	9252					4,454.40			
88	BP	1200				28/02/2013	Debit card	340.00	68.00		Y	408.00	N		
		88	7502	0	Stationery			340.00	68.00	T1		408.00			
89	BP	1200				28/02/2013	BACS	16,780.00	0.00		Y	16,780.00	R		28/02/2013
		89	7000	0	Wages			16,780.00	0.00	T9		16,780.00 -			
90	BR	1200				28/02/2013	10742	5,000.00	0.00		Y	5,000.00	N		
		90	3000	0	Share capital			5,000.00	0.00	T9		5,000.00 -			
91	BP	1200				28/02/2013	122995	4,000.00	800.00		Y	4,800.00	R		28/02/2013
		91	0030	0	Colour printer			4,000.00	800.00	T1		4,800.00	N		
97	CP	1230				28/02/2013	PC104	5.00	0.00		Y	5.00	-		
		97	7501	0	Postage stamps			5.00	0.00	T2		5.00	N		
98	CP	1230				28/02/2013	PC105	4.00	0.80		Y	4.80	-		
		98	5003	0	Packing tape			4.00	0.80	T1		4.80	N		
103	BR	1235				28/02/2013	10745	720.00	144.00		Y	864.00	-		
		103	4000	0	Hardware sales			600.00	120.00	T1		720.00	N		
		104	4001	0	Software sales			120.00	24.00	T1		144.00	N		
109	BP	1200				28/02/2013	BANK	50.00	0.00		Y	50.00	R		28/02/2013
		109	7901	0	Bank charges			50.00	0.00	T2		50.00	N		

Task 4

Backup

| Backup Company | Advanced Options | Previous Backups |

Company Details

You are about to create a backup of:

Company Name: Pronto Supplies Limited

Found In: C:\DOCUMENTS AND SETTINGS\ALL USERS\APPLICATION
DATA\SAGE\ACCOUNTS\2012\COMPANY.000\

Where do you want the company backed up to?

Please click Browse to select a location to save this backup to. We have suggested a filename for this backup. If you are happy with this suggestion, click OK to save the backup.

Backing Up to removable media? Insert the device before clicking OK.

Backing Up to CD? Refer to the Help now.

Filename : Chapter 11 end

Location : F:\Sage backups

Browse...

Note: Your filename and location may be different.

OK   Cancel   Help

Chapter 12

Task 3

Pronto Supplies Limited

Period Trial Balance

To Period: Month 2, February 2013

N/C	Name	Debit	Credit
0020	Plant and Machinery	35,000.00	
0030	Office Equipment	19,760.00	
0040	Furniture and Fixtures	30,000.00	
1100	Debtors Control Account	2,853.60	
1200	Bank Current Account	36,934.64	
1230	Petty Cash	2.80	
1235	Cash Register	9,948.00	
2100	Creditors Control Account		12,048.00
2200	Sales Tax Control Account		31,918.00
2201	Purchase Tax Control Account	36,521.16	
2300	Loans		35,000.00
3000	Ordinary Shares		80,000.00
4000	Computer hardware sales		139,380.00
4001	Computer software sales		29,914.00
4002	Computer consultancy		2,640.00
4904	Rent Income		456.00
5000	Materials Purchased	93,362.00	
5003	Packaging	4.00	
6201	Advertising	22,600.00	
7000	Gross Wages	33,010.00	
7100	Rent	9,000.00	
7103	General Rates	800.00	
7200	Electricity	150.00	
7201	Gas	158.00	
7501	Postage and Carriage	30.00	
7502	Office Stationery	567.00	
7550	Telephone and Fax	585.00	
7701	Office Machine Maintenance	19.80	
7901	Bank Charges	50.00	
	Totals:	331,356.00	331,356.00

Interlingo Limited Extended Exercise: Activity 2

Task 3

Interlingo Translation Services

Day Books: Customer Invoices (Detailed)

| Date From: | 01/07/2013 | | | | | | | | | | Customer From: | | | |
| Date To: | 31/07/2013 | | | | | | | | | | Customer To: | ZZZZZZZZ | | |

| Transaction From: | 1 | | | | | | | | | | N/C From: | | | |
| Transaction To: | 99,999,999 | | | | | | | | | | N/C To: | 99999999 | | |

| Dept From: | 0 | | | | | | | | | | | | | |
| Dept To: | 999 | | | | | | | | | | | | | |

Tran No.	Type	Date	A/C Ref	N/C	Inv Ref	Dept.	Details	Net Amount	Tax Amount	T/C	Gross Amount	V	B
1	SI	06/07/2013	RS001	9998	10010	0	Opening Balance	850.00	0.00	T9	850.00	-	-
2	SI	12/07/2013	PL001	9998	10011	0	Opening Balance	795.00	0.00	T9	795.00	-	-
3	SI	17/07/2013	RT001	9998	10012	0	Opening Balance	1,210.00	0.00	T9	1,210.00	-	-
4	SI	19/07/2013	HD001	9998	10013	0	Opening Balance	345.00	0.00	T9	345.00	-	-
5	SI	20/07/2013	SC001	9998	10014	0	Opening Balance	800.00	0.00	T9	800.00	-	-
							Totals:	4,000.00	0.00		4,000.00		

Task 6

Interlingo Translation Services

Day Books: Supplier Invoices (Detailed)

| Date From: | 01/07/2013 | | | | | | | | | | Supplier From: | | | |
| Date To: | 31/07/2013 | | | | | | | | | | Supplier To: | ZZZZZZZZ | | |

| Transaction From: | 1 | | | | | | | | | | N/C From: | | | |
| Transaction To: | 99,999,999 | | | | | | | | | | N/C To: | 99999999 | | |

| Dept From: | 0 | | | | | | | | | | | | | |
| Dept To: | 999 | | | | | | | | | | | | | |

Tran No.	Type	Date	A/C Ref	N/C	Inv Ref	Dept	Details	Net Amount	Tax Amount	T/C	Gross Amount	V	B
6	PI	07/07/2013	TD001	9998	2347	0	Opening Balance	780.00	0.00	T9	780.00	-	-
7	PI	08/07/2013	BB001	9998	9422	0	Opening Balance	420.00	0.00	T9	420.00	-	-
							Totals	1,200.00	0.00		1,200.00		

Interlingo Limited Extended Exercise: Activity 3

Task 2

Interlingo Translation Services

Period Trial Balance

To Period: Month 2, August 2013

N/C	Name	Debit	Credit
0020	Plant and Machinery	5,000.00	
0030	Office Equipment	2,500.00	
0040	Furniture and Fixtures	3,000.00	
1100	Debtors Control Account	4,000.00	
1200	Bank Current Account	7,085.00	
2100	Creditors Control Account		1,200.00
2200	Sales Tax Control Account		814.00
2201	Purchase Tax Control Account	623.00	
2300	Loans		5,000.00
3000	Ordinary Shares		15,000.00
4000	Sales Type A		3,660.00
4001	Sales Type B		456.00
4002	Sales Type C		950.00
5000	Materials Purchased	300.00	
5001	Materials Imported	750.00	
6201	Advertising	550.00	
7000	Gross Wages	2,000.00	
7100	Rent	250.00	
7103	General Rates	129.00	
7200	Electricity	61.00	
7501	Postage and Carriage	86.00	
7502	Office Stationery	471.00	
7550	Telephone and Fax	275.00	
	Totals:	27,080.00	27,080.00

Task 3

Interlingo Translation Services

Period Trial Balance

To Period: Month 2, August 2013

N/C	Name	Debit	Credit
0020	Office computers	5,000.00	
0030	Office Equipment	2,500.00	
0040	Furniture and Fixtures	3,000.00	
1100	Debtors Control Account	4,000.00	
1200	Bank Current Account	7,085.00	
2100	Creditors Control Account		1,200.00
2200	Sales Tax Control Account		814.00
2201	Purchase Tax Control Account	623.00	
2300	Loans		5,000.00
3000	Ordinary Shares		15,000.00
4000	Translation services income		3,660.00
4001	Sales of language books		456.00
4002	Sales of language CDs		950.00
5000	Purchases of books	300.00	
5001	Purchases of CDs	750.00	
6201	Advertising	550.00	
7000	Gross Wages	2,000.00	
7100	Rent	250.00	
7103	General Rates	129.00	
7200	Electricity	61.00	
7501	Postage and Carriage	86.00	
7502	Office Stationery	471.00	
7550	Telephone and Fax	275.00	
	Totals:	27,080.00	27,080.00

Interlingo Limited Extended Exercise: Activity 4

Task 3

Interlingo Translation Services

Day Books: Customer Invoices (Detailed)

Date From:	01/08/2013	
Date To:	31/08/2013	
Transaction From:	1	
Transaction To:	99,999,999	
Dept From:	0	
Dept To:	999	

Customer From:		
Customer To:	ZZZZZZZ	
N/C From:		
N/C To:	99999999	

Tran No.	Type	Date	A/C Ref	N/C	Inv Ref	Dept.	Details	Net Amount	Tax Amount	T/C	Gross Amount	V	B
50	SI	10/08/2013	HD001	4000	10015	0	Translation of sales contracts	520.00	104.00	T1	624.00	N	-
51	SI	16/08/2013	PL001	4000	10016	0	Translation of sales literature	120.00	24.00	T1	144.00	N	-
52	SI	20/08/2013	RS001	4000	10017	0	Translation of shipping docs	100.00	20.00	T1	120.00	N	-
53	SI	20/08/2013	RT001	4000	10018	0	Translation of sales contracts	320.00	64.00	T1	384.00	N	-
54	SI	22/08/2013	SC001	4000	10019	0	Translation of sales contracts	160.00	32.00	T1	192.00	N	-
							Totals:	1,220.00	244.00		1,464.00		

Interlingo Translation Services
Day Books: Customer Credits (Detailed)

Date From:	01/08/2013	Customer From:
Date To:	31/08/2013	Customer To: ZZZZZZZZ
Transaction From:	1	N/C From:
Transaction To:	99,999,999	N/C To: 99999999
Dept From:	0	
Dept To:	999	

Tran No.	Type	Date	A/C Ref	N/C	Inv Ref	Dept.	Details	Net Amount	Tax Amount	T/C	Gross Amount	V	B
55	SC	31/08/2013	HD001	4000	501	0	Refund of 10% discount , invoice	52.00	10.40	T1	62.40	N	-
							Totals:	52.00	10.40		62.40		

Interlingo Limited Extended Exercise: Activity 5

Task 3

Interlingo Translation Services
Day Books: Supplier Invoices (Detailed)

Date From:	01/08/2013	Supplier From:
Date To:	31/08/2013	Supplier To: ZZZZZZZZ
Transaction From:	1	N/C From:
Transaction To:	99,999,999	N/C To: 99999999
Dept From:	0	
Dept To:	999	

Tran No.	Type	Date	A/C Ref	N/C	Inv Ref	Dept	Details	Net Amount	Tax Amount	T/C	Gross Amount	V
56	PI	15/08/2013	TD001	5001	2561	0	Beginners French CDs	500.00	100.00	T1	600.00	N
57	PI	15/08/2013	TD001	5001	2561	0	Advanced Italian CDs	300.00	60.00	T1	360.00	N
58	PI	20/08/2013	BB001	5000	11231	0	German First Course	297.00	0.00	T0	297.00	N
59	PI	20/08/2013	BB001	5000	11231	0	French Second Course	267.75	0.00	T0	267.75	N
60	PI	15/08/2013	AB001	5100	72/554	0	Miscellaneous deliveries	100.00	20.00	T1	120.00	N
							Totals	1,464.75	180.00		1,644.75	

Task 4

Interlingo Translation Services
Day Books: Supplier Credits (Detailed)

Date From:	01/08/2013	Supplier From:
Date To:	31/08/2013	Supplier To: ZZZZZZZZ
Transaction From:	1	N/C From:
Transaction To:	99,999,999	N/C To: 99999999
Dept From:	0	
Dept To:	999	

Tran No.	Type	Date	A/C Ref	N/C	Inv Ref	Dept	Details	Net Amount	Tax Amount	T/C	Gross Amount	V	B
61	PC	28/08/2013	TD001	5001	1919	0	Beginners French CDs	50.00	10.00	T1	60.00	N	-
							Totals	50.00	10.00		60.00		

Interlingo Limited Extended Exercise: Activity 6

Task 2

Interlingo Translation Services

Day Books: Customer Receipts (Summary)

						Customer From :	
Transaction From:	1					Customer To:	ZZZZZZZZ
Transaction To:	99,999,999						

Bank 1200   **Currency**   Pound Sterling

No	Type	Date	Account	Ref	Details	Net £	Tax £	Gross £	B	Bank Re
62	SR	10/08/2013	HD001	100110	Sales Receipt	345.00	0.00	345.00	N	
63	SR	17/08/2013	PL001	100112	Sales Receipt	795.00	0.00	795.00	N	
64	SR	24/08/2013	RS001	100114	Sales Receipt	850.00	0.00	850.00	N	
65	SR	24/08/2013	RT001	100114	Sales Receipt	1,210.00	0.00	1,210.00	N	
66	SR	31/08/2013	SC001	100116	Sales Receipt	800.00	0.00	800.00	N	
					Totals £	4,000.00	0.00	4,000.00		

Task 4

Interlingo Translation Services

Day Books: Bank Receipts (Detailed)

Transaction From:	1	
Transaction To:	99,999,999	

Dept From:	0	
Dept To:	999	

Bank: 1200   **Currency:**   Pound Sterling

No	Type	N/C	Date	Ref	Details	Dept	Net £	Tax £	T/C	Gross £	V	B
67	BR	4000	10/08/2013	100111	Translations	0	96.00	19.20	T1	115.20	N	N
68	BR	4002	10/08/2013	100111	CDs	0	240.00	48.00	T1	288.00	N	N
69	BR	4001	10/08/2013	100111	Books	0	160.00	0.00	T0	160.00	N	N
70	BR	4000	17/08/2013	100113	Translations	0	116.00	23.20	T1	139.20	N	N
71	BR	4002	17/08/2013	100113	CDs	0	180.00	36.00	T1	216.00	N	N
72	BR	4001	17/08/2013	100113	Books	0	107.00	0.00	T0	107.00	N	N
73	BR	4000	24/08/2013	100115	Translations	0	104.00	20.80	T1	124.80	N	N
74	BR	4002	24/08/2013	100115	CDs	0	220.00	44.00	T1	264.00	N	N
75	BR	4001	24/08/2013	100115	Books	0	84.00	0.00	T0	84.00	N	N
76	BR	4000	31/08/2013	100117	Translations	0	82.00	16.40	T1	98.40	N	N
77	BR	4002	31/08/2013	100117	CDs	0	190.00	38.00	T1	228.00	N	N
78	BR	4001	31/08/2013	100117	Books	0	113.00	0.00	T0	113.00	N	N
						Totals £	1,692.00	245.60		1,937.60		

Interlingo Limited Extended Exercise: Activity 7

Task 2

Interlingo Translation Services
Day Books: Supplier Payments (Summary)

Date From:	01/08/2013				**Bank From:**	1200
DateTo:	31/08/2013				**Bank To:**	1200
Transaction From:	1				Supplier From:	
Transaction To:	99,999,999				Supplier To:	ZZZZZZZZZ

Bank 1200   **Currency** Pound Sterling

No	Type	Date	Supplier	Ref	Details	Net £	Tax £	Gross £	B	Bank Re
79	PP	06/08/2013	TD001	120006	Purchase Payment	780.00	0.00	780.00	N	
80	PP	06/08/2013	BB001	120007	Purchase Payment	420.00	0.00	420.00	N	
					Totals £	1,200.00	0.00	1,200.00		

Task 4

Interlingo Translation Services
Day Books: Bank Payments (Detailed)

Transaction From:	1				**N/C From:**	
Transaction To:	99,999,999				**N/C To:**	99999999
Dept From:	0					
Dept To:	999					

Bank: 1200   **Currency:** Pound Sterling

No	Type	N/C	Date	Ref	Details	Dept	Net £	Tax £	T/C	Gross £	V	B
81	BP	0040	07/08/2013	120009	Office furniture	0	140.00	28.00	T1	168.00	N	N
82	BP	6201	08/08/2013	120010	Advertising	0	600.00	120.00	T1	720.00	N	N
83	BP	7100	15/08/2013	120011	Rent	0	250.00	50.00	T1	300.00	N	N
84	BP	7502	17/08/2013	120012	Stationery	0	126.00	25.20	T1	151.20	N	N
85	BP	7103	20/08/2013	120013	Rates	0	129.00	0.00	T2	129.00	N	N
86	BP	7550	22/08/2013	120014	Telephone	0	186.00	37.20	T1	223.20	N	N
87	BP	7200	24/08/2013	120015	Electricity	0	84.00	16.80	T1	100.80	N	N
88	BP	7501	30/08/2013	120016	Postages	0	45.60	0.00	T2	45.60	N	N
89	BP	7000	31/08/2013	BACS	Wages	0	2,240.00	0.00	T9	2,240.00	-	N
					Totals £		3,800.60	277.20		4,077.80		

Interlingo Limited Extended Exercise: Activity 8

Task 3

Interlingo Translation Services

Day Books: Cash Payments (Detailed)

| Date From: | 01/08/2013 | | | | | | | | | |
| DateTo: | 31/08/2013 | | | | | | | | | |

| Transaction From: | 1 | | | | N/C From: | |
| Transaction To: | 99,999,999 | | | | N/C To: | 99999999 |

| Dept From: | 0 |
| Dept To: | 999 |

Bank: 1230 **Currency:** Pound Sterling

No	Type	N/C	Date	Ref	Details	Dept	Net £	Tax £	T/C	Gross £	V	B
92	CP	7502	07/08/2013	0001	A4 paper	0	16.00	3.20	T1	19.20	N	-
93	CP	7501	07/08/2013	0002	Postage stamps	0	24.00	0.00	T2	24.00	N	-
94	CP	7502	15/08/2013	0003	Box files	0	20.00	4.00	T1	24.00	N	-
95	CP	7501	22/08/2013	0004	Postage stamps	0	12.00	0.00	T2	12.00	N	-
					Totals £		72.00	7.20		79.20		

Interlingo Limited Extended Exercise: Activities 9 & 10

Activity 9 Task 1

Activity 9 Task 4, Activity 10 Task 2 (trial balance extract)

N/C	Name	Debit	Credit
0020	Office computers	5,000.00	
0030	Office Equipment	2,500.00	
0040	Furniture and Fixtures	3,140.00	
1100	Debtors Control Account	1,401.60	
1200	Bank Current Account	7,608.90	
1230	Petty Cash	0.80	
2100	Creditors Control Account		1,584.75
2200	Sales Tax Control Account		1,302.80
2201	Purchase Tax Control Account	1,077.40	
2300	Loans		5,000.00
3000	Ordinary Shares		15,000.00
4000	Translation services income		5,226.00
4001	Sales of language books		920.00
4002	Sales of language CDs		1,780.00
4902	Commissions Received		48.00
5000	Purchases of books	864.75	
5001	Purchases of CDs	1,500.00	
5100	Carriage	100.00	
6201	Advertising	1,150.00	
7000	Gross Wages	4,240.00	
7100	Rent	500.00	
7103	General Rates	258.00	
7104	Premises Insurance	98.50	
7200	Electricity	145.00	
7501	Postage and Carriage	167.60	
7502	Office Stationery	633.00	
7550	Telephone and Fax	461.00	
7901	Bank Charges	15.00	
	Totals:	30,861.55	30,861.55

Interlingo Limited Extended Exercise: Activity 10

Task 1

Interlingo Translation Services
Bank Reconciliation

Page: 1

Bank Ref:	1200			Date To:	31/08/2013
Bank Name:	Bank Current Account			Statement	31 08 13
Currency:	Pound Sterling				

Balance as per cash book at 31/08/2013: 7,608.90

Add: Unpresented Payments

Tran No	Date	Ref	Details	£
87	24/08/2013	120015	Electricity	100.80
88	30/08/2013	120016	Postages	45.60
				146.40

Less: Outstanding Receipts

Tran No	Date	Ref	Details	£
				0.00

Reconciled balance : 7,755.30

Balance as per statement : 7,755.30

Difference : 0.00

Task 2

Interlingo Translation Services
Aged Debtors Analysis (Summary)

Report Date:	31/08/2013		Customer From:	
Include future transactions:	No		Customer To:	ZZZZZZZ
Exclude later payments:	No			

** NOTE: All report values are shown in Base Currency, unless otherwise indicated **

A/C	Name		Credit Limit	Turnover	Balance	Future	Current	Period 1	Period 2	Period 3	Older
HD001	Hill & Dale & Co, Solicitors	£	0.00	813.00	561.60	0.00	561.60	0.00	0.00	0.00	0.00
PL001	Playgames PLC	£	0.00	915.00	144.00	0.00	144.00	0.00	0.00	0.00	0.00
RS001	RS Export Agency	£	0.00	950.00	120.00	0.00	120.00	0.00	0.00	0.00	0.00
RT001	Rotherway Limited	£	0.00	1,530.00	384.00	0.00	384.00	0.00	0.00	0.00	0.00
SC001	Schafeld Ltd	£	0.00	960.00	192.00	0.00	192.00	0.00	0.00	0.00	0.00
		Totals:		5,168.00	1,401.60	0.00	1,401.60	0.00	0.00	0.00	0.00

Interlingo Translation Services
Audit Trail (Detailed)

Date From:	25/08/2013		Customer From:	
Date To:	31/08/2013		Customer To:	ZZZZZZZ
Transaction From:	1		Supplier From:	
Transaction To:	99,999,999		Supplier To:	ZZZZZZZ
Exclude Deleted Tran:	No			

No	Type	A/C	N/C	Dept	Details	Date	Ref	Net	Tax	T/C	Pd	Paid	V	B	Bank Rec. Date
55	SC	HD001				31/08/2013	501	52.00	10.40		N	0.00	-		
		55	4000	0	Refund of 10%			52.00	10.40	T1		0.00	N		
61	PC	TD001				28/08/2013	1919	50.00	10.00		N	0.00	-		
		61	5001	0	Beginners French			50.00	10.00	T1		0.00	N		
66	SR	SC001				31/08/2013	100116	800.00	0.00		Y	800.00	R		31/08/2013
		66	1200	0	Sales Receipt			800.00	0.00	T9		800.00	-		
					800.00 to SI 5	31/08/2013	10014					800.00			
76	BR	1200				31/08/2013	100117	385.00	54.40		Y	439.40	R		31/08/2013
		76	4000	0	Translations			82.00	16.40	T1		98.40	N		
		77	4002	0	CDs			190.00	38.00	T1		228.00	N		
		78	4001	0	Books			113.00	0.00	T0		113.00	N		
88	BP	1200				30/08/2013	120016	45.60	0.00		Y	45.60	N		
		88	7501	0	Postages			45.60	0.00	T2		45.60	N		
89	BP	1200				31/08/2013	BACS	2,240.00	0.00		Y	2,240.00	R		31/08/2013
		89	7000	0	Wages			2,240.00	0.00	T9		2,240.00	-		
100	BP	1200				25/08/2013	STO	15.00	0.00		Y	15.00	R		31/08/2013
		100	7901	0	Albion Bank			15.00	0.00	T2		15.00	N		
101	BR	1200				25/08/2013	STO	12.00	2.40		Y	14.40	R		31/08/2013
		101	4902	0	Worldwide			12.00	2.40	T1		14.40	N		

Task 3

Interlingo Translation Services
Customer Activity (Detailed)

Date From:	01/01/1980		Customer From:	HD001
Date To:	31/08/2013		Customer To:	HD001
Transaction From:	1		N/C From:	
Transaction To:	99,999,999		N/C To:	99999999
Inc b/fwd transaction:	No		Dept From:	0
Exc later payment:	No		Dept To:	999

** NOTE: All report values are shown in Base Currency, unless otherwise indicated **

A/C: HD001   **Name:** Hill & Dale & Co, Solicitors   **Contact:**   **Tel:**

No	Type	Date	Ref	N/C	Details	Dept	T/C	Value	O/S	Debit	Credit	V	B
4	SI	19/07/2013	10013	9998	Opening Balance	0	T9	345.00		345.00		-	-
50	SI	10/08/2013	10015	4000	Translation of sales contracts	0	T1	624.00 *	624.00	624.00		N	-
55	SC	31/08/2013	501	4000	Refund of 10% discount ,	0	T1	62.40 *	-62.40		62.40	N	-
62	SR	10/08/2013	100110	1200	Sales Receipt	0	T9	345.00			345.00	-	R
					Totals:			561.60	561.60	969.00	407.40		

Amount Outstanding	561.60
Amount Paid this period	345.00
Credit Limit £	0.00
Turnover YTD	813.00

Task 4

Interlingo Translation Services
Supplier Activity (Detailed)

Date From:	01/01/1980		Supplier From:	TD001
Date To:	31/08/2013		Supplier To:	TD001
Transaction From:	1		N/C From:	
Transaction To:	99,999,999		N/C To:	99999999
Inc b/fwd transaction:	No		Dept From:	0
Exc later payment:	No		Dept To:	999

** NOTE: All report values are shown in Base Currency, unless otherwise indicated **

A/C: TD001   **Name:** TDI Wholesalers   **Contact:**   **Tel:**

No	Type	Date	Ref	N/C	Details	Dept	T/C	Value	O/S	Debit	Credit	V	B
6	PI	07/07/2013	2347	9998	Opening Balance	0	T9	780.00	0.00		780.00	-	-
56	PI	15/08/2013	2561	5001	Beginners French CDs	0	T1	600.00 *	600.00		600.00	N	-
57	PI	15/08/2013	2561	5001	Advanced Italian CDs	0	T1	360.00 *	360.00		360.00	N	-
61	PC	28/08/2013	1919	5001	Beginners French CDs returned	0	T1	60.00 *	-60.00	60.00		N	-
79	PP	06/08/2013	120006	1200	Purchase Payment	0	T9	780.00	0.00	780.00		-	R
					Totals:			900.00	900.00	840.00	1,740.00		

Amount Outstanding	900.00
Amount paid this period	780.00
Credit Limit £	0.00
Turnover YTD	1,530.00

Task 5

Hill & Dale & Co, Solicitors
17 Berkeley Chambers
Penrose Street
Mereford
MR2 6GF

Playgames PLC
Consul House
Viney Street
Mereford
MR2 6PL

RS Export Agency
46 Chancery Street
Mereford
MR1 9FD

Rotherway Limited
78 Sparkhouse Street
Millway
MY5 8HG

Schafeld Ltd
86 Tanners Lane
Millway
MY7 5VB

Answers to activities

CHAPTER 2: LOOKING AFTER THE COMPUTER AND THE DATA

2.1 Passwords, which should not be revealed to unauthorised parties, enable access to computer systems and to specific programs, eg computer accounting packages. Access rights operate within software packages and restrict employees to certain types of transaction. Computer accounting packages normally contain very sensitive information, eg details of customers (how much they owe and how good they are at paying), payroll (how much employees earn), all of which needs to be protected against unauthorised access. Passwords protect the data from outsiders and unauthorised employees; access rights further protect sensitive data from employees.

2.2 The system date is the date that the computer thinks the date is. It will normally be allocated to any transaction carried out or file created on that date. The program date is different from the system date. It can be allocated to a set of transactions, eg a series of cheques paid into the bank last week which you want to carry that date from the previous week. In short: system date = actual date, program date = date you are allocating.

2.3 Back-up disks could include: a set locked up on the premises at the close of business each day, a set taken home by an employee at the close of business each day.

2.4 You should carry out a 'restore' routine from the latest set of back-up disks. This will unfortunately mean that you will have to re-input the transactions since the last back-up, but it is better than losing the whole lot.

2.5 Install anti-virus software which will create a firewall to protect your system against virus invasion. Update the software regularly. Warn employees against opening up 'spam' emails with attachments which might contain viruses.

CHAPTER 3: SETTING UP THE COMPANY IN SAGE

3.1 Wizards, computer manual, on-screen Help.

3.2 Company details, financial year, VAT details, passwords and access rights.

3.3 **(a)** Customers
  (b) Suppliers
  (c) Nominal

CHAPTER 4: SETTING UP RECORDS FOR CUSTOMERS AND SUPPLIERS

4.1 False.

4.2 **(a)** A customer who has bought on credit and who owes money
  (b) A supplier who supplies on credit and who is owed money

4.3 **(a)** Sales Ledger
  (b) Purchases Ledger

4.4 **(a)** The total amount owed by receivables (debtors) – ie customers

(b) The total amount owing to payables (creditors) – ie suppliers

4.5 A trade discount is an agreed percentage reduction in the selling price of goods or services given to regular customers.

A settlement (or 'cash') discount is an agreed percentage reduction in the selling price of goods or services given when early payment is made within a specified time period.

4.6 Trial balance.

4.7 Account reference - needed for input into the accounting system.

Credit limit - needed to ensure that the level of credit given to the customer can be monitored and controlled.

4.8 Only if there are no transactions on it.

CHAPTER 5: SETTING UP THE NOMINAL LEDGER

5.1 A list of accounts, classified into various function areas, covering the accounting needs of a business.

5.2

Categories	Description
Sales	income from the sale of goods or services - accounts can be allocated for different types of sales
Purchases	items bought to produce goods to sell - accounts can be allocated for different types of purchases
Direct expenses	expenses incurred which are directly related to producing the goods
Overheads	expenses which have to be paid and which are not directly related to producing the goods
Fixed assets	items which are bought to keep in the business in the long-term
Current assets	items owned, or owed to, the business in the short term
Current liabilities	items owed by the business in the short-term
Long-term liabilities	items owed by the business in the long-term
Capital & reserves	the financial investment of the owner(s) of the business

5.3
(a) &
(b)

account name	account number	category
Freehold Property	0010	fixed assets
Office Equipment	0030	fixed assets
Motor Vehicles	0050	fixed assets
Materials Purchased	5000	purchases
Bank Current Account	1200	current assets
Creditors Control	2100	current liabilities
Directors Salaries	7001	overheads
Electricity	7200	overheads
Share Capital	3000	capital & reserves

CHAPTER 6: SELLING TO CUSTOMERS ON CREDIT

6.1 Purchase order, delivery note, invoice, credit note, statement, cheque.

6.2 False.

6.3 False.

6.4 The two most important are the amount to be paid and when it has to be paid.

6.5 Customers who have bought on credit from the business.

6.6 Sales Ledger ('Customers' in Sage).

6.7 The batch totals should be checked against the invoice or credit note totals calculated by the computer from the input.

6.8 Customer account number, date, invoice number, details of invoice, net amount and tax code.

6.9 The tax code input will automatically calculate the amount of VAT due on the invoice goods total. The VAT amount which shows on the computer screen should be carefully checked with the VAT total on the invoice and adjusted if necessary.

CHAPTER 7: BUYING FROM SUPPLIERS ON CREDIT

7.1 Suppliers who supply on credit and who are owed money.

7.2 Purchases Ledger ('Suppliers' in Sage). This shows how much is owed to each supplier.

7.3   Purchases relate to materials or items bought to produce or provide the actual product of the business; expenses are running costs incurred (note that these are not the same as 'direct expenses' in the Chart of Accounts); capital items are items bought for long-term use in the business. It is important to identify each of these types so that the correct account number (and therefore Chart of Accounts category) can be allocated.

7.4   See text on page 89 for input procedure. Note the importance of checking the VAT on screen.

The invoices should be checked for irregularities before input and any problems identified and dealt with.

After input the batch total should be checked against the computer total - a Day Book Report could be printed to provide this figure.

CHAPTER 8: CUSTOMER AND SUPPLIER PAYMENTS

8.1   Payment icon = cash (ie non-credit) payment to a supplier

Supplier icon = payment to a supplier who has sold on credit terms

Receipt icon = cash (ie non-credit) payment from a customer

Customer icon = payment from a customer who has bought on credit

8.2   If no remittance advice is received for a BACS payment receipt the business will not know - until the bank statement arrives - that the payment has been received. The remittance advice will be needed to provide input details (amount, date, references) for the business.

8.3   Payment from a credit customer - accounting entries are: a debit to the bank account, which will increase, and a credit to the customer account, which will decrease (owe less).

Payment to supplier (assuming credit is given) - accounting entries are: a credit to the bank account, which will decrease, and a debit to the supplier account, which will decrease (the business will owe less).

8.4   A Supplier Payments Day Book Report will show the total of cheques issued to suppliers on any given day. It is important that this is printed out and its total checked against the manual listing and total of the cheques issued to suppliers on that day.

CHAPTER 9: CASH RECEIPTS AND PAYMENTS

9.1   Receipt.

9.2   Payment.

9.3   **(a)**   £120.00 to Bank Account, £100.00 to Sales Account, £20.00 to Sales VAT Account.

(b)   £160.00 to Purchases VAT Account, £960.00 to Bank Account, £800.00 to Purchases Account.

9.4   Remember that 'cash' can include cheque payments. Examples include: capital invested by the owner, loans, grants, rent received.

CHAPTER 10: BANK ACCOUNTS AND RECURRING ENTRIES

10.1 **(a)** Payments in: Transfer screen from Bank, transfer from Bank Current Account 1200 to Petty Cash Account 1230.

(b) Payments out: Bank Payments screen from Bank, payment from Petty Cash Account 1230 to appropriate Nominal Account.

10.2 **(a)** There is no VAT on stamps - code T2 (VAT exempt) should be used.

(b) There is VAT on stationery at standard rate (T1). The VAT can be calculated either manually, or by using the 'Calc Net' button at the bottom of the screen.

(c) The voucher should be referred to a higher authority; it cannot be processed if the transaction is unauthorised.

10.3 **(a)** Daily takings should be entered as Receipts (in Bank). Record payments into the bank account as a Transfer from Cash Register Account to Bank Current Account, using the paying-in slip as the source document.

(b) Security risk. The money could be better employed on the bank account, paying bills etc.

10.4 Recurring entries are normally for BACS (automated bank) regular receipts and payments. Receipts include items such as rent received and payments include items such as rates, loan repayments and insurance premiums.

CHAPTER 11: REPORTS AND ROUTINES

11.1 To monitor and maintain the accuracy of the double-entry bookkeeping system: the two columns should always agree.

11.2 A computer accounting system is a single entry system: a debit always generates an equal credit (or credits) and vice versa and so the total of debits and credits will always automatically be the same.

11.3 A trial balance provides management with useful information such as the balance of the bank account, the level of sales and individual expenses of the business.

11.4 Input order.

11.5 **(a)** An aged debtor analysis shows the amounts that individual customers owe and how long the debt has been outstanding. It enables management to identify the customers that need to be chased up and any bad debts that may have to be written off.

(b) An aged creditor analysis shows the amounts that are owing to individual suppliers and how long each debt has been outstanding. It enables the business to schedule payments to suppliers and make the most of credit granted.

11.6 **(a)** £2,433.60

(b) Debtors Control Account

(c) The account is in arrears (assuming a 30 day credit period). A customer statement.

11.7 **(a)** £36,934.64

(b) Cash receipts £9,948.00 plus petty cash £2.80 = £9,950.80

(c) Total sales (hardware, software, consultancy) = £171,934.00

11.8 Provide printout as requested. See Customer List on page 149.

CHAPTER 12: CORRECTIONS AND ADJUSTMENTS

12.1 **(a)** Write off, Refunds and Returns Wizard - Customer Cheque Returns function.

(b) Journal entry (debit Advertising Account, credit Stationery Account).

(c) Write off, Refunds and Returns Wizard – Write off Customer Accounts.

AAT Sample Assessment

This sample Assessment is reproduced by kind permission of the AAT.

Instructions to candidates

This assessment asks you to input data into a computerised accounting package and produce documents and reports. There are 14 tasks and it is important that you attempt all tasks.

The time allowed to complete this Computerised accounting assessment is **2 hours**.

Additional time up to a maximum of 1 hour may be scheduled by your tutor to allow for delays due to computer issues, such as printer queues and uploading documents to LearnPlus.

It is important that you print **all** reports and documents specified in the tasks so your work can be assessed. A checklist has been provided at the end of the assessment to help you check that all documents and reports have been printed. All printed material should be **titled** and marked with your **name** and **AAT membership number**.

If your computerised accounting system allows for the generation of PDFs, these can be generated instead of hard copy prints. Screenshots saved as image files are also acceptable.

If you are using print-outs as evidence, the only document you are required to upload at the end of the assessment is your assessment book. If you have generated PDFs or screenshots instead of printing, these documents should be uploaded to LearnPlus with your assessment book. Your assessor will tell you which option to use.

Data

This assessment is based on an existing business, **Campbell Kitchens**, an organisation that supplies kitchen furniture and equipment. The owner of the business is **Kitty Campbell** who operates as a sole trader.

At the start of business Kitty operated a manual bookkeeping system but has now decided that from **1 May 20XX** the accounting system will become computerised.

You are employed as an accounting technician.

You can assume that all documentation has been checked for accuracy and authorised by Kitty Campbell.

Cash and credit sales are to be analysed in **two** ways:

- Kitchen furniture
- Kitchen equipment

Some nominal ledger accounts have already been allocated account codes. You may need to amend or create other account codes.

The business is registered for VAT. The rate of VAT charged on all goods and services sold by Campbell Kitchens is **20%**.

All expenditure should be analysed as you feel appropriate.

Before you start the assessment you should:

- Set the system software date as **31 May of the current year**
- Set the financial year to start on **1 May of the current year**
- Set up the company details by entering the name **Campbell Kitchens** and the address: **47 Landsway Road, Stotton, ST4 9TX**.

This set-up does not form part of the assessment standards, so your training provider may assist you with this.

Task 1

Refer to the **customer listing** below and set up customer records to open sales ledger accounts for each customer, entering opening balances at 1 May 20XX.

Customer Listing

Customer name and address	Customer account code	Customer account details at 1 May 20XX
Fraser Designs 291 Tower Way Stotton ST7 4PQ	FRA001	Opening balance: £2,017.60 Payment terms: 30 days
Fry and Partners 9 Carters Lane Brigtown BG1 3QT	FRY002	Opening balance: £1,597.60 Payment terms: 30 days
SCL Interiors 14 Dingle Street Stotton ST4 2LY	SCL001	Opening balance: £1,906.50 Payment terms: 30 days

Task 2

Refer to the **supplier listing** below and set up supplier records to open purchases ledger accounts for each supplier, entering opening balances at 1 May 20XX.

Supplier Listing

Supplier name and address	Supplier account code	Supplier account details at 1 May 20XX
Hart Ltd 3 Lion Street Stotton ST8 2HX	HAR001	Opening balance: £1,012.75 Payment terms: 30 days
Jackson Builders 75 Stevens Street Brigtown BG5 3PE	JAC001	Opening balance: £456.35 Payment terms: 30 days
Vanstone plc 404 Larchway Estate Brigtown BG9 7HJ	VAN001	Opening balance: £2,097.40 Payment terms: 30 days

Task 3

Refer to the **list of nominal ledger accounts** below:

(a) Set up nominal ledger records for each account, entering opening balances at 1 May 20XX and making sure you select, amend or create appropriate nominal ledger account codes.

(b) Generate a trial balance, check the accuracy of the trial balance and, if necessary, correct any errors. **You do not need to print the trial balance.**

List of nominal ledger accounts as at 1 May 20XX

Account names	Debit balance £	Credit Balance £
Motor vehicles	20,067.10	
Bank current account	4,916.26	
Petty cash	68.24	
VAT on sales		1,497.68
VAT on purchases	909.23	
Capital		26,416.85
Drawings**	350.00	
Sales – kitchen furniture		456.20
Sales – kitchen equipment		119.30
Goods for re-sale	224.00	
Sales ledger control* see note below	5,521.70	
Purchases ledger control* see note below		3,566.50

* Note

As you have already entered opening balances for customer and suppliers the software package you are using may not require you to enter these balances.

** You may need to set up an account for drawings. Use nominal code 3050.

Task 4

Refer to the following summary of sales invoices and summary of sales credit notes and enter these transactions into the computer.

Summary of sales invoices

Date 20XX	Customer Name	Invoice No.	Gross £	VAT £	Net £	Kitchen furniture £	Kitchen equipment £
7 May	Fry and Partners	523	2,011.68	335.28	1,676.40	1,676.40	
21 May	Fraser Designs	524	852.24	142.04	710.20		710.20
	Totals		2,863.92	477.32	2,386.60	1,676.40	710.20

Summary of sales credit notes

Date 20XX	Customer Name	Credit note No.	Gross £	VAT £	Net £	Kitchen furniture £	Kitchen equipment £
14 May	Fry and Partners	61	500.16	83.36	416.80	416.80	
	Totals		500.16	83.36	416.80	416.80	0.00

Task 5

Refer to the following purchases invoices and the purchases credit note and enter these transactions into the computer.

Purchases invoices

Jackson Builders
75 Steven Street, Brigtown, BG5 3PE
VAT Registration No 321 3726 89
INVOICE NO 5/219
Date: 12 May 20XX

Campbell Kitchens	
47 Landsway Road	
Stotton	
ST4 9TX	
	£
Repairs to building	909.25
VAT @ 20%	181.85
Total for payment	1,091.10
Terms: 30 days	

Vanstone plc
404 Larchway Estate, Brigtown, BG9 7HJ
VAT Registration No 119 0799 52

I N V O I C E   N O   2017

Date: 18 May 20XX

Campbell Kitchens
47 Landsway Road
Stotton
ST4 9TX

	£
Supplying goods for re-sale	2,146.80
VAT @ 20%	429.36
Total for payment	2,576.16

Terms: 30 days

Purchases credit note

Vanstone plc
404 Larchway Estate, Brigtown, BG9 7HJ
VAT Registration No 119 0799 52

CREDIT NOTE   N O   426

Date: 20 May 20XX

Campbell Kitchens
47 Landsway Road
Stotton
ST4 9TX

	£
Return of goods supplied for re-sale	612.75
VAT @ 20%	122.55
Total for payment	735.30

Terms: 30 days

Task 6

Refer to the following BACS remittance advice notes received from customers and enter these transactions into the computer, making sure you allocate all amounts as shown on each remittance advice note.

SCL Interiors BACS Remittance Advice
To: Campbell Kitchens   15 May 20XX
An amount of £1,906.50 has been paid directly into your bank account in payment of the balance outstanding at 1 May.

Fry and Partners BACS Remittance Advice
To: Campbell Kitchens   25 May 20XX
An amount of £1,097.44 has been paid directly into your bank account in payment of the balance outstanding at 1 May and including credit note 61.

Task 7

(a)   Refer to the following summary of payments made to suppliers and enter these transactions into the computer, making sure you print a remittance advice as shown in (b) **and** allocate all amounts correctly as shown in the details column.

(b)   **Print** a remittance advice to accompany the payment made to Hart Ltd.

Cheques paid listing

Date 20XX	Cheque number	Supplier	£	Details
12 May	006723	Vanstone plc	1,200.00	Payment on account
24 May	006724	Hart Ltd	1,012.75	Payment of opening balance

Task 8

(a)   Refer to the following email from Kitty Campbell and enter this transaction into the computer.

Email
From: Kitty Campbell **To:**   Accounting Technician **Date:**   10 May 20XX **Subject:**   Premises insurance
Hello I have today paid our annual premises insurance of £819.40 by business debit card. Please record this transaction. VAT is not applicable. Thanks, Kitty

(b)   Refer to the following cash sales listing and enter this transaction into the computer.

Cash sales listing

Date 20XX	Payment method	Details	Amount
24 May	Cheque	JL Green – kitchen equipment	£474.00 including VAT

Task 9

Refer to the following standing order schedule:

(a)   Set up a recurring entry as shown in the standing order schedule below.

(b)   **Print** a screen shot of the screen setting up the recurring entry.

(c)   Process the first payment.

Standing order schedule

Details	Amount	Frequency of payment	Total number of payments	Payment start date 20XX	Payment finish Date 20XX
Rent - VAT not applicable	£750	One payment every 2 months	3	2 May	2 September

Task 10

(a)   Refer to the following petty cash re-imbursement slip and enter this transaction into the computer.

Petty Cash Reimbursement PCR No 29	
Date: 1 May 20XX	
Cash from the bank account to restore the petty cash account to £150.00.	£81.76

(b)   Refer to the following petty cash vouchers and enter these transactions into the computer.

Petty Cash Voucher	
Date 7 May 20XX	**No** PC212
Printer paper – including VAT	£ 45.60
Receipt attached	

Petty Cash Voucher	
Date 18 May 20XX	**No** PC213
Rail fare VAT not applicable	£ 37.90
Receipt attached	

Task 11

Refer to the following journal entries and enter them into the computer.

Journal entries - 24 May 20XX	£	£
Premises insurance	10.00	
Bank		10.00
Being an error in the amount shown on Kitty Campbell's email of 10 May for premises insurance.		
Drawings	600.00	
Bank		600.00
Being cash withdrawn from the bank by Kitty Campbell for personal use		

Task 12

Refer to the following bank statement:

(a) Enter the bank interest received (no VAT) which has not yet been accounted for.

(b) Reconcile the bank statement. If the bank statement does not reconcile check your work and make the necessary corrections. **You do not need to print a bank reconciliation statement.**

Rowley Bank plc
505 High Street
Stotton
ST1 9VG

Campbell Kitchens
47 Landsway Road
Stotton
ST4 9TX

Account number 62082176   31 May 20XX

STATEMENT OF ACCOUNT

Date 20XX	Details	Paid out £	Paid in £	Balance £
01 May	Opening balance			4,916.26C
01 May	Cash	81.76		4,834.50C
02 May	James Holdings Ltd - Rent	750.00		4,084.50C
10 May	FH Insurance plc	829.40		3,255.10C
12 May	Cheque 006723	1,200.00		2,055.10C
15 May	BACS - SCL Interiors		1,906.50	3,961.60C
24 May	Cash withdrawn	600.00		3,361.60C
25 May	BACS - Fry and Partners		1,097.44	4,459.04C
28 May	Bank interest received		24.20	4,483.24C
	D = Debit C = Credit			

Task 13

(a)   Use the password 'CPAGp1' to protect your accounting data and **print** a screenshot of the screen showing the entry of the password into the computer.

If it is not possible to enter the password given in the assessment, print a screenshot showing the entry of your password (eg at the login stage).

(b)   Use a file name made up of your name followed by 'CKbackup' and back up your work to a suitable storage medium. **Print** a screenshot of the backup screen showing the file name and location of back up data. If, for example, your name is Helen Smith you should use the file name 'HelenSmithCKbackup'. Your assessor will tell you what storage medium you should use.

If it is not possible to enter the filename given in the assessment, print a screenshot of the backup screen showing your own filename together with the location of the backup data.

Task 14

Print the following reports:
- the purchases day book (supplier invoices)
- an aged trade payables analysis
- all sales ledger accounts (customer accounts), showing all transactions within each account
- a trial balance at 31 May 20XX
- the sales ledger control account in the nominal ledger, showing all transactions within the account
- an audit trail, showing full details of all transactions, including details of receipts/payments allocated to items in customer/supplier accounts and details of items in the bank account that have been reconciled.

Please note the accounting package you are using may not use exactly the same report names as those shown above, so some alternative names are shown in brackets.

Before you finish your work use the checklist below to make sure you have printed all documents and reports as specified in the assessment.

Checklist

Documents and reports	Task	✓ when printed
Remittance advice	7	☐
Screenshot of the recurring entry set up screen	9	☐
Screenshot showing the entry of the password	13	☐
Screenshot showing the file name and location of backup data	13	☐
Purchases day book (supplier invoices)	14	☐
Aged trade payables analysis	14	☐
Sales ledger accounts (customer accounts), showing all transactions within each account	14	☐
Trial balance at 31 May 20XX	14	☐
Sales ledger control account in the nominal ledger, showing all transactions within the account	14	☐
Audit trail, showing full details of all transactions, including details of receipts/payments allocated to items in customer/supplier accounts and details of items in the bank account that have been reconciled	14	☐

Sample answers

The answers that are provided by the AAT are given below, although these are not exhaustive. The answers provided are indicative of relevant content within the audit trail, the exact format of which will differ according to the computerised accounting package used. We have reproduced the required documents using Sage 50 and included them on the following pages.

Task	Transaction type	Account(s)		Date 20XX	Net Amount £	VAT £	Allocated against receipt/ payment ✓	Reconciled with bank statement ✓
1	Customer O/bal	FRA001		01 May	2,017.60			
	Customer O/bal	FRY002		01 May	1,597.60		✓	
	Customer O/bal	SCL001		01 May	1,906.50		✓	
2	Supplier O/bal	HAR001		01 May	1,012.75		✓	
	Supplier O/bal	JAC001		01 May	456.35			
	Supplier O/bal	VAN001		01 May	2,097.40			
3	Dr	Motor vehicles		01 May	20,067.10			
	Dr	Bank current account		01 May	4,916.26			✓
	Dr	Petty cash		01 May	68.24			
	Cr	VAT on sales		01 May	1,497.68			
	Dr	VAT on purchases		01 May	909.23			
	Cr	Capital		01 May	26,416.85			
	Dr	Drawings		01 May	350.00			
	Cr	Sales – kitchen furniture		01 May	456.20			
	Cr	Sales – kitchen equipment		01 May	119.30			
	Dr	Goods for re-sale		01 May	224.00			
	Dr	Sales ledger control*		01 May	5,521.70			
	Cr	Purchases ledger control* *If appropriate		01 May	3,566.50			
4	Sales inv	FRY002	Sales- Kitchen furniture	07 May	1,676.40	335.28		
	Sales inv	FRA001	Sales- Kitchen equip	21 May	710.20	142.04		
	Sales CN	FRY002	Sales- Kitchen furniture	14 May	416.80	83.36	✓	
5	Purchases inv	JAC001	Repairs	12 May	909.25	181.85		
	Purchases inv	VAN001	Goods	18 May	2,146.80	429.36		
	Purchases CN	VAN001	Goods	20 May	612.75	122.55		
6	Customer receipt	SCL001	Bank	15 May	1,906.50			✓
	Customer receipt	FRY002	Bank	25 May	1,097.44			✓
7	Supplier payment on a/c	VAN001	Bank	12 May	1,200.00			✓
	Supplier payment	HAR001	Bank	24 May	1,012.75			
8	Bank payment	Bank	Premises insurance	10 May	819.40			✓
	Bank receipt	Bank	Sales – Kitchen equip	24 May	395.00	79.00		
9	Bank payment	Bank	Rent - SO/DD	02 May	750.00			✓
10	Dr	Petty cash		01 May	81.76			
	Cr	Bank		01 May	81.76			✓
	Cash payment	Petty cash	Stationery	07 May	38.00	7.60		
	Cash payment	Petty cash	Travel	18 May	37.90			
11	Journal debit	Insurance		24 May	10.00			
	Journal credit	Bank		24 May	10.00			✓
	Journal debit	Drawings		24 May	600.00			
	Journal credit	Bank		24 May	600.00			✓
12	Bank receipt	Bank	Bank interest received	28 May	24.20			✓

Task 7

Campbell Kitchens
47 Landsway Road
Stotton
ST4 9TX

Tel :

VAT Reg No.

REMITTANCE ADVICE

Date	24/05/2013
Account Ref	HAR001
Cheque No	006724

Hart Ltd
3 Lion Street

Stotton

ST8 2HX

NOTE: All values are shown in Pound Sterling

Date	Ref	Details	Debit	Credit
01/05/2013	Opening bala	Opening Balance		1,012.75

	Amount Paid
£	1,012.75

Task 9

Task 13

Task 13

Backup ☒

Backup Company	Advanced Options	Previous Backups

Company Details

You are about to create a backup of:

Company Name: Campbell Kitchens

Found In: C:\DOCUMENTS AND SETTINGS\ALL USERS\APPLICATION
DATA\SAGE\ACCOUNTS\2012\COMPANY.000\

Where do you want the company backed up to?

Please click Browse to select a location to save this backup to. We have suggested a filename for this backup. If you are happy with this suggestion, click OK to save the backup.

Backing Up to removable media? Insert the device before clicking OK.

Backing Up to CD? Refer to the Help now.

Filename :   CKbackup

Location :   F:\

Browse...

OK   Cancel   Help

Task 14

Campbell Kitchens

Day Books: Supplier Invoices (Summary)

Date From:		01/01/1980				Supplier From:		
Date To:		31/12/2019				Supplier To:		ZZZZZZZZ
Transaction From:		1						
Transaction To:		99,999,999						

Tran No.	Item	Type	Date	A/C Ref	Inv Ref	Details	Net Amount	Tax Amount	Gross Amount
4	1	PI	01/05/2013	HAR001	Opening	Opening Balance	1,012.75	0.00	1,012.75
5	1	PI	01/05/2013	JAC001	Opening	Opening Balance	456.35	0.00	456.35
6	1	PI	01/05/2013	VAN001	Opening	Opening Balance	2,097.40	0.00	2,097.40
30	1	PI	12/05/2013	JAC001	5/219	Repairs to building	909.25	181.85	1,091.10
31	1	PI	18/05/2013	VAN001	2017	Good for resale	2,146.80	429.36	2,576.16
						Totals	6,622.55	611.21	7,233.76

Campbell Kitchens

Aged Creditors Analysis (Summary)

Report Date:	31/05/2013			**Supplier From:**	
Include future transactions:	No			**Supplier To:**	ZZZZZZZ
Exclude Later Payments:	No				

** NOTE: All report values are shown in Base Currency, unless otherwise indicated **

A/C	Name	Credit Limit		Turnover	Balance	Future	Current	Period 1	Period 2	Period 3	Older
JAC001	Jackson Builders	£	0.00	1,365.60	1,547.45	0.00	1,091.10	456.35	0.00	0.00	0.00
VAN001	Vanstone plc	£	0.00	3,631.45	2,738.26	0.00	640.86	2,097.40	0.00	0.00	0.00
	Totals:			4,997.05	4,285.71	0.00	1,731.96	2,553.75	0.00	0.00	0.00

Campbell Kitchens

Customer Activity (Detailed)

Date From:	01/01/1980			**Customer From:**	
Date To:	31/05/2013			**Customer To:**	ZZZZZZZZ
Transaction From:	1			**N/C From:**	
Transaction To:	99,999,999			**N/C To:**	99999999
Inc b/fwd transaction:	No			**Dept From:**	0
Exc later payment:	No			**Dept To:**	999

** NOTE: All report values are shown in Base Currency, unless otherwise indicated **

| A/C: | FRA001 | Name: | Fraser Designs | | Contact: | | | | Tel: | | | |

No	Type	Date	Ref	N/C	Details	Dept	T/C	Value	O/S	Debit	Credit	V	B
1	SI	01/05/2013	Opening	9998	Opening Balance	0	T9	2,017.60 *	2,017.60	2,017.60		-	-
28	SI	21/05/2013	524	4001	Kitchen equipment	0	T1	852.24 *	852.24	852.24		N	-
					Totals:			2,869.84	2,869.84	2,869.84			

Amount Outstanding	2,869.84
Amount Paid this period	0.00
Credit Limit £	0.00
Turnover YTD	2,727.80

| A/C: | FRY002 | Name: | Fry and Partners | | Contact: | | | | Tel: | | | |

No	Type	Date	Ref	N/C	Details	Dept	T/C	Value	O/S	Debit	Credit	V	B
2	SI	01/05/2013	Opening	9998	Opening Balance	0	T9	1,597.60			1,597.60	-	-
27	SI	07/05/2013	523	4000	Kitchen furniture	0	T1	2,011.68 *	2,011.68	2,011.68		N	-
29	SC	14/05/2013	61	4000	Kitchen furniture	0	T1	500.16			500.16	N	-
34	SR	25/05/2013	BACS	1200	Sales Receipt	0	T9	1,097.44			1,097.44	-	R
					Totals:			2,011.68	2,011.68	3,609.28	1,597.60		

Amount Outstanding	2,011.68
Amount Paid this period	1,097.44
Credit Limit £	0.00
Turnover YTD	2,857.20

| A/C: | SCL001 | Name: | SCL Interiors | | Contact: | | | | Tel: | | | |

No	Type	Date	Ref	N/C	Details	Dept	T/C	Value	O/S	Debit	Credit	V	B
3	SI	01/05/2013	Opening	9998	Opening Balance	0	T9	1,906.50			1,906.50	-	-
33	SR	15/05/2013	BACS	1200	Sales Receipt	0	T9	1,906.50			1,906.50	-	R
					Totals:			0.00	0.00	1,906.50	1,906.50		

Amount Outstanding	0.00
Amount Paid this period	1,906.50
Credit Limit £	0.00
Turnover YTD	1,906.50

Campbell Kitchens
Period Trial Balance

To Period: Month 1, May 2013

N/C	Name	Debit	Credit
0050	Motor Vehicles	20,067.10	
1100	Debtors Control Account	4,881.52	
1200	Bank Current Account	3,944.49	
1230	Petty Cash	66.50	
2100	Creditors Control Account		4,285.71
2200	Sales Tax Control Account		1,970.64
2201	Purchase Tax Control Account	1,405.49	
3000	Capital		26,416.85
3050	Drawings	950.00	
4000	Sales Kitchen furniture		1,715.80
4001	Sales Kitchen equipment		1,224.50
4906	Bank interest received		24.20
5000	Materials Purchased	1,758.05	
7100	Rent	750.00	
7104	Premises Insurance	829.40	
7400	Travelling	37.90	
7502	Office Stationery	38.00	
7800	Repairs and Renewals	909.25	
	Totals:	**35,637.70**	**35,637.70**

Campbell Kitchens
Nominal Activity

Date From:	01/01/1980		N/C From:	1100
Date To:	31/05/2013		N/C To:	1100
Transaction From:	1			
Transaction To:	99,999,999			

| N/C: | 1100 | | Name: | Debtors Control Account | | | | Account Balance: | | 4,881.52 DR |

No	Type	Date	Account	Ref	Details	Dept	T/C	Value	Debit	Credit	V	B
1	SI	01/05/2013	FRA001	Opening	Opening Balance	0	T9	2,017.60	2,017.60		-	-
2	SI	01/05/2013	FRY002	Opening	Opening Balance	0	T9	1,597.60	1,597.60		-	-
3	SI	01/05/2013	SCL001	Opening	Opening Balance	0	T9	1,906.50	1,906.50		-	-
27	SI	07/05/2013	FRY002	523	Kitchen furniture	0	T1	2,011.68	2,011.68		N	-
28	SI	21/05/2013	FRA001	524	Kitchen equipment	0	T1	852.24	852.24		N	-
29	SC	14/05/2013	FRY002	61	Kitchen furniture	0	T1	500.16		500.16	N	-
33	SR	15/05/2013	SCL001	BACS	Sales Receipt	0	T9	1,906.50		1,906.50	-	R
34	SR	25/05/2013	FRY002	BACS	Sales Receipt	0	T9	1,097.44		1,097.44	-	R
							Totals:		8,385.62	3,504.10		
							History Balance:		4,881.52			

Campbell Kitchens
Audit Trail (Detailed)

Date From:	01/01/1980			Customer From:	
Date To:	31/12/2019			Customer To:	ZZZZZZZZ
Transaction From:	1			Supplier From:	
Transaction To:	99,999,999			Supplier To:	ZZZZZZZZ
Exclude Deleted Tran:	No				

No	Type	A/C	N/C	Dept	Details	Date	Ref	Net	Tax	T/C	Pd	Paid	V	B	Bank Rec. Date
1	SI	FRA001				01/05/2013	Opening	2,017.60	0.00		N	0.00	-		
		1	9998	0	Opening Balance			2,017.60	0.00	T9		0.00	-		
2	SI	FRY002				01/05/2013	Opening	1,597.60	0.00		Y	1,597.60	-		
		2	9998	0	Opening Balance			1,597.60	0.00	T9		1,597.60	-		
					500.16 from SC 29	14/05/2013	61					500.16			
					1097.44 from SR 34	25/05/2013	BACS					1,097.44			
3	SI	SCL001				01/05/2013	Opening	1,906.50	0.00		Y	1,906.50	-		
		3	9998	0	Opening Balance			1,906.50	0.00	T9		1,906.50	-		
					1906.50 from SR 33	15/05/2013	BACS					1,906.50			
4	PI	HAR001				01/05/2013	Opening	1,012.75	0.00		Y	1,012.75	-		
		4	9998	0	Opening Balance			1,012.75	0.00	T9		1,012.75	-		
					1012.75 from PP 36	24/05/2013	006724					1,012.75			
5	PI	JAC001				01/05/2013	Opening	456.35	0.00		N	0.00	-		
		5	9998	0	Opening Balance			456.35	0.00	T9		0.00	-		
6	PI	VAN001				01/05/2013	Opening	2,097.40	0.00		N	0.00	-		
		6	9998	0	Opening Balance			2,097.40	0.00	T9		0.00	-		
7	JD	0050				01/05/2013	O/Bal	20,067.10	0.00		Y	20,067.10	-		
		7	0050	0	Opening Balance			20,067.10	0.00	T9		20,067.10	-		
8	JC	9998				01/05/2013	O/Bal	20,067.10	0.00		Y	20,067.10	-		
		8	9998	0	Opening Balance			20,067.10	0.00	T9		20,067.10	-		
9	JD	1200				01/05/2013	O/Bal	4,916.26	0.00		Y	4,916.26	-		31/05/2013
		9	1200	0	Opening Balance			4,916.26	0.00	T9		4,916.26	-		
10	JC	9998				01/05/2013	O/Bal	4,916.26	0.00		Y	4,916.26	-		
		10	9998	0	Opening Balance			4,916.26	0.00	T9		4,916.26	-		
11	JD	1230				01/05/2013	O/Bal	68.24	0.00		Y	68.24	-		31/05/2013
		11	1230	0	Opening Balance			68.24	0.00	T9		68.24	-		
12	JC	9998				01/05/2013	O/Bal	68.24	0.00		Y	68.24	-		
		12	9998	0	Opening Balance			68.24	0.00	T9		68.24	-		
13	JC	2200				01/05/2013	O/Bal	1,497.68	0.00		Y	1,497.68	-		
		13	2200	0	Opening Balance			1,497.68	0.00	T9		1,497.68	-		
14	JD	9998				01/05/2013	O/Bal	1,497.68	0.00		Y	1,497.68	-		
		14	9998	0	Opening Balance			1,497.68	0.00	T9		1,497.68	-		
15	JD	2201				01/05/2013	O/Bal	909.23	0.00		Y	909.23	-		
		15	2201	0	Opening Balance			909.23	0.00	T9		909.23	-		
16	JC	9998				01/05/2013	O/Bal	909.23	0.00		Y	909.23	-		
		16	9998	0	Opening Balance			909.23	0.00	T9		909.23	-		
17	JC	3000				01/05/2013	O/Bal	26,416.85	0.00		Y	26,416.85	-		
		17	3000	0	Opening Balance			26,416.85	0.00	T9		26,416.85	-		
18	JD	9998				01/05/2013	O/Bal	26,416.85	0.00		Y	26,416.85	-		
		18	9998	0	Opening Balance			26,416.85	0.00	T9		26,416.85	-		
19	JD	3050				01/05/2013	O/Bal	350.00	0.00		Y	350.00	-		
		19	3050	0	Opening Balance			350.00	0.00	T9		350.00	-		
20	JC	9998				01/05/2013	O/Bal	350.00	0.00		Y	350.00	-		
		20	9998	0	Opening Balance			350.00	0.00	T9		350.00	-		
21	JC	4000				01/05/2013	O/Bal	456.20	0.00		Y	456.20	-		
		21	4000	0	Opening Balance			456.20	0.00	T9		456.20	-		
22	JD	9998				01/05/2013	O/Bal	456.20	0.00		Y	456.20	-		
		22	9998	0	Opening Balance			456.20	0.00	T9		456.20	-		
23	JC	4001				01/05/2013	O/Bal	119.30	0.00		Y	119.30	-		
		23	4001	0	Opening Balance			119.30	0.00	T9		119.30	-		
24	JD	9998				01/05/2013	O/Bal	119.30	0.00		Y	119.30	-		
		24	9998	0	Opening Balance			119.30	0.00	T9		119.30	-		
25	JD	5000				01/05/2013	O/Bal	224.00	0.00		Y	224.00	-		

continued...

Campbell Kitchens
Audit Trail (Detailed)

No	Type	A/C	N/C	Dept	Details	Date	Ref	Net	Tax	T/C	Pd	Paid	V	B	Bank Rec. Date
		25	5000	0	Opening Balance			224.00	0.00	T9		224.00	-		
26	JC	9998				01/05/2013	O/Bal	224.00	0.00		Y	224.00	-		
		26	9998	0	Opening Balance			224.00	0.00	T9		224.00	-		
27	SI	FRY002				07/05/2013	523	1,676.40	335.28		N	0.00	-		
		27	4000	0	Kitchen furniture			1,676.40	335.28	T1		0.00	N		
28	SI	FRA001				21/05/2013	524	710.20	142.04		N	0.00	-		
		28	4001	0	Kitchen equipment			710.20	142.04	T1		0.00	N		
29	SC	FRY002				14/05/2013	61	416.80	83.36		Y	500.16			
		29	4000	0	Kitchen furniture			416.80	83.36	T1		500.16	N		
					500.16 to SI 2	14/05/2013	Opening balance					500.16			
30	PI	JAC001				12/05/2013	5/219	909.25	181.85		N	0.00	-		
		30	7800	0	Repairs to building			909.25	181.85	T1		0.00	N		
31	PI	VAN001				18/05/2013	2017	2,146.80	429.36		N	0.00	-		
		31	5000	0	Good for resale			2,146.80	429.36	T1		0.00	N		
32	PC	VAN001				20/05/2013	426	612.75	122.55		N	0.00	-		
		32	5000	0	Goods for resale			612.75	122.55	T1		0.00	N		
33	SR	SCL001				15/05/2013	BACS	1,906.50	0.00		Y	1,906.50	R		31/05/2013
		33	1200	0	Sales Receipt			1,906.50	0.00	T9		1,906.50	-		
					1906.50 to SI 3	15/05/2013	Opening balance					1,906.50			
34	SR	FRY002				25/05/2013	BACS	1,097.44	0.00		Y	1,097.44	R		31/05/2013
		34	1200	0	Sales Receipt			1,097.44	0.00	T9		1,097.44	-		
					1097.44 to SI 2	25/05/2013	Opening balance					1,097.44			
35	PA	VAN001				12/05/2013	006723	1,200.00	0.00		N	0.00	R		31/05/2013
		35	1200	0	Payment on Account			1,200.00	0.00	T9		0.00	-		
36	PP	HAR001				24/05/2013	006724	1,012.75	0.00		Y	1,012.75	N		
		36	1200	0	Purchase Payment			1,012.75	0.00	T9		1,012.75	-		
					1012.75 to PI 4	24/05/2013	Opening balance					1,012.75			
37	BP	1200				10/05/2013	Debit card	819.40	0.00		Y	819.40	R		31/05/2013
		37	7104	0	Premises insurance			819.40	0.00	T2		819.40	N		
38	BR	1200				24/05/2013	Cheque	395.00	79.00		Y	474.00	N		
		38	4001	0	Cash sales kitchen			395.00	79.00	T1		474.00	N		
39	BP	1200				02/05/2013	SO	750.00	0.00		Y	750.00	R		31/05/2013
		39	7100	0	Rent			750.00	0.00	T9		750.00	-		
40	JC	1200				01/05/2013	PCR 29	81.76	0.00		Y	81.76	R		31/05/2013
		40	1200	0	From bank to petty			81.76	0.00	T9		81.76	-		
41	JD	1230				01/05/2013	PCR 29	81.76	0.00		Y	81.76	-		
		41	1230	0	From bank to petty			81.76	0.00	T9		81.76	-		
42	CP	1230				07/05/2013	PC212	38.00	7.60		Y	45.60	-		
		42	7502	0	Printer paper			38.00	7.60	T1		45.60	N		
43	CP	1230				18/05/2013	PC213	37.90	0.00		Y	37.90	-		
		43	7400	0	Rail fare			37.90	0.00	T0		37.90	N		
44	JD	7104				24/05/2013	JNL01	10.00	0.00		Y	10.00	-		
		44	7104	0	Value error K			10.00	0.00	T9		10.00	-		
45	JC	1200				24/05/2013	JNL01	10.00	0.00		Y	10.00	R		31/05/2013
		45	1200	0	Value error K			10.00	0.00	T9		10.00	-		
46	JD	3050				24/05/2013	JNL02	600.00	0.00		Y	600.00	-		
		46	3050	0	K Campbell drawings			600.00	0.00	T9		600.00	-		
47	JC	1200				24/05/2013	JNL02	600.00	0.00		Y	600.00	R		31/05/2013
		47	1200	0	K Campbell drawings			600.00	0.00	T9		600.00	-		
48	BR	1200				28/05/2013		24.20	0.00		Y	24.20	R		31/05/2013
		48	4906	0	Interest earned			24.20	0.00	T2		24.20	N		

INDEX